MY LIFE FOR THE BOOK

MY LIFE
IVAN D. SYTIN
FOR THE BOOK

THE MEMOIRS OF A RUSSIAN PUBLISHER

TRANSLATED, EDITED, AND ANNOTATED
BY CHARLES A. RUUD AND MARINA E. SOROKA

McGILL-QUEEN'S UNIVERSITY PRESS

Montreal & Kingston · London · Ithaca

© McGill-Queen's University Press 2012
ISBN 978-0-7735-4024-8

Legal deposit third quarter 2012
Bibliothèque nationale du Québec

Printed in Canada on acid-free paper that is 100% ancient forest free
(100% post-consumer recycled), processed chlorine free

McGill-Queen's University Press acknowledges the support of the Canada
Council for the Arts for our publishing program. We also acknowledge the
financial support of the Government of Canada through the Canada Book
Fund for our publishing activities.

This book has been published with the help of a grant from the J.B. Smallman
Publication Fund, Faculty of Social Science, Western University.

Library and Archives Canada Cataloguing in Publication

Sytin, Ivan Dmitrievich, 1851–1934
My life for the book : the memoirs of a Russian publisher / Ivan D. Sytin ;
translated, edited, and annotated by Charles A. Ruud and Marina E. Soroka.

Translated from the Russian.
Includes bibliographical references and index.
ISBN 978-0-7735-4024-8

1. Sytin, Ivan Dmitrievich, 1851–1934. 2. Publishers and publishing–Russia
(Federation)–Biography. I. Ruud, Charles A., 1933– II. Soroka, Marina E.
III. Title.

Z368.S9A313 2012   070.5092   C2012-901956-9

This book was designed and typeset by studio oneonone in Sabon 10.3/14

CONTENTS

INTRODUCTION[1]

This book offers a portrait of a remarkable Russian, Ivan Dmitrievich Sytin (1851–1934). Part I, the first nine chapters, consists of those parts of Sytin's memoirs that were omitted from Soviet-era publications. They were found in 1992 after lying for years on a shelf in the State Publishing House (Gosizdat), acquired, and given to the I.D. Sytin Exhibition Center in Moscow by Sytin's grandson, the late Dmitry Ivanovich Sytin. They showed no signs of having been classified or arranged by an archivist or an editor. We have compiled them for publication with the permission and assistance of the director of the Sytin Exhibition Center, Natalya N. Alëshina.

Part II, the last three chapters, includes an unpublished description of Sytin and his family by Sergei Sokolov, Sytin's nephew, as well as four descriptions of Sytin published earlier in Russian.

Sytin wrote these recollections of his life in the second half of the 1920s, when his vast projects were well behind him and his businesses had been nationalized. His memoirs recall his successes in mass-market publishing and his links with some of the great writers of his time. They also make clear his central place in the attempt – little recognized in Russia and seldom-explored by scholars – to bring the Russian peasant into modern life. This effort, which has been largely ignored in Soviet historical and cultural studies and by Soviet and Western scholars, who have focused instead on the decades-long political struggle between the revolutionary opposition and the tsarist government, was a true cultural offensive aimed at educating the class from which Sytin came. Sytin drew into that cause a multitude of writers, printers, philanthropists, scholars, artists, teachers, military officers, journalists, and even political figures. Understanding how they worked together and how they failed provides a fresh perspective on the history of Russian culture in the decades before the Revolution of 1917.

Sytin was no mere businessman bent only on profit. He revelled in meeting challenges, especially those involved in attracting well-known writers to help enlighten the unlettered and the newly literate Russian peasants. He promoted Russian culture by issuing Tolstoy's Mediator series, encyclopaedias that are still valued today, fine schoolbooks for classroom use, manuals on agriculture and mechanics, and popular children's stories. Through him, the collected works of Russian and Western authors were made available in inexpensive editions that allowed them to reach a wider audience. Even his calendars contained useful information. His daily newspaper, *Russian Word*, reached the largest number of readers in the history of Russia. Sytin worked to broaden distribution networks for printed literature across Russia. And he used every means possible to distribute what he published: peddlers on foot and horseback, trains, kiosks, bookstores, and reading rooms. Although sometimes forced to bow to censors and other tsarist authorities, he managed to advance his projects.

Sytin wrote his memoirs in a second-story apartment above Tverskaia Street in central Moscow, not far from where he had concluded his greatest business triumphs and where a monument to his acumen still stands – a section of his newspaper building, adjacent to the *Izvestiia* building. By the time he wrote, Soviet officials had stripped him of both his wealth and, more important to him, the opportunity to work – they could never see the dethroned capitalist as one of "them." Idled, Sytin turned to reflecting on his life, hoping to show the masters of the new "battle engine," as he called it, the enormous contribution he had made to Russia. And, in a Tolstoyan frame of mind, he wished to explain his life to himself and to others before it came to an end.

Because he wrote what he called "cameos," Sytin ruminated on some periods of his life more than once and sometimes provides several versions of the same events. The original manuscript does not offer clues to the precise dates or circumstances under which its various parts were written, leaving us to judge only by the content. His sentences – colourful, vigorous, and full of pithy folk expressions – are also rambling and lack proper punctuation and capitalization. He wrote in a folk vernacular of the nineteenth century, now unfamiliar to most Russians. The problems of editing Sytin's manuscripts are compounded by his scrawling handwriting, ungrammatical phrasing, misspellings, and a tendency to insert spaces within words and omit word endings. He said of himself that he was "not literate" – and he did so without embarrassment. He liked to remind himself and others of his humble peasant origins in order to bolster his legitimate pride in his achievements. And, because the gentry and intelligentsia who surrounded him during his career idealized the Russian peasant, it did the astute Sytin no harm to take this tack. Another Russian peasant boy who did very well, becoming the first secretary of the Soviet Communist Party – Nikita S. Khrushchev – also liked to advance his purposes by presenting himself as a simple village fellow.

Sytin's memoirs reflect the preoccupations that assailed him in his old age. Solitude, quiet, and inactivity were new problems for him. For his entire business career, as a deeply involved hands-on manager of a huge enterprise, he had been involved in an array of different problems and projects. Writing on his own was a special challenge for a man old, ill, and rejected. Sytin's pages consist partly of a memoir written by the patriarch of a large family to teach moral lessons to his children and grandchildren by recalling his accomplishments and the effort required to achieve them. When his pages are placed in approximate chronological order, at their end, in the poignant section on his life from 1918 on under Soviet rule (his business was nationalized in 1917), is an appeal to the Soviet government to abandon the legal proceedings they had instigated against him, a venerable Russian publisher, for alleged involvement in a money-making scheme. The final paragraphs betray his fear and bitterness at finding himself treated as a criminal and stripped of his personal savings. It is possible that he began his memoirs as part of an emotional appeal for mercy to the Soviet authorities that would base his defence on his lifetime service to the people, and then gradually became preoccupied with his memories and turned more and more to the golden times of his life. Even though he ostensibly wrote to share his personal experiences and thoughts with his children, he may also have had a larger public in mind, even as the attitudes of Soviet authorities made that prospect increasingly unlikely.

As he recounts the memorable episodes of his life, Sytin recalls in detail his contacts with major Russian literary figures. He felt justifiable pride in these connections and wanted others to know that the simple lad from the provinces had had long and fruitful dealings with such celebrated writers as Anton Chekhov, Maksim Gorky, and Leo Tolstoy. He also wrote about them because it seemed right that anyone who had worked with writers of such eminence should leave a testimonial for posterity. But, considering Sytin's lifelong habit of staying on the right side of arbitrary authorities, his repeated allusions to his closeness to the great icons of Russian culture may also have been his way of shielding himself from the usual Soviet accusations that he had been a right-wing conservative and profiteer. He also describes a number of leading figures of the Imperial regime. Sytin approached several highly placed figures to secure support for his plan to improve peasant literacy; they in turn tried to enlist Sytin to promote public opinion favourable to the government. He met and talked with Tsar Nicholas II and Prime Minister Sergei Yu. Witte. The memoirs contain a record of his meetings with Konstantin P. Pobedonostsev, the procurator of the Holy Synod, and with Prime Minister Petr A. Stolypin. He recalls a brief encounter with Rasputin. With the exception of his meeting with Stolypin, these recollections do not flatter the pre-Revolution rulers of Russia.

In Russian, Sytin's writing conveys a subtle irony in the way he reproduces his own deferential, supplicatory tone when meeting with men of high standing and the rudeness or brusqueness of his interlocutors. Despite his wealth and accomplishments, throughout his life he remained a peasant bowing before his betters. Recognizing that men of high status took for granted that they inspired awe in persons of lesser status, Sytin may even have exaggerated his humbleness to win such men's favour, using a form of flattery to get what he wanted from them. He used his relations with the Holy Synod's publishing program to neutralize the anger of its omnipotent head, K.P. Pobedonostsev, against Sytin's Mediator enterprise. Memoirs of Pobedonostsev by his social peers or superiors describe him as a courteous, kindly, mild old man, always ready with a friendly word and smile. Sytin's memoir is unique in that it shows what this high official could be like with those beneath him.[2]

Sytin was exacting in describing business triumphs: his story showed the world what a Russian peasant could accomplish, even in the face of obstacles. His recollections of these matters decades after they occurred show the focused memory of an elderly man with few reference materials at hand who remembered the details of transactions and the first names, patronymics, and last names of persons he had dealt with over a half a century before. We know that one of his sons gave him some, although slight, assistance while he wrote and that he had in his possession a copy of the commemorative book, *A Half Century for the Book (Polveka dlia Knigi)*, that his company had published in 1916, which would have been a useful reference work. Sytin's writing, however, shows that he was working mainly on his own in assessing the happenings and central preoccupations of his past.

Sytin's publishing activities were summarized in *A Half-Century for the Book*, whose 610 pages commemorated his golden jubilee in the publishing business. It includes a short essay titled "From the Past: Autobiographical Sketches by the Anniversary Hero," a piece undoubtedly written by others. In it, Sytin says that he had decided on the celebration as a morale-booster for fellow Russians suffering from the increasingly difficult conditions of world war. The gala affair, however, actually promoted Sytin and provided a fine meal for his staff in one of Moscow's finest restaurants, the Praga.

The memoirs of Ivan Sytin[3] were published by the official Soviet press in 1960. They had, however, been thoroughly reviewed by Soviet censors, who omitted sections in which he reflected on religion as well as those on his rise from a "boy" in a tiny shop to a millionaire because such writing contradicted the official Soviet stance that there had been no opportunities for peasants under the tsarist regime and that a true man of the people, as he was portrayed, was not interested in making money. Including such materials would have made publication of the memoirs impossible.

The excluded reminiscences published here reveal Sytin as a religious man – a believer who became a pillar of his church, a promoter of projects to benefit mankind, and someone who engaged in daily spiritual exploration of his soul. Here is a "capitalist" whose life force was religious.[4]

Sytin's religion was that of the Russian Eastern Orthodox Church.

He found the ancient variant of Russian Orthodoxy, the faith of the Old Believers, especially attractive, as he makes clear here.[5] He saw the peasant of the north of Russia as the purest expression of the Old Believers' faith, believing that this sturdy, benevolent, and hard-working countryman was the future of Russia. The Russian peasant, he believed, stood alone spiritually, strong and permanent, like a rock. But such peasants were still mired in ignorance and awaited enlightenment. He understood the peasants from his own origins, but the meaning of their lives became clear to him through his contact with Chekhov and Tolstoy. It is this Sytin who is apparent in his unpublished memoirs, where he counts himself – as in no other document – as a Tolstoyan.

Sytin's view of the printed word and of his own mission originated in his religious beliefs. He embraced "the book" in quite a different way than the Soviet rulers of Russia, who saw publishing as a weapon in the class war. Printing was not a traditional tool of Russian propaganda. As Boris Uspensky notes, "According to the medieval concept, the world is a book, i.e., the text represents in itself the Divine idea. The book – and not a semantic or grammatical system – is the symbol of the world. The text itself is from God."[6] The poet Marina Tsvetayeva echoes the importance of "the book" to Russians: "Russia always approached writers, or rather went in search of writers as a peasant *muzhik* went in search of the tsar – for the sake of finding the truth."[7] There is no better example of the religious power of the "book," than Avvakum's *Life*, which was the revolutionary inspiration of the Old Believers whom Sytin accepted as the true Russians. Avvakum's seventeenth-century work is a powerful spiritual document with few parallels in any language in which he summons his followers to a life of unbending worship.[8] The Russian peasant of the north preserved Avvakum's dedication to the True Faith and won Sytin's permanent devotion. Seminal books such as Avvakum's retained a powerful hold on the religious imagination of the Russian peasant. Sytin grew up in that culture and retained a profound reverence for books.

Because he had risen to wealth from lowly beginnings, Sytin's life was in a sense a "fairy tale." But later in life he felt that he had to make amends because he had spent his life acquiring wealth and property. He told the writer Nicholas Teleshov, "I have seen the fruits of my work and life, and it is enough for me," saying that he planned to spend his last days in a monastery.[9] The reader can see his doubts in the pages published here and perhaps they provide an explanation for the ease with which he yielded his massive printing and publishing empire to the Soviet nationalisers. Unlike many other well-off Russians, he did nothing to frustrate the new leadership but decided to help it. He was ready to work with the new rulers for the betterment of Russia, although nowhere does he say that he approves of the "socialist experiment." His acceptance of the new order was rooted in his belief that it might lead to a better life for the Russian people, overlaid with his life-long pragmatism. He had worked with the autocracy; he would now work with the Soviets.

Sytin was born 24 January 1851 in the depths of rural Russia in the village of Gnezdnikovo in Kostroma province, not far from town of Soligalich. He died in Moscow on 23 November 1934 as Stalin, by means of the brutal collectivization and Five-Year Plans, was tightening his grip on the Communist Party and transforming Russian life.

During his eighty-three years, Sytin witnessed upheavals that greatly influenced the development of modern Russia: the liberation of the serfs in 1861, the assassination of Alexander II twenty years later; the industrialization of Russia in the next two decades; the Revolutions of 1905 and 1917; and the installation of the Soviet order. Among the punishing conflicts that provided a back-drop to these events were the Crimean War of 1854–56, the near-constant battles in the Caucasus and with the tribesmen of Central Asia, the Russo-Turkish War (1877–78), the Russo-Japanese War (1904–05), the First World War , and the Russian Civil War following the Revolution.

After a beginning as an apprentice to a bookseller in Moscow and the eventual advance to owning his own very small shop, Sytin began to publish his own cheap books and calendars and developed a network of peddlers (called *ofenia* or *ofeni* in Russian), an army of salesmen who walked or rode horseback from Moscow deep into the countryside, the only way to reach distant villages. Sytin's printing business depended on them because they carried his calendars, pictures, and books – along with icons, thread, needles, buttons – to the peasant domiciles, where they proffered their wares through the windows. Any publisher serious about selling his works to the peasants first had to sell them to the peddlers, who insisted on books with bright and lively pictures because so many of their customers either could not read or read haltingly. Nor would the peddlers accept any item that contained a printed price, for they, like their customers, liked to haggle. Sytin cultivated the peddlers and used them more extensively and effectively than any other publisher. He used the peddlers, for instance, as a source of marketing information about peasant tastes. He recruited only honest and sober peddlers, extended credit to them, and helped them select publications that had not yet been sold in the area that the peddlers planned to visit.

One critic rightly said that Sytin's *lubki* (the Russian word for publications for the peasant market) were slipshod productions. In some the title had nothing to do with the contents, and the pictures might not relate to either. Sentences were often ungrammatical and the printer might leave great gaps in the text in order to stretch his type to fill the pages. The paper was thin, soft, and absorbent so the impression made by the type – which was usually substandard in any case – was blurred. But it was through just such publications that Sytin laid the foundations for his publishing empire.[10]

His rise toward success began in the 1880s. Tolstoy and a group of his followers, loosely known as the Tolstoyans, decided to create a series of small books of high quality and with a clear moral message that would be sold to the peasants. One of the group, Vladimir Chertkov, approached Sytin in the winter of 1884 to serve as their printer because of his well-known success in distributing his own works to the vast peasant market. The Tolstoyans had declared war on such cheap popular literature but they needed Sytin to get their quite-different publications into the hands of the peasants. Attempts to circulate their little books through the St Petersburg Committee on Literacy – made up largely of well-meaning aristocrats – had been disappointing. What the Tolstoyans needed most from Sytin was marketing savvy as well as the collaboration of an ambitious publisher who could be interested in publishing works of high quality.

In reaching a deal with Chertkov, Sytin insisted that each book sell for no more than two kopecks, a price within the reach of the peasant buyer. For their part, the Tolstoyans demanded that their books resemble Sytin's only in price and format. Not only would they provide the contents but they would also donate layout, editing, and proofreading services – three stages of production that Sytin routinely neglected. Altruistic writers, Tolstoy included, wrote simple tales reflecting the teachings of Christ; such well-known artists as Gay, Kramskoi, and Repin contributed illustrations. On the distinctively red-bordered cover of the books appeared the motto, "God is not in might, but in truth."

Assigning himself the role of intermediary between the intelligentsia and peasant reader, Sytin chose the name Mediator (Posrednik) to designate the series. Suddenly he was on the side of the good and righteous. Although his other ventures were commercial, he was to remind his critics, "Mediator is like a prayer; it is for the soul." Sytin was quick to adopt the language of religious idealism in dealing with Chertkov and other Tolstoyans. The extraordinarily pious Tolstoyan Paul Biriukov accepted Sytin at face value and anointed him a Tolstoy acolyte. He described Sytin as a "divine spark" who provided the energy for the great business of enlightenment against the "dark forces" bent on keeping the masses of the people in ignorance.[11]

Sometime in 1885, Sytin first met Tolstoy, who recognized that there were commercial considerations in Sytin's relationship with Mediator and had already categorized him as an ordinary but well-off businessman who deserved no special credit for printing Mediator at a small profit. He chided Chertkov for idealizing the shrewd publisher. Sytin, said Tolstoy, got back more in prestige than he ever sacrificed in earnings.

Without question, Mediator gave Sytin a crucial boost with intellectuals and writers. As he himself would recall, "genuine writers and genuine literature" had been in "a world unattainable to us" until "through chance [becoming publisher for Mediator] ... everything turned out as in a magical tale."[12] Following his association with Mediator, he issued the works of such leading authors as N.S. Leskov, G.I. Uspensky, A.I. Ertel', A.V. Grigorovich, and – especially important to Sytin – A.P. Chekhov. Although the peasants paid less heed to the books than had been hoped, Mediator books had caught the imagination of populist intellectuals and attracted them to the Moscow publisher.

Sytin in turn recruited well-known authors for his own publications, all the while becoming less dependent on the Tolstoyans. Biriukov remarked in a letter to Chertkov that Sytin had calculated the advantages Mediator offered him: "Sytin, who is more intelligent and farseeing than other popular publishers, has understood that the golden time [for *lubki*] has passed irrevocably."[13] He believed that Sytin had "seized on Mediator ... so that under its influence ... he would little by little change the character of his own publications." Once again, Sytin had seen opportunity and seized it. He would use a similar strategy in later years when he started a daily paper.

Still, the collaboration continued because the Tolstoyans valued it, and in October 1888 Chertkov sought to mollify Tolstoy over repeated delays. By this time the publisher's attitude had changed. Sytin, he explained, "does not now especially need such small books and is terribly slow in printing them"; so great was the disorder in his shops "that some manuscripts are being mislaid and we have to replace them with our copies." Chertkov, however, counselled against "unpleasantness with Sytin, who I like and in [whom] lies all the mechanical strength of our venture." Rather, he favoured "gentle patience and unremitting insistence so that ... all the material provided by me will be printed, although only a full year after I have received it from the author."[14] The Moscow publisher had tumbled in the estimation of the Tolstoyans from the spiritual pedestal he had once occupied and had become the amiable but inefficient printer on whom the project depended.

By the end of four years of collaboration between Sytin and the Tolstoyans, at the close of 1888, press runs of Mediator books had totalled an impressive twelve million copies. Sytin would continue printing the series until early in the twentieth century, but sales of his own publications in that period far outnumbered those of the Mediator books. Furthermore, he was getting ominous signals from government censors that the procurator of the Holy Synod, K.P. Pobedonostsev, objected to the promotion of Tolstoy's moral views through Mediator; Sytin made at least two trips to St Petersburg to call on the powerful official in attempts to mollify him – as he would later travel to Petrograd to see Lenin. He describes his difficulties,

including an interview with Pobedonostsev, in the pages here. Aware
that annoyance over Mediator within the government could frustrate
his other publishing ventures, in 1893 Sytin turned down a proposal
for a new series of books for an urban readership by advising the
Tolstoyans to use other printing plants in order to get their works done
"more expeditiously."[15] The break was complete by 1904. By then,
thanks in good measure to the Tolstoy connection, Sytin ranked among
the half dozen largest publishers in Russia.

By then, as well, Sytin had benefited from his contacts with another
preeminent writer, Anton Chekhov, whom Sytin had first met in 1893.
The correspondence and the dealings between the two men reveal
Sytin's wish to form a personal relationship decidedly closer than that
between Sytin and Tolstoy. Sytin especially cherished the fact that
Chekhov valued him for his publishing on behalf of the peasants.

Chekhov says that he regarded Sytin as a shallow but still intelligent and intriguing character whose very real power as a publisher
could and should be put to good use. Chekhov wrote to I.I. Pavlovsky,
"He is an interesting man. A great, but completely unlettered publisher
who came from the people. A bundle of energy together with slack-
ness ... and lack of firmness."[16] This said, Chekhov genuinely valued
Sytin for having risen so far above his beginnings in the countryside
and for establishing the only printing company "where the Russian
spirit reigned."[17]

Like the Tolstoyans, Chekhov admired Sytin's ability to get the
printed word out to the people; and, like the Tolstoyans, Chekhov
channelled that skill. The rough-hewn Sytin had the means and
machinery for educating the masses but needed the guidance of cultivated minds to achieve it. Toward that end, Chekhov advised Sytin to
create a popular liberal newspaper in Moscow, a city dominated by
conservative merchants and press.

Such a venture posed serious obstacles. Sytin would need official
approval to publish a newspaper from a government that had tagged
him as a "dirty liberal" for printing the Mediator books. Secondly, he
was wholly inexperienced. "I didn't know the newspaper business and
feared greatly its extraordinary complexity and difficulty. But A.P.
Chekhov ... told me: 'Sytin ought to publish a paper.'"[18]

Chekhov provided the strategy that worked, one that, the writer
understood, would be compatible with the publisher's "lack of firm-

ness." Sytin would not tackle the authorities head-on, but would launch a conservative paper and gradually make it into a liberal one. In other words, he would present himself to the government as one kind of publisher and, without official permission, transform himself into another. In 1894, Sytin proposed to A.A. Aleksandrov, the editor of a Moscow literary review well liked by the government, that he petition to start a daily newspaper with Sytin as unnamed backer. Aleksandrov, a former instructor in Russian literature, was a protégé of Pobedonostsev, whose influence went well beyond his official sphere into censorship and other areas of government policy.

Aleksandrov agreed to Sytin's proposal and soon won approval as editor and publisher for a new Moscow daily, *Russian Word*, which would not be subject to preliminary censorship.[19] Sytin and several other backers of his choosing stayed behind the scenes. From *Word*'s start in 1895, however, Aleksandrov showed no understanding of the daily newspaper business, failed to attract sufficient readership, and steadily lost money. Sytin deplored a tone in *Russian Word* that was "drum roll and unbearably vulgar." Losses mounted and the paper faced bankruptcy. "In a condition of melancholy and depression," Sytin recalled, "I took some of my usual medicine – I went to talk to A.P. Chekhov." Chekhov reassured him: "This editorial staff is not permanent … It is necessary only to await its natural death and to substitute another." Chekhov reminded Sytin that the first goal had been to "to secure the right to an uncensored paper, even if it was acceptable to circles of conservative tendencies." Sytin must await a "more enlightened time and the possibility of reforming *Word*."[20]

Russian Word's fortunes continued to plunge, and Sytin concluded that he would have to become the official publisher in order to get the management out of Aleksandrov's hands. The government agreed to the change on the condition that Aleksandrov stay on as editor. Once again, Chekhov offered his congratulations and then his old advice: "Change the editor and the matter will be in the bag." That change and many others in the staff followed, transforming *Word* onto a recognizably liberal paper by 1902.

A main purpose of a good newspaper, Chekhov maintained, was not only to inform but also to promote reading, and Sytin quotes him as saying, "A newspaper reader ought to grow into a book reader. From where else will he learn about books … which book to buy?"[21]

Chekhov had touched a chord that resonated with Sytin and justified on cultural grounds the many columns of advertisements in *Russian Word* and other periodicals that promoted Sytin's books. By invoking Chekhov, Sytin blunted charges that he kept *Word* going for strictly self-promotional reasons. Not so, Sytin always contended. His first calling was his mission from Chekhov to edify the Russian people.

In February 1917, on the occasion of his fiftieth anniversary in the publishing business, Sytin proudly proclaimed that he had founded *Word* under the inspiration and guidance of Chekhov. The illness and death of Chekhov, he said, "was extraordinarily painful ... Everything that he proposed, counselled, and told me was sacred. And now, looking back on my past life, I can say only one thing: 'Forgive me, dear spirit of A.P. [Anton Pavlovich Chekhov] if I have sinned in any way before you.'"[22]

Sytlin's relations with Vlas Doroshevich, a journalist who became editor of *Russian Word*, were quite different than those he had with Chekhov. Sytin relied on Chekhov for political and moral guidance in business affairs; he depended on Doroshevich to create a new *Russian Word*. Between 1900 and the Revolution of 1917, the name of Vlas Doroshevich was as close to a household name as that of any Russian writer. Doroshevich was "king of the feuilletonists" and widely emulated by other journalists.[23]

Although Sytin's son-in-law F.I. Blagov[24] had become executive editor of *Russian Word*, Doroshevich edited the paper from 1901 until he stepped aside in 1912 and yielded his chair to N.V. Valentinov, a Social Democrat to whom Sytin turned to shift he paper slightly to the left, although without transforming it into a party paper. Doroshevich insisted on a high salary to make *Word* a first-rate daily; he finally persuaded Sytin that he was worth every kopeck. (Doroshevich's commanding position on the paper is fully reflected in his letters to Sytin, chapter 11. Sytin recounts his hiring in chapter 4.)

Doroshevich came to journalism naturally. He was born in 1864 to a liberated woman who supported herself by writing romances for the popular press.[25] Doroshevich was little interested in school and at the age of seventeen became a proof reader with a paper and then moved to the rank of reporter. He was a journalistic celebrity at a succession of Russian papers until he finally settled at *Word* in 1901 because Sytin gave him everything he wanted – an enormous salary and complete editorial control of the paper. Wrote Doroshevich: "I was invited to take the newspaper in my hands. This means it must follow my course."[26] That meant several departures for Russian journalism.

Doroshevich opposed taking sides along party lines, and he strenuously and successfully resisted the ties sought by the opposition Constitutional Democratic Party and by the Stolypin government. Even after Doroshevich left the paper in 1917 for reasons of health, the tradition of the daily as an illuminator of events rather than advocate of political programs remained alive. In its final days, *Word* championed non-partisan democracy until its final closure by the Bolsheviks in November 1917.

Doroshevich kept his distance from the publisher while insisting on absolute freedom to control *Word*'s content and Sytin had little choice but to accede. Doroshevich's daughter quotes her father's explosive words over rumours that Sytin at one point planned to sell the paper: "This little merchant has got it into his head to sell my newspaper and me with it ... Keep in mind that neither *Russian Word* nor Doroshevich is for sale to any party for any price."[27]

Doroshevich insisted on good taste and rigorous editing. Regarding the paper's Sunday supplement, for example, he wrote, "I see how inanities and vulgarisms are creeping in. And I know from experience on magazines that if you do not cut this short, immediately with a cruel, iron hand – a whole river will pour in and you will be choked before you realize what is happening." Similarly, he was scathing about typographical errors. "The proof- reading is disgusting ... [readers] ought to fling this paper away after the second column of the first article and say, 'some illiterate person has the cheek to continue to publish this paper.'"[28] In line with his goal of providing local, national, and international coverage, he recruited a series of able correspondents and sent them to Russian cities and to foreign capitals. Twenty reporters, some near the front lines, provided unprecedented coverage of the Russo-Japanese War in 1904–05.

✺

Sytin's best years in terms of both profit and prestige came in the second decade of the twentieth century, for by 1910 he had fully recovered from a fire during the Revolution of 1905 that had consumed most of his book publishing plant in Moscow. At the same time he began questioning the worth of immense material success even as he succeeded in acquiring it. He wrote the priest and journalist Gregory Petrov in 1909 that his thinking had become "tangled" and he wondered if Peter Struve was correct in viewing A.I. Ertel's renunciation of literary life to become a simple worker in the fields as an act of religious meaning. The death of Leo Tolstoy in 1910 focused his thought even more on Tolstoy's call for common cause with the people. At least to some extent for altruistic reasons, Sytin was to make possible, at some personal expense, the great writer's bequests of his works to the public domain and his estate to the peasants who lived there.

From this private altruism came, however, a business deal of great benefit to him: he negotiated an agreement whereby his company paid 300,000 rubles for the rights to the first posthumous edition of Tolstoy's complete works. At the same time, but off the record, he privately paid another 147,000 rubles to Tolstoy's widow for copies of published but unsold works that Tolstoy had granted her during his lifetime but rescinded in his will. This last sum went to help purchase the estate lands from Sofia Andreevna and distribute them among the peasants who lived on them.

During the two years that Sytin and the A.F. Marks Company of St Petersburg made bids and counterbids for Tolstoy's work, each offer included a sum for the widow for her rights to copies of the pre-1881 works that Tolstoy, in his will, had placed in the public domain. Finally, in late 1912, as the executors held out for 300,000 rubles plus the amount for the books in the warehouse, the Marks company at first agreed and then declared that it could not pay that amount and withdrew as a contender. Sytin, as lone bidder, accepted a contract that had been negotiated by the representatives of the Marks Company. He seems to have understood early on that the prices being asked by the executors would cause the Marks Company to withdraw from the negotiations and that he would be the beneficiary. Cunning negotiator that he was, Sytin actually expressed some pleasure during the negotiations when Marks tried to assume the total cost itself. He believed that the two negotiators sent from St Petersburg had overreached themselves and that the Marks company would not accept the deal.

As Sytin explained the actual financial transaction, his company paid 300,000 rubles for the rights to Tolstoy's works. Aleksandra Lvovna, Tolstoy's daughter and one of the executors, testified that she purchased the land for the peasants on 26 February 1913 and paid 400,000 rubles to her mother on that day.[29] (Sytin's own account, printed here as chapter 5, shows that the publisher paid the additional 147,000 rubles for the books in the widow's possession.)

Sytin's capacity for mass production led another writer to work with him – Maksim Gorky. Although Gorky had had no use for Sytin or his publications in the first years of the century, by 1910 he was cultivating the Moscow publisher and seeking to collaborate with him. Gorky did not at first like either Sytin's penuriousness or his politics. He wrote in 1901 to Leonid Andreev, who had just agreed to a 350-ruble honorarium for a first edition of his stories: "Your publisher [Sytin] is a swindler and a son-of-a-bitch, for he has cleaned you out shamelessly, ruthlessly. My friends behave that way only at nights on lonely streets ... because they want to eat; your publisher is sated"[30] Gorky convinced Andreev to publish instead with his company, Knowledge (Znanie). Later, the grateful Andreev said he would have perished from heavy newspaper work if he hadn't been rescued from Sytin's claws.

In 1901, Gorky felt that Sytin's goals – for instance getting rich and boosting Orthodoxy and autocracy – made him irredeemable. He railed over what he called the chauvinism of *Russian Word*, especially the articles of Fr Gregory Petrov, who signed himself, "The Russian." Such Russians of *Russian Word* and other people of sanctimonious spirit, Gorky wrote, "can simply be called scum for Christ's sake, not a genuine Christ but a Church-police Christ who has recommended rendering to God and the Tsar equally." Gorky classed Sytin with the "plasterers who smear over the cracks in the old structure of our life."[31]

By 1909, Sytin had risen in Gorky's estimation. For one thing, Sytin had undertaken to recruit highly respected writers to publish original works in his *Russian Word*. Novels, poetry, critical essays, and even critical social commentary began to appear in the columns of his paper. Among those he persuaded to write for him were Dmitry Merezhkovsky, Aleksandr Blok, Leonid Andreev, Ivan Bunin – and Gorky.

Necessity also compelled Gorky to re-evaluate Sytin, for Gorky was facing financial shortfalls in his own publishing company, Knowledge, and his literary miscellany of the same name. Government confiscations and a slumping book market had cut into his profits and, in contrast to his public acclaim at the start of the century, his celebrity as a writer had faded. In 1901, Gorky had scorned Sytin; in 1909, he was ready to ask for his backing not only for Knowledge but for other projects that he had in mind: an encyclopaedia of Siberia, for instance, and – related to his hope to found a new political party to take positions between the liberals and radical revolutionaries – a new political paper.

Gorky soon came to admire Sytin's energy, initiative, and love of work – characteristics that were not "Russian," no matter what the social level, and traits that Russia sorely needed to raise the cultural and material level of all the people. "The Russian," he wrote, "admires energy but finds it hard to believe in it." He is, most often, a "poor worker [who] ... takes no satisfaction in the building of his life and the process of work gives him no joy; he would like – as it is said in the folk stories – to build cathedrals and palaces in three days and, in general, he loves to do everything at once; and, if not at once, if he cannot succeed right away, he throws the whole matter over." Blaming this attitude on the religious belief that rewards come not in this life but "beyond the grave," Gorky wanted Russians to discover the error of this terrible "eastern truth." He saw Sytin as providing a great example of the rewards of wholehearted effort.[32]

In the summer of 1909, in self-imposed exile on Capri, Gorky invited Sytin for discussions. (Sytin describes two visits to Gorky on Capri in chapter 8.) Gorky, however, was mistakenly and naively optimistic about Sytin's willingness to deal and to do so on Gorky's terms. For one thing, Sytin did not passively invest in other men's companies. With Sytin's capital went Sytin's control and his dovetailing of projects. As well, Sytin was less interested in Gorky's projects than he was in having Gorky's by-line in *Russian Word* along with those of others who published in Knowledge.

Rather than visit Gorky in the summer of 1910, Sytin took his wife for twenty days to the spa at Carlsbad for treatment for obesity. But he was sorry that he had gone because he found the disciplined hours for rising, sleeping, and meals appalling. "Whoever is boss has devised a bastardly regime of the Devil." He added, "It's no good us trying to copy Germans."[33]

Sytin finally made it to Capri two years later, in March 1911, but it was an encounter that mainly benefited Sytin. As Sytin tells it, he shared

tea with Gorky and two of his collaborators on Gorky's terrace on
Capri and discussed pleasantly how best to educate the Russian people.
Gorky, in contrast, wrote his wife that at the end of two days he had worn
himself out "snarling uninterruptedly like a borzoi on the hunt."[34]

Gorky and his friends were surprised to hear Sytin's proposal to
restructure Knowledge as a joint-stock company. Sytin would invest
10,000 rubles to become principal stockholder and director of the
"practical side of the business." He also insisted on a share of the profits on works already in print. Gorky said no. Sytin, Gorky concluded,
was best kept at arm's length, for "if one falls into the hands of such
a *muzhik*, he quickly extorts from you all the living spirit, crystallizing
it in the form of rubles and books, and you will be tossed aside like a
squeezed lemon."[35]

During 1912, Sytin presumed to suggest to Gorky that he submit
everything he wrote to *Russian Word*. When the two met again on
Capri in May 1913, one firm agreement resulted, a good one for Sytin.
He would pay 1,200 rubles to serialize Gorky's autobiographical
Childhood in *Russian Word* during 1913 and 1914 and would pay
another 1,500 rubles to publish the book version. Gorky felt placing
Childhood in Sytin's daily rather than in Marks's monthly magazine,
Nivá, which he had also considered, would have the advantage of
reaching a greater circulation. "To have a connection with a paper so
widely distributed is not so bad."[36] Gorky also hoped that his obvious
good will in letting the publisher have *Childhood* would nudge Sytin
into backing Knowledge publications, for that company was still having financial difficulties.

Relations between the two men were now cordial, and Gorky laid
plans to publish a democratic newspaper in St Petersburg with Sytin's
backing. When he returned to Russia in December 1913, he stayed
at Sytin's estate, Bersenevka, for three weeks early in 1914 and visited Sytin's printing plant in Moscow – an occasion marked by a
photograph showing Gorky standing among workers in the plant.

Shortly after Gorky returned to Russia, he learned that Sytin, because
of other commitments, was not going to finance a history of Russia
they had been discussing. Nor had Sytin shown any interest in an encyclopaedia about Siberia that Gorky had proposed, focusing his time
and resources instead on an encyclopaedia of military affairs. (This
encyclopaedia, an immense project undertaken in collaboration with

a number of young military officers, remains an important source of information on Imperial Russian military affairs, although not all the planned volumes were published.) Instead, Sytin instead offered Gorky 200,000 rubles for his collected works, to be published in an edition of 40,000 copies, but he added so many conditions that Gorky refused. He further offended Gorky by not providing financial backing for his projected newspaper, which was to be called *Ray*. Sytin was shifting to the right politically and had lost his taste for involvement with democratic publishing. In June 1914, Gorky wrote that Sytin "is dragging out negotiations [on *Ray*], hindering me from beginning the matter with other people. I am determined to have a decisive explanation from him."[37] Whatever Sytin replied, *Ray* remained in the planning stages. In November 1916, Gorky wrote his wife, "It seems they are giving me rubbish ... it seemed that everything was ready, and suddenly everything went to pieces. That damned Sytin does not let himself get caught, like a fish."[38]

In contrast, Sytin was very willing to back a literary review, and he made possible publication of Gorky's *Chronicle* (*Letopis'*) from 1915 to 1917, even though its low circulation (8,000 subscribers) caused him to lose about 50,000 rubles. Sytin also backed Gorky's new publishing house, Sail, in 1915 and gave him several editorial jobs with Sytin & Co. in the last two years before the Revolution. Gorky was still negotiating over the purchase of his complete works and the projected daily newspaper when the assassination of the Archduke Francis Ferdinand on 28 June opened the door to war.

As a publisher, Sytin capitalized on wars, even as he saw how profoundly the Great War and what he called its "bloody mindlessness" threatened Russia. Following the October Revolution in 1917 that brought the Bolsheviks to power, Sytin took bold steps to continue publishing under the new government. He visited Lenin (his three different accounts of the visit are included here) to appeal to him for a place in the publishing industry under the new Socialist order. Having reached an agreement with Lenin to collaborate with the regime, Sytin embarked on several projects in the early 1920s, including an official trip to Germany to secure financial backing for the Soviet paper industry and one to America to promote Russian art.[39] His descent to the status of pensioner and widower followed in 1924, the year of the death of both Lenin and Sytin's wife, trusted confidante and advisor of forty-seven years, Evdokia Ivanovna. Deprived of her and of what had been his army of editors, he had no one to refine his rough prose when he wrote his memoirs in the second half of the 1920s.

Sytin's memoirs include his comments on history, religion, politics, and social problems. He provides critical and astute assessments of historical developments in Russia between the liberation of the serfs in 1861 and the First World War, surprising from a man of the business world. He believed that the liberation of serfs by Alexander II had religious meaning. It was the momentous event in the history of his country, liberating not only the person of the peasant but the human spirit. In a moving description of villagers assembling at their church to render thanks for what had occurred, Sytin reveals his belief that religion is deeply bound up with the thought and character of the Russian people, a theme that he returns to again and again in these memoirs.

Sytin connected many of the difficulties of post-Emancipation Russia to government neglect of the freed peasants. He thought that educated Russians had also lost their moorings and were drifting. The intelligentsia, he believed, had a sacred task to speak the truth. Writers were the guardians of spiritual values in a new, more secularized Russia. Their vocation was the same as that of monks in pre-Petrine Russian society: their writings were sermons. Given this, writers had to teach, to give moral guidance. This is what the people expected from them, but they had failed in this task. Sytin believed that they, including Tolstoy and Kropotkin, had fallen into the trap of substituting themselves for God; they had come to think of their words as absolute. He felt that it was more important that they provide words that individuals can live by.

Sytin criticizes Westernized Russian intellectuals, feeling that they had led Russian youth astray by promoting dreams of impossible socialist utopias, ideas had injected a kind of poison into Russian life because the young had become so completely disillusioned with their own country that they were unable to play a constructive role in its development. Too many young people were leaving university without job prospects and falling under the influence of intellectuals who spent their time criticizing the government, did not know what they want, and had "no practical skills to accompany [their] teaching."

Sytin's personality included competing psychological impulses that paralleled the fissures in Russian society. He was buffeted from all sides due to Russia's deep-seated problems. His spectacular successes in business, once deeply satisfying now left him adrift in the collapsing social and political conditions of revolutionary Russia. His hope of transforming his publishing company into a vast project that would help to educate the peasants was repeatedly blocked by Imperial officials. His aristocratic partners abandoned him. His fellow businessmen were only interested in protecting themselves. On the left, Sytin withdrew from Gorky, who was seeking to advance his own political agenda. The publisher could not find common cause either on the left or the right.

The pages censored from the published memoirs show Sytin from many sides. Many found him elusive, difficult to understand. A number would have shared Chekhov's view that his principal trait was "wishy-washiness." This is perhaps another way of saying that Sytin cannot be defined by a single psychological trait: some thought him honest, others dishonest; some thought him a true Russian *muzhik*, a peasant, others a businessman of the American type. Some thought him a liberal publisher, others a reactionary cultivator of nationalistic instincts in Russians. The testimony of those who knew him reveals that although many understood his larger purposes, others, both before and after the Revolution, saw him as a threat to their cherished views.

As the documents in this volume show, Sytin's character had many facets and how he was described depended on the angle of vision of the describer. He owned no single "truth" but many truths. As a man of the village making his way in the new competitive environment of Russia/Europe he had many conflicting drives, motivations, and aspirations. His story is the manner in which he dealt with them.

The village of Gnezdnikovo in the north of Kostroma province where Ivan Sytin was born and lived the first years of his life. The view is of the main street running through the middle of the village. This picture, taken in the 1980s, shows that vehicular traffic is virtually nonexistent. The only transportation to the village from the town of Soligalich is by trailer hauled by a tractor. The village has the look of a village of the Russian north: the houses, or *izbas*, as they are called, are built of wood with corrugated metal roofs. The wide spacing among them is to inhibit the spread of fire. (Photo by Aleksei V. Sytin)

A bust of the village's most famous son, Ivan Sytin, mounted in a prominent location on the main street of Gnezdnikovo. (Photo by Aleksei V. Sytin)

A monastery located in northern Kostroma near Sytin's home
village. Sytin's high opinion of the role of monasteries in the
life of Russian peasants was probably based on his knowledge
of the importance of this one. (Photo by Aleksei V. Sytin)

Housed in this building in Soligalich, the town nearest to Sytin's
native village, was a local printing plant founded by merchants.
Sytin contributed the mechanical equipment for the plant.
(Photo by Aleksei V. Sytin)

This building in Soligalich evidently contains a chapel because it is said to be the place where Ivan Sytin was christened in the faith of Russian Orthodoxy. (Photo by Aleksei V. Sytin)

The principal street (Merchants' Row) of Soligalich. The stone buildings show that trade had produced a level of wealth that was far above the meager standards of the usual Russian village. Historically, the wealth of the town was based on the salt industry. At one time, Soligalich supplied the salt for the whole of Russia and Scandinavia. The town was not far from Sytin's home village of Gnezdnikovo and might well have been in Sytin's mind when he wrote in his memoirs that the peasant villager rarely had need to visit a town. (Photo by Aleksei V. Sytin)

P.N. Sharapov, the Moscow merchant who sold pictures to the peasants and welcomed the fourteen-year-old Ivan Sytin into his shop in Moscow. Sytin received his basic business education as Sharapov's apprentice. Sharapov was the first of several men Sytin credited with giving him a boost in his life and career.
(Photo: Sytin Exhibition Centre)

Sytin's wife, Evdokia Ivanovna Sytina, in a formal photograph published in but taken some years before the publication of the commemorative volume *Half-Century for the Book*. She does not figure in Sytin's memoirs but is described by her nephew Sergei Sokolov in his reminiscences which appear in this volume.
(*Polveka dlia Knigi*)

Vladimir G. Chertkov was among those who figured predominantly in Sytin's life and career. Chertkov, a close collaborator of Leo Tolstoy, brought Sytin into the Mediator project and had a role in Sytin's publication of the first posthumous edition of Tolstoy's works. The portrait, painted around 1890, is by Ilya Repin. (Yandex)

An early Mediator book showing both the front and back cover. It is a dramatization of Tolstoy's tale, "The Imp and the Crust," which was also published as a play titled *The First Distiller*, a comedy in six acts. The typically eye-catching cover is of the Devil on his throne directing one of his imps to make haste to complete the corruption of a peasant. The peasant is finally induced to distill his corn crop into vodka. The back cover shows the results of the imp's work, a peasant passed out from drink. The chief devil and imp look on with pleasure. (*Polveka dlia Knigi*)

Sytin declared both publicly and in his writings that he owed a special debt to the writer Anton Chekhov, shown here in the 1890s, about the time that he met Sytin. The debt was for more than useful advice in the launching of the newspaper, *Russian Word* – Chekhov deeply influenced Sytin's understanding of the publishing business as having spiritual purpose. (Yandex)

Vlas Doroshevich, peripatetic journalist and editor of outstanding talent, who took into his hands the creation of Russia's largest and finest daily newspaper before the Revolution of 1917, *Russian Word*. Doroshevich ran the paper as though it was his own, and he insisted, as his letters to Sytin show, that he would brook no interference in editorial matters. *Russian Word* was the most widely read newspaper in Russia before the Revolution of 1917. (Yandex)

The editorial offices of *Russian Word*, facing Tverskaia
Street in downtown Moscow. Sytin's apartment was
on the third floor. A description of the interior is given
by Sergei Sokolov in his memoir of the Sytin family
in chapter 12. This section of the building looks very
similar today and, although no longer used for publishing
operations, it is immediately in front of the newspaper
plant of *Izvestiia*, the Russian daily newspaper.

The printing plant of I.D. Sytin on Piatnitskaia street, opened in 1904. Sytin published books and pictures in this plant. It was badly damaged by fire during the revolutionary events of 1905 but later repaired and has been in continuous use as a printing facility to this day. The plant was a model industrial enterprise for its day and included an infirmary for workers. Sytin also opened a newspaper plant in 1905, located on Tverskaia, the main street of Moscow.

Ivan D. Sytin at his desk in his publishing company. Although commanding a vast business enterprise, Sytin remained a hands-on manager. His projects were varied and included not only newspaper and book publishing but a magazine, an experimental farm on his estate near Moscow, and several philanthropic projects. (Sytin Exhibition Centre)

Ivan Sytin and directors of Sytin & Co. in the boardroom on Piatnitskaia Street. At the opposite end of the table from Sytin is M.T. Soloviev, who sold his printing company to Sytin and then joined him as a board member and director of mechanical operations. (Sytin Exhibition Centre)

A rotary press at Sytin & Co., probably at the newspaper printing plant on Tverskaia Street in central Moscow. The large rolls of newsprint show that this press is designed for newspaper printing rather than books. The press was likely purchased in Germany where Sytin bought most of his up-to-date printing equipment. The pressroom is remarkable for its cleanliness and natural light. (Sytin Exhibition Centre)

The Niznhii Novgorod bookstore of the I.D. Sytin company. Sytin opened a series of bookstores after the government shut down the peddler system that he had used to reach peasant customers for his books. The two large signs identify the store as trading in books and pictures. (Sytin Exhibition Centre)

An idyllic summer scene at the Bersenevka estate where three families spent the warm months. This picture was taken in front of the main manor house. The estate was close to Moscow and located near to the railway line to St Petersburg so Sytin could conveniently come out from the city after work. Sergei Sokolov describes summer activities in his memoir, "Bersenevka," chapter 12.
(Sytin Exhibition Centre)

Sytin and workers on his estate inspecting a McCormack mowing machine at his estate at Bersenevka. Sytin ran a productive farm on the estate and experimented with crops.
(Sytin Exhibition Centre)

Sytin, pictured on one of his walking tours around the
estate, very likely early on Sunday morning. The buildings
on the estate were built mainly in the old Russian style,
using logs, boards, and thatched roofs. The small
windows are also characteristic. (Sytin Exhibition Centre)

After the start of the First World War, Sytin made the "wooden dacha" at Bersenevka available to the recovering wounded from the war zones. There was space for thirty invalids at the dacha and they are shown here with doctors and nurses. (Sytin Exhibition Centre)

Дача И. Д. Сытина, гдѣ помѣщается 30 раненыхъ.

During the First World War Sytin's Bersenevka estate housed wounded soldiers from the Russian Army. The caption at the bottom of the original photo says that thirty wounded lived in the "wooden dacha." (Sytin Exhibition Centre)

The "brick dacha" at Bersenevka described by Sergei
Sokolov in the memoir published as chapter 12. It provided apartments for two families, and Sokolov spent
summers there with his siblings. (Sytin Exhibition Centre)

The main manor house at Bersenevka after 1917 when
the estate had been nationalized by the new Soviet
government. The house was allowed to fall into
disrepair and was finally destroyed by fire in the 1930s.
(Sytin Exhibition Centre)

Having a discussion with Sytin on the veranda of his
country house at Bersenevka is F.I. Blagov, Sytin's son-in-
law and editor-in-chief of the newspaper *Russian Word*.
Even in these informal surroundings, the two men are
carefully dressed. Sytin made it a point to dress well
and many have remarked on his neat appearance.
(Sytin Exhibition Centre)

Sytin and his wife, Evdokia Ivanovna, over tea at the main house at Bersenevka. The picture was probably taken on a Sunday morning after Sytin's early walk around the estate followed by lunch on the veranda. (Sytin Exhibition Centre)

I.D. Sytin in his last years, posing with unknown persons. The photo is undated but very likely taken about the time that he was writing his memoirs. (Sytin Exhibition Centre)

PART I

MEMOIRS

IVAN D. SYTIN

1

BY WAY OF INTRODUCTION

My sweet childhood, where are you? You, dear, have put me on the path of a happy and abundant life. And your wise and sweet lesson became my guiding star throughout my life. And I have kept it as a sacred gift of your extraordinary bounty to me. At the end of my long and happy life, my merciful and holy star, I see you and feel you and I beseech you. Let me open my sinful soul to you in the hope of your mercy. Give me the wisdom to express truthfully what you have given me, a small illiterate twelve-year-old village boy. It is a seventy-six-year-young old man who is standing before you and he still feels and sees everything as if his soul were still that of a child. I am asking you, my gracious and merciful star, give me the wisdom to pour out all my uneducated and simple soul to my children, and to anyone who would like to know of your great kindness to me.

Everything is yours in my life, my work, in my experience, knowledge, my behaviour and actions ... There is no limit. I am nothing and everything of mine belongs to you and everything of yours belongs to me. I am you. That's how, all-merciful and kind star, you have guided me during my long and happy life.

They say that there should be three periods in a man's life. [In] his youth he must be prepared so as to be able to enter life sensibly, reasonably, with great sincerity and purity. And if your supervisor offers you the opportunity and strength for this second [period] of your life, go forward boldly, never forget your boss; remember that you are simply the executor of his will. You are just a boy and you grow according to your boss's will, which you must not oppose. And, in the meantime, your strength and will are growing, you see them and are getting used to them, they are teaching you while you hear and feel them. The old, bright companion has been with you since childhood.[1] Do not discard him, his path is the true one. The third and the last of my lifetime companions: again I am a boy by the grace of my boss, except that I am not twelve but seventy-six years old, and beginning again like a child.

There I sit and think: "What shall I do now?" There am I, having lived out my life, there is not much left, perhaps a very short but most precious time. What did you learn and have you done all that you had to do? Give an account of yourself. The most important final [is at hand] and I have to justify myself. So I have filled a small copybook with what I have done and what I lived for. Perhaps it will provide material for someone to write about. All my life I traded in, and published books on, life's situations and problems – a very daring thing to do. Why did I do it? I will try to justify it. I will write of what I have witnessed and participated in in my lifetime.

Childhood

Russia is a land out of a fairy-tale: great, wild, and boundless. Only its little corner is in touch with the European culture while three-quarters of her people are primitive aborigines. Only sixty years have passed since serfdom collapsed, when a man's value was less than that of a puppy and when he could be bought and sold like cattle. I am a witness to serfdom and to liberation from it.

Dear childhood: the memories of it remain with me as long as I live. Ostensibly our family was well-off. The fact that father worked as a secretary of the volost'[2] – the new administrative body instituted at the time when the liberation of the peasants was being prepared – gave us a somewhat higher status in relation to the children of ordinary peasants, but it was also a trying experience for me as a child.

Under serfdom a volost' secretary was considered to be somewhat more literate than a simple peasant. We were not serfs, but "economic peasants," belonging to the Crown.[3] My father, a peasant, completed elementary school, then went to a district school[4] and was appointed

volost' secretary in the village of Gnezdnikovo, near the town of Soligalich in the government of Kostroma.

We outsiders lived in the village, in rented quarters, in more straitened
circumstances than an average peasant family. We had nothing but the
20 rubles of my father's pay for the upkeep of the whole family and for
rent. As I grew, I went to school at the same place, the *volost'* office,
as the peasant children. The following subjects were taught at the
elementary school: the Slavonic alphabet, the Book of Hours (in
Slavonic), the four rules of arithmetic, introduction to Catechism, and
calligraphy – that was all. The subjects were all taught in Slavonic,
with the exception of arithmetic, which was taught in Russian. Three
years of such dreary studies left a residue of sadness, boredom, and
total dullness upon pupil and teacher alike. There were forty of us
village boys in the class; the teacher did his job like an automaton: he
shouted, ordered us about, made us kneel, even flogged us, but to no
avail. Everything was done mechanically and carelessly and punish-
ments made no difference. There was no control over the operation of
the school; it was run in an arbitrary manner before the emancipation
of the peasantry.

All the boys in the village are masters of the whole farm economy:
they own a horse, a cow, some sheep, and all sorts of fowl. And there
am I, alone, without property; I own nothing, a pauper, with no opportunity to make my little contribution. I wander around, look into the
farmyards, see the boys taking an interest in everything that goes on,
helping to feed the horse, the cow. Whenever they can, they watch how
the grown-ups do things.

I am eleven years old. I go to school with them, they share among
themselves the joys of their work but I am the odd-man-out and I weep
in frustration. How lucky they are, they have everything. They run
over to the meadow to make hay and when threshing comes that is
the happiest time of all. To thresh, to winnow, to sweep the kiln, to
take the horses out for the night and to look after them! To go everywhere with your father. "Hey, Vanka, here are the reins, we'll take you
for a drive, get in with me," he shouts. My friend teases me and shows
off his ability to handle horses. I run up to him, climb aboard, but in
my heart feel a pang of bitterness – here I am a superfluous little fellow – this stirs my imagination; I get on with feelings of shame and

pain. Why is my father not a peasant, what does he want to do administration for? "My dear dad, why are you a secretary? It is so good to
have your own land and a horse."

"Yes, my dear, but not everyone can be a peasant. My father was a
peasant but he made me a secretary. This is his will. But you can
become a peasant. When liberation comes you can take an allotment
and be a peasant." [So] my dear dad has made me a peasant. "Yes,
you are a peasant. When you grow up, settle down and work, first as
hired help and later get your own farm. And settle on the land as a peasant. Work, plough, thresh, and do everything that life teaches you."
This was the sweetest hope of my dreams; liberation was drawing near
and then, suddenly, the Manifesto of 19th February [1861].⁵ Father
says to me: "Well, peasant, let's go and pray. Today is the great day in
the life of our whole nation."

My dad says to me. "Well, Vanya, let's go to church. Let us go – this
is a day of great celebration. In the town, our parish church of Sts
Boris and Gleb floods the whole square with the festive ringing of its
bells, marking the great feast of liberation. People from all the neighbouring villages congregate at the church. The great celebration begins,
the service goes on in a solemn and deeply prayerful mood. The people pray tearfully, on their knees, in a spiritually exalted frame of mind.
At the end of the Liturgy the priest comes from the altar with the cross
and proclaims, "Rejoice, ye Orthodox Russian people! This is a great
and blessed day in your life. I am proclaiming the Monarch's Manifesto granting the peasants freedom from serfdom." At this point he
reads the Manifesto and then continues, "Let us pray to the Lord,
bringing him our prayers and our hopes. May the Lord help us to
accept this day of liberation for our own good and to the glory and
power of our Mother Russia. May the Lord fortify us all in strength,
justice, and the True Faith."

After again reading from the Manifesto – "Let the Orthodox Russian people bless themselves with the sign of the cross!" These words
evoke great sobbing and tears. The whole church is filled with the
sounds of prayerful weeping, so that it is hard to hear the priest, who
is weeping with the people. The reading of the Manifesto is followed
by a Thanksgiving service: people follow the solemn words of the prayer
in tears, on their knees. After the service the whole church, friends and
strangers, embrace and kiss each other as if this was the happiest day

in our lives. After our return home immense joy spreads to all the villages, all are caught up in the great festive mood. In the town, all the village people who had come to the church went about kissing those they knew and those they did not know, as if it were Easter. Then the surveying of land and its division into allotments [plots] began. The happy mood of the people and, particularly, of the children of my age with whom I went to school weighed heavily on my little soul: "When am I going to be so lucky as to work on my own land, milk my own cow, look after the lambs and the piglets?"

All this happiness around me all day and here I am walking about like a shadow, seeing it all, but not participating in anything. My friends are sorry for me and, now and again, try to help. They make me fetch water and give the calf a drink, bed the sheep with straw, or take me along when putting the horse out to pasture for night. But all this was done as a favour and this bothered and saddened me as I felt my total uselessness.

II

I did not do well at school. My poor memory and hyperactive personality did not permit me to concentrate, and my absent-mindedness and flippant attitude manifested themselves constantly. It was a sad childhood. The [financial] need and the constant worry about what to do with myself so as not to be a burden to my family made this time difficult for me. I was just a tool, a little piece of construction material. I needed to be taken somewhere to be put to work under supervision. So my uncle sent me to the Nizhnii [Novgorod] Fair[6] to peddle fur collars by going to hotel rooms and offering samples to the buyers of locally made fur collars. The whole trick in dealing with out-of-town buyers was to appear to be a polite, honest, and pleasant seller – an extremely simple matter – but the main thing was to present oneself as deserving of attention, so as to interest the buyer and make a good impression. This was a practical school, with me providing direct service to the customer, even though it involved insignificant goods. This service, given its initial results, might pay off in the future. My modest but honest and friendly approach brought me close to this group of merchant buyers, so that contacts were made and one would recommend me to another: "That boy is nice, not very experienced but polite and honest, so buy from him, brother, and help the kid."

In this manner, with my uncle's help, I got started in my little business. After the fair I did not feel like going home to face boredom and need. I went to Moscow with my great new friend, whom I served devotedly. He was a merchant from Kolomna who manufactured fur collars at the Fair. When the fair was closing, V.K. Begletsov said to me: "What, brother Vanya, do you want to go back to Galich for? Let's go to my place at Kolomna, I will set you up as a "boy" with some merchant in his shop; it will be better for you than hanging around in the village." This saved me. So I went with him, first to Kolomna, and later he fixed me up in Moscow, in Sharapov's shop.

So here I am in Moscow, in Sharapov's little picture shop, in a shed near the Ilinsky Gate, the main centre for trade in woodcut prints and pictures that sold for five kopeks per hundred. This was in 1863; my deeply felt remembrance goes to you, my beloved boss, Petr Nikolaevich [Sharapov]. We came to Moscow from Kolomna with my boss, the fur trader, on the eve of Holy Cross Day, 13 September. As we left the railway station at six in the evening, all Moscow was filled with the ringing of the bells. (As is usual, on the eve of a great feast.) As we walked toward the center we met throngs of shop assistants who had just finished work. We needed a place to stay for a night and we went to see an acquaintance of my boss who was a cook in a house on Taganka where she gave a us tiny corner and she let us sleep in that corner of her room. In the morning, we went to Ilinsky Gate. The wooden hut where Sharapov did his business was locked. We waited in the next-door chapel to see if the shop would open later. At ten the shop opened. We entered. I handed the clerk the letter and he asked me to wait until the boss came. I stood next to the door of the shop and waited; people were gathering in the shop on the occasion of the Holy Cross feast. All the friends of the old master were there. At eleven, the master arrived at the entrance. He took off his hat, made the sign of the cross, bowed to the icon, and then greeted all his employees and the guests who had come to have tea with him in a small tavern on the occasion of the feast. I shyly handed him the note from my boss. With a commanding air the severe old man took the message and passed it on to his senior clerk. "Read it." Vasily Nikitich read the proposal – to take me as an apprentice as long as the master thought it convenient. "Well, Vasily Nikitich, I promised V.K." "Well, my boy, this is your boss." And he pointed to his senior clerk, Vasily Nikitich. "Serve well and you won't be sorry. I find you too big. Well, nothing to do about that. If you serve me well, you will not be sorry."

This was my induction ceremony, without specifying the time that I would stay as an apprentice, without specifying any set time that I would stay as an errand boy. (Usually, three to five years.) I bowed respectfully and went to stand next to the door. That's how I began my career.

From a village, without having studied anywhere but in the most basic semi-Slavonic school, barely literate, without school knowledge and ignorant, I entered straight into a marvellous university under the supervision of a respectable and venerable old man of sixty-five who was very partial to the Old Belief. He was a strict observer of religious rules. He worshipped only in the most ancient church tradition. He remained celibate all his life. He was strict in his devotion to the patriarchal traditions. He loved everything from ancient times. He read only very ancient books and he had two businesses. His main business was in furs. He inherited the book trade after his brother's death and he only looked after it for his niece and nephew, but he treated it as nonsense. As for himself, he tried to learn as much as he could, sympathizing with and surrounding himself with Old Believers and people knowledgeable in the old rites. He kept a special assistant for acquiring and restoring ancient icons and this area was his main labour of love; he did it for his soul.

Where am I? Among everything that I see, where are the books? I saw only woodcuts of the lowest quality and smallest size, of fairy tales, lives of the saints, garishly coloured pictures for peasants at five kopecks per hundred. The pictures were coloured by hand in the villages, there was no author's name attached to them, and they were all bought by the peddlers and sold in the market places. That's how my career began. And how else could it have been? I was already fourteen and I had to work somewhere. Thanks to Vasily Kuzmich, from the fair, I got to Moscow where I got employment.

The first two or maybe three years I worked for free. Later, I was paid 5 or 10 rubles per month. This was already a career. I began a new life of strict subordination. Two clerks and a boy older than me who had already served here for three years and had experience. They all were above me. I was everybody's errand boy. The meekest servant of all. I immediately got many duties. My rights were to be the first to get up, to bring water from the well, to start the samovar for tea, to go to the market or to the shop to buy everything that was needed (milk and everything needed in the kitchen), to bring in the wood, clean the kitchen, and take all the garbage to the dump. All the morning chores had to be finished by eight in the morning. In the evening, I had to polish the boots and rubber galoshes of the two clerks and the boss. I had to tidy up the rooms, lay the table, and serve the clerks. I did all this conscientiously for three years. It became such a routine that it seems odd today. How patriarchal and simple the life and customs were then.

The family consisted of the boss, his charwoman, two clerks, the senior errand boy of seventeen, myself at fourteen, and the cook – we all lived like a real, close family. We all were very close to one another. The business was small and nobody thought of going after big money. Sharapov's book-selling business did all the printing and book selling. All his book-selling enterprises, including printing and sales, brought in 25,000 rubles. But the expenses were also very low. The relations among us were very close and friendly.

At that time selling books to the people was in the hands of Manukhin, Presnov, Leupkin, Morozov, Abramov. They had nothing to do with schools or with the general book market. They made their money by selling the lowest quality and cheapest woodcuts or some of the Church Slavonic publications that came from Kiev, from the Monastery of the Caves, and, later, from Moscow. They always sold only the most wretched woodcuts, which they themselves despised. They sold woodcuts at an incredibly cheap price but they produced them incredibly cheaply.

It is hard to imagine what those times were like and what those people were like. Illiterate men were at the helm of publishing for the people. There was not a single even more or less self-respecting author. All of the authors were drunken, mediocre, talentless, cheap, and phony. One of this small group was Suvorov, a former low-ranking official who became an alcoholic, who would supply any booklet for 3 rubles. Evstigneev would adopt or re-write anything that you wanted for 10-15 rubles. And there were a dozen more of this kind of writers. Instead of attracting the reader, they only inspired an aversion to reading.

III

> On a number of occasions in his memoirs Sytin tries to assess the
> significance of the liberation of the serfs. Generally, he thought it had
> been a missed opportunity because the government failed to take
> adequate steps to prepare the peasants for their new life. As is usually
> the case when he tries to write in a more philosophical vein, Sytin is
> not very clear and his prose contains an especially large number of
> ungrammatical phrases and instances of unclear syntax.

Remembering my childhood and that great Russia of my childhood, the operation of serfdom, ruled by the gentry, and the masses – grey, illiterate, and savage. The Orthodox Church with the autocratic monarch, and later zemstvo schools.[7] The development of literacy could have been achieved so simply, had things been different during this time. At this moment, it would have been very easy to give them both literacy and development, but long ago something had begun to rot in the people themselves because for centuries they had been immobilized and morally deformed and the government thought that they were unready for development.

The liberation of the serfs. The Tsar, influenced by a bunch of liberals, granted it and then it was as if he got cold feet. What he needed at that moment was to have around him a vanguard of committed men, a bold, united troop, in solidarity with the people, who would set off on the wide road of popular education and work out a concrete program for the new school of life. On the crest of this great uplift the Tsar should have surrounded himself with able people, including the populists[8] among the gentry, of whom there were dozens still available. But instead of becoming something heroic, it all ended in a terribly, cowardly way; instead of strengthening the state's power, it became more a final stage in the collapse of the power of faint-hearted authorities. And the oppressive atmosphere resulted in grief and the demoralization of society.

The great bright deed of freedom and liberation became so tarnished due to the lack of one guiding principle of leadership and of purpose in Russian society that to an observer [it appeared] like an absurd remnant of the whole great history of the Russian Empire; [some would say] that this [place], where a nation of 150 million has been struggling helplessly for centuries, is a complete madhouse. That's the excuse, but if this, the ancient Rus',[9] if it has become so rotten, where is the knight in shining armor [the Varangian][10] [where is] the true, genuine Rus'? He is in the tundra, in the wilderness, in a remote area that is wild, covered in moss. What prevented him from coming out into the world? The routine of serfdom, heavy and devoid of freedom. If, at the moment of liberation, he had been granted schooling, been really uplifted and enlivened, as I have entreated, there would have been cottage industry and artisans in every village, as is happening in [the regions of] Viatka, Perm', and a few others. But ninety percent [of peasants] remain idle, illiterate, in brutal conditions. Days change into each other as do hours, months, and years and we lazy, cowardly [people] remain in place, we move slowly to the end of our life, which is so precious. After all, life cannot be lived over again; an individual is insignificant, but it is sad to waste a country like Russia. The Russian people have formidable stubborn endurance within themselves, and, even at this terrible hour of trial, the people's voice is silent but it has not been lost.

IV

N.I. Protas'ev pulls up at Sharapov's shop, opens his carriage window, and yells: "Hey, there, young fellow, call the boss." Sharapov comes running, taking off his cap. "Give me the money, here is the invoice, send someone for the goods tomorrow." Standing by the carriage, Sharapov pulls out the money, hands it over, bowing and offering his thanks. "Thank you, Sir, Nikolai Ivanovich." The carriage turns around and drives away. All newsprint factories belonged to landowners [although there were also non-noble *raznochintsy*[11] producers in the cottage industry].[12] All industrial construction developed after the 1870s, until then, the unmistakable smell of nobles was everywhere.

Things went badly for the first ten years [after 1861]: little changed, school education was just beginning, there were two kinds of censorship – the ecclesiastical and the civil – without which not even one printed character could be set.[13]

But the life of the younger and progressive nobility was changing somewhat; the zemstvo, led by progressive nobility, was just beginning to stir. In the world of books, "holy tranquility" reigned. Five publishers, working entirely with woodcuts, fed the whole of Russia through Moscow and the country fairs, eking out their miserable existence. In Moscow only Ferapontov and, in Petersburg, Chudov dealing in Church Slavonic [texts]. In general literature, Salaev and Glazunov in Moscow and Glazunov [and] Wolff in Petersburg. Then, all of a sudden, the zemstvo and zemstvo schools, [which began] when I was a boy of fourteen to eighteen [During that time] I went to the fairs at Nizhnii Novgorod at Epiphany, at Kharkov and Rostov during the first week in Lent, to Simbirsk and to Kiev for the *kontrakty*[14] after Epiphany.

In those years books were not really considered commercial goods: the trade was in either the cheapest, simplest popular woodcut pictures made in the villages and, partly, in towns, or in books in Church Slavonic – the Psalter, Church calendars, the Book of Hours   that was all. All dealers sold, at a minimum profit, only to the itinerant peddlers and to small merchants operating at markets in towns. It was during this dreary period, so disastrous for the book trade, that the Committees for Literacy in Moscow and Petersburg began their activities selling books, from 5 to 10 kopecks each. All the benefactors of the people, great orators at conferences, looked down on woodcuts [such as] "Bova," "Eruslan," "Konek-gorbunok," "Zhar-ptitsa" and "Ivan-Tsarevich," which lived their own lives in the villages.[15] These were not read by the city folk nor, most importantly, by the young noble and city merchant [bourgeois] intelligentsia. But nevertheless the woodcut printers were providing them to the Committees for Literacy. The people wanted to educate themselves through newly developed reading and literacy. I was most fortunate that I became involved toward the end, almost at the beginning of the demise of this great undertaking by our heroic intelligentsia. The Moscow Committee for Literacy [headed by] A.N. Strekalov, the Society for the Distribution of Useful Books, and Tolstoy's school at Yasnaia Poliana were slowly dying, but the meetings still continued.[16] I was informed about all the plans and proposals before the Committee. Something new had to be created; after all it was high time that we started because we had this whole bunch of projects. About ten books [titles] had been distributed over the year and six had been published. This was the time when Chertkov[17] became active in the cause of the people with a completely new proposal. A new man appeared, one who did not write himself, but was ready to serve the cause as a middle-man between the reader and the writer. Fresh, unprejudiced, filled with the desire to serve for the benefit and welfare of the people, my contribution was commitment and zeal.

Both of us set off on the same course at the same time. His searchings and mine were so close to each other that they resulted in a magnificent achievement. Our mutual cooperation was such that when he set [before us] the task to take all that is best in literature, from whatever source, everything became possible for us, there were no protestations or arguments. The phrase "it can't be done" ceased to exist, as did the problems of price, ownership, rights, or personalities. All this disappeared. Everything was for the cause, for the benefit of the cause, and a great and sacred service to the cause resulted: the appearance of a series of books at 75 to 100 [kopecks]. This amounted to 5 to 10 [kopecks] per copy. Everyone was amazed, more so as time went on. In the shops dealing in prints there appeared, at the same price as woodcuts such as the eternal "Bova," "Eruslan," and "St. Nicholas," the finest literary works by Tolstoy, Leskov, or Korolenko with attractive titles, such as "What Does Man Live By?" or "Christ on a Visit to a Muzhik" … This innovation complemented rather than replaced earlier editions. And, along with the introduction and development of the new kind of books, a new type of reader was gradually maturing, perfecting his consciousness. It was all taking place almost imperceptibly, so that many years were needed for the hundred millions of illiterate people to absorbed it into their lives. Fifty years after the liberation of the people, their education was still woefully inadequate. People got little literacy out of school. The schools were poor, half of them run by church parishes and the other half teaching only reading and writing. The fear of the masses becoming literate worked against any improvement in this regard. How regrettable it is that so much was not understood. Where is happiness …

2

PARTING WITH SHARAPOV AND THE BIRTH OF MEDIATOR

Sytin oversaw the production and distribution of Sharapov's publications and skillfully cultivated sales among peasant stall keepers at fairs. He spent long hours of hard work at his master's business and learned Sharapov's methods inside and out. Moscow was staunchly Russian in outlook and business practices. One of the traditional values that Sharapov upheld was responsibility for the material and moral well-being of his apprentices. He advised Sytin on ways to save his soul. He helped the promising young man start a business of his own. When Sytin married (as a result of Sharapov's match-making), it was time for the young man to open his own shop.

The exhibition ended. I received a silver medal. As a peasant I was not entitled to anything better.[1] After the exhibition Sharapov said to me: "You, brother, are advancing further and further. I have no strength to carry on with a large business. This is something for the bold entrepreneurs with ambitious plans. I am happy with the business that I have. You will be better off on your own, without interference. I'll give you goods to the value of five thousand r[ubles] to get you started. Go with my blessing and build your own business." And so I took over a little shop of his and began to trade. I started on 20 December 1883, and opened on 1 January 1884.

I write elsewhere[2] about the arrival of Doroshevich, which occurred before the opening.[3] The year 1884 gave me much. [It gave me] my own real business. The dear old little man Sharapov saw my confused

and somewhat hectic work as a dangerous result of my being seduced
by the new-fangled heresy of publishing learned nonsense. Everything
liberal was seen as evil and harmful. So he and I parted, but as friends.
At first the old man would drop in on me for a friendly chat over a
cup of tea. For the first few months my business was slow. Suddenly
word spread among my friends that my shop now existed independently. V.G. Chertkov called on me. His offer and our conversation are
described below. The appearance of the first Mediator books and of
popular pictures made a lot of noise in the worlds of [book] trade and
literature. In Moscow and Petersburg we printed [editions of] one hundred thousand at one kopeck per book, which the Committee for
Literacy sold for seven kopecks.

II
Meeting Chertkov and Mediator

In the little shop, just opened and beginning its business, far from the
centre on Old Square, V.G. Chertkov appeared. The son of a tsar's general, Chertkov had been destined for a brilliant career in the military.
After some mishap he came under the influence of L.N. Tolstoy, who
attracted him strongly by his deeply spiritual sermon on non-resistance
to evil and by his Yasnaia Poliana booklets for the peasants. (These
were published by the St Petersburg Literacy Committee for the price
of five to ten kopecks.)

The ardent and energetic young Chertkov saw a group of publishers circling around Tolstoy, hoping to get his books. Among them was
V.N. Marakuev,[4] who was interested in cheap and accessible booklets
and hoped to distribute them to the people. Chertkov became terribly
excited and carried away by this idea. As he had lost everything and
was completely at sea, he grabbed the idea of enlightening the people
as a lifeline. His soul had been prepared by his family's connection to
Pashkov. Chertkov's mother was born Pashkova and was a passionate
follower and preacher of Pashkov's evangelical doctrine.[5] This family
background in following evangelical teaching prepared Chertkov to
fall under Tolstoy's influence.

Chertkov kept asking Marakuev which publishers he should talk to
in order to print cheaply truly good books that would replace wood-

cuts, in order to take over the woodcut market. Chertkov wanted to start this business on a large scale. Marakuev gave Chertkov all the addresses of the folk publishers and among others he mentioned my fledgling business on Staraya Ploshchad (Old Square). A tiny shop, 5 x 10 arshin.[6] On a frosty winter day in 1884 appeared a young, elegant, handsome, and refined gentleman in a fur coat and a beaver hat. Extremely modestly and kindly he said that he wanted to talk to publisher Sytin.

I came up and asked "What is your pleasure? I am Sytin."

"You are Sytin. That's nice. How do you do? You are so young, just a beginner. That's even better because I am a beginner, too. Let's begin together." He then said in a melodious voice, "I have been directed to you by Marakuev. My name is Chertkov. I come to you with the proposal of my partnership to publish a series of cheap books for the people by our famous authors. I have here with me beautiful works by L.N. Tolstoy."[7]

He took out the booklets and showed them to me while he surveyed the wretched little shop, under the vaults, lit only by the entrance door. It was cold there in winter and this happened to be early December.

"Can you print them as cheaply and as nicely as possible so that our quality literary booklets would be the cheapest? We want to sell them at the same price as the woodcuts. I have here with me three samples: 'What People Live By,' 'Two Old Men,' and 'Christ Visiting a Peasant's House' by Leskov."

[I replied:] "My God, how nice. Thank you very much. We have long awaited a visit from someone like you.[8] It is time that we should begin to give the people real, intelligent fiction. Until now, it has been the opposite. Nobody came to us [the publishers]; authors were disgusted by the people and the woodcuts [they were producing]. "I will gladly do everything that you wish. Here is [one of] our woodcuts." I showed Chertkov a printed booklet. "Its price is 90 kopecks per hundred, less than a kopeck [for each one]."

[Chertkov asked me:] "What price would you fix for these books?"

"And what price do you want, V[ladimir] G[rigor'evich]? We sell books of that size and quality of paper to the people [peddlars] at 80 kopecks per hundred, but we pay the authors three and five rubles per printer's signature."[9]

"Well, this is exactly what I want, which is for you to agree to publish these books and the same size ones that will follow and sell them as ordinary pamphlets at 80 [kopecks] per hundred."

"This would give me great pleasure. I will agree to everything provided you help me. Here is our series of pamphlets: fairy tales and religious [subjects]. They are all thirty-six pages and sell for 80 k[opecks] per hundred, which is the unit of rural trade. They are bought at market prices in tens for one-half kopeck for the villagers. They read them and, when finished, tear them up for cigarette paper."[10]

Chertkov laughed: "Maybe our books will have better luck and the customers will want to read them ten times. I am also glad to see your love for a good book. You and I will be happy working together."

This is what we decided for a start: I was to take three books free of charge. In the future, books sold at a higher price would compensate for the ones given away free. They would be sold at 80 kopecks per hundred, replacing the woodcut picture books. This is how the great work of Mediator began.

[Chertkov explained:] "We don't want anything for the first three booklets, but we would like them to be done in nicer-looking, more elegant type and on a better kind of paper."

[Sytin answered:] "Let's do it then. I will make this first set of booklets exactly as you wish."

[Chertkov:] "And put some artistic drawings on the cover."

[Sytin:] "We will fulfill all your requirements, we'll improve the type, outward appearance, and paper. You are doing the people such a great favor that I see it as my duty to make it a labour of love as you are doing, to respond positively to everything and to give you your order free of charge. We refuse any advance benefits with regard to profits and will undertake this common sacred project."

[Chertkov:] "I am very glad that you are so considerate. As well, we need this series to stand out and to be published under its own name, Mediator, so that all these books can be printed without copyright. If we pay 50 or 100 rubles for some of them, these expenses will be covered by the free printing of other titles."[11]

Chertkov was genuinely pleased and became even more elated when, about five days later, I gave him the galleys and the first page proofs. Three days later he got the booklets themselves. We printed fifty thousand copies of each. They were perfect, three by Tolstoy and one by Leskov, illustrated with artistic drawings. They were put on the market together with the rest, at the price of 90 kopecks per hundred. Chertkov and L.N. [Tolstoy] himself were in raptures. Right away they [the books] became the subject of conversation in literary circles; everyone was amazed at their cheapness and elegant appearance. The success exceeded all expectations. However the newspapers were silent and some people were hostile toward the project – there was a buzzing that the anti-Christ was going to the people: the heretic Tolstoy and his apostles. One had to be cautious in order to protect oneself: the books were published after strict censorship as the publications of Mediator were common [public] property.[12] As soon as a book appeared, anyone could re-publish it for free. A hundred thousand were printed [of each title] and from then on everything carried on in the spirit of affection, joy, and happiness. They [the Tolstoy group] began to accept books for Mediator after choosing them carefully and offices were opened in Petersburg and Moscow. P.I. Biriukov was the first to join [the staff], followed by numerous others.[13] Subsequent authors were paid. The quality of the work was what mattered. The problem of free material no longer existed, as we paid the authors whatever [sum] was asked. All the editorial work was done by Chertkov, Biriukov, and A.K. Gitrikh. This mutual cooperation of authors, collaborators [editors], and publishers meant that the enterprise operated like a private family cause.

The business side was most cordial. Chertkov was jubilant. He fussed over Sytin like a child with a new toy and we treated all the writers and artists as if they were our close family. In three years' time the business had expanded and began to cause serious concern to the Synod – and that was when Konstantin Petrovich [Pobedonostsev][14] began to stir.

The St Petersburg depot was maintained on profits from the sale of books where cost was 30 percent below the sale price. The authors and the artists designing the covers and drawings were paid by the publishers. All this was covered by profit from the sale of the books. Detailed financial reports were produced by the office for all this. The project paid for itself, enabling us to meet all the expenses and to expand the business on the sale profits. All the profits were directed toward expansion of the list and increasing the size of the editions. My own business had already expanded greatly thanks to other projects. Even before this [the Mediator project], the Moscow Literacy

Committee began to prepare, with my participation, a series of book-lets. After Chertkov [became involved], the business attracted increasing attention because Tolstoy, Leskov,[15] Garshin,[16] and many others joined immediately ... Chertkov, disillusioned with aristocratic life, had gone to Tolstoy and became his closest follower and friend as well as an indefatigable worker for the cause of Mediator. Our agreement in this respect was most cordial. We began to accept [manuscripts], but only after we studied them closely, and then published them. Proprietary rights did not exist. Our printing shop was small at that time, with four machines; the editorial board consisted of Chertkov's followers: P.I. Biriukov, I.I. Gorbunov-Posadov, Al'demirova,[17] and some others. This project, like the other ones, was brilliantly successful. Following Chertkov, Baroness V.I. Uxkhüll'[18] came to inspect the books.

I remember the happy meeting with Vsevolod Mikhailovich on the Nevsky [Prospect in St Petersburg]. "Good day to you, I.D., but I have a grievance against you: Why did you put my story "The Scarlet Flower" into a literary calendar?" "Dear Vsevolod Mikhailovich, the Calendar was put together by your friends Gol'tsev and Remizov.[19] It is their fault that they didn't ask you."

"Well, yes, I am not angry with you. I want to tell you that I will never refuse you anything. But ask me first and then I shall be happier to have some of my own [work] in your publications. However, I have to punish you: for doing that you shall be made a lifelong member of our circle, pay 10 rubles per year, and come to see me tomorrow together with Vlad. Grigor'evich."

The next day Chertkov and I went to see him upstairs on the fourth floor. We found him at breakfast. He treated us to some eggs and talked about general matters. V.M. was very gloomy. (Mediator had published a few of his books.) He worked on the railway.

When we left him, going out of the door onto the staircase I noticed the small landing with a protective railing consisting of just one iron bar over a deep stairwell. I said to Chertkov: "Isn't it scary? Look into this gaping abyss. How dangerous. A moment of inattention and a man is gone."

A few days later V.M. threw himself down from the landing and died all broken up.[20]

III

For Sytin, collaboration with the Tolstoyans meant entry into the world of respectable book publishers and also of the intellectuals who worked under Tolstoy's religious inspiration and leadership. Chertkov came to see Sytin as one of them. Sytin, although he never forgot the financial side, was pleased and flattered by Chertkov's good opinion and friendliness. He may have seen Chertkov's exaltation and senti-mentalism as slightly comic, but overall he respected the Tolstoyans' activity.

[One day I told Chertkov] "Vladimir Grigor'evich, I would like to visit you at Krokshino. When would that be convenient?"

"Please, suit yourself," said Chertkov. "I would very much like you to come, any time. Get off [the train] at the Ol'ginskaia station, beyond Voronezh. It is twelve versts[21] from the station to us. If you let us know ahead of time, we will send horses for you. At the worst you'll always find a cabby at the station, for pennies. There are always cab drivers there."

One week later I wrote to Chertkov and went. When I arrived at the station a young man wearing a very modest short fur coat got off the train with me. He carried a bag over his shoulder, like a religious pilgrim. He inquired about catching a lift to Chertkov's Krokshino. We went together in one cart and introduced ourselves. He was about to start work at the editorial office of the Mediator on recommenda-tion of [Biriukov]. It was I.I. Gorbunov-Posadov. Now he was going [to Krokshino] on invitation by Vlad. Gr. I asked him if he had already worked [for them] before. "No," he said, "I have only been selling the Mediator books. Now I am going to help with the editorial work."

We were received warmly. The sweet little cozy household shared the life of the village. The farm was operated by M.I. Chistiakov, friend of the writer Ertel'[22] with whom I maintained a close friendship. Chis-tiakov was very close to both of us in his actions and his ideas and a true natural household manager. The farm was abundantly equipped with equipment and livestock. It employed twenty workers including the female servants. A complete working farm, with arable land. More than ten oxen, five cows, plenty of fowl. The whole way of life and the natural setting engendered joy and inspired optimism. At the foot of the hill was a magnificent huge ravine, covered for tens of versts, up and down, with a tall forest. In the middle of this was a huge lake, on the shore of which was V.G.'s lakeshore vegetable garden and a small house with an orchard. This was the abode of Vladimir Grigor'evich, sheltered from the wind and always cool. A truly quiet and tranquil life. And all around, for tens of versts in all directions, stretched the blessed broad steppe with swaying orchards and fields sown with bountiful wheat, its ears billowing prettily like sea waves.

The surrounding steppes were large and uninhabited. There, sixty-five thousand desiatin[23] belonged to Chertkov, containing nine farms with fine-fleeced sheep, one thousand head or more per farm. Chertkov's steward had the reputation in neighboring gubernias[24] of being most capable. He had worked for sixty years without replacement. He had been brought from abroad by old Chertkov. He had a perfect grasp of the local climatic conditions and was renowned throughout Russia as a very capable agronomist.

I spent three happy days in that blessed virgin country and was invited to come again, to live there at a different season of the year.

This happened at the beginning [of my stay], when Chertkov and I went for a walk at 4 o'clock in the morning, to enjoy the full beauty of the steppe at its awakening: At the first light of dawn we ascended a high hill and saw first the shining rays, followed, in an instant, by the appearance of the luminous face of the divine sun. It lit up everything with its bright radiance. Chertkov fell down on this knees and I followed his example. In a powerful voice, he sang the hymn to the Divine power, glory, and greatness. Only here, in our own immense southern steppe, can one see such beauty and richness, with no human being for hundreds of versts. I said this to Chertkov [who replied]: "Yes, brother, we have all that and much more, but too little wisdom."

I bade goodbye to Vlad. Gr. on the day after the next. I.I. [Gorbunov] remained. I mentioned to Chistiakov[25] that their group [Tolstoyans] was growing. "Yes, brother," he says, "they are a special kind. They [feel they have to teach everyone], they spend their entire lives teaching others, but know nothing themselves. Come back, brother, now that you know the way. I am happy to see you. With them I have nothing to talk about, but you feel and understand it all. You should see in winter how the steppe wolves visit us at night."

IV

The famine of 1891–92 in Russia began after a prolonged drought in the Volga region and then extended to the Black Sea region and the Urals. It was followed by a cholera epidemic and caused close to a million deaths, according to some sources. Early government measures were not on the scale needed to meet the situation and the Tolstoy society organized volunteer help to the affected regions. Sytin's contribution to the anti-famine effort was through printing a portrait of Alexander III and he also sent a wagonload of food supplies to the Volga region.

Countess M.E. Kleinmikhel'[26] and R.R. Golike[27] arrived from Petersburg and came to the little shop on Old Square. "Well, Ivan Dmitrievich," says R.R., "only you can do what the countess is going to propose." I willingly offered my services. The countess, a painter, had painted a picture of Alexander III with his entourage and wanted it to be elegantly reproduced, by chromolithographic process, in ten thousand copies. She wanted to sell them herself, with the aid of the provincial governors, for the benefit of famine-afflicted peasants. I willingly consented and thanked the countess for having entrusted me with this undertaking. "We would like you to do it urgently, Ivan Dmitrievich" [she said].

"I will try to create an exact copy within two weeks, the price depends on the time factor – [how] cheap it will be."

This was a noble project. There was a famine and Nicholas, the heir to the throne, chaired the committee of [aid to the victims of] the famine. We parted on friendly terms. I took the picture, ordered it to be copied urgently, and one week later took the proofs to the countess [in St Petersburg]. She was delighted with them and asked for the finished copies to be sent in as soon as possible. A week later I brought her the completed print job. The Countess was happy and asked how much she owed me for the ten thousand pictures. I told her: "Countess, the peasants are starving. I am a peasant myself, I have a greater right to feed them than you have. Therefore give everything you earn on the pictures to the starving. Your picture and my copying of it are both free of charge."

She was so surprised that she asked me if she should try to obtain a medal for me for this. [I said]: "I am even less entitled to that than to a financial reward. One can only give to the starving people, not take anything from them."

She was so impressed that she became my great friend. She invited me to her dinner party and also invited I.N. Durnovo.[28] It was painful, excruciating, for me to be in such exalted company, but it all ended in a miracle. I remembered that I had been prevented from selling books in Kiev and said, "Well, Countess, you've been so kind as to promise to help me in need. They do not allow me to trade in books in Kiev. Be so kind as to help me, Countess, be my guarantor."

She turned to Durnovo who was the head of the Police Department: "Ivan Nikolaevich, how is it possible to refuse Sytin permission? He is a most reliable man. Give me your word that you'll do it." He gave his word and I received the permit. Every cloud has its silver lining.

V

The prestige and contacts that Sytin gained through his association with the Tolstoyans and charitable organizations were considerable. He published "respectable" authors, including some of Russian classics, and this brought him in contact with the living Russian authors, among them Anton P. Chekhov.

My own favorite reading was closest to the popular taste (what the people [narod] were reading): the weeklies The Alarm Clock (Budil'-nik), Amusement (Razvlechenie), Light and Shadows (Svet i teni) in which diverse authors described, in a humorous way, amusing details of everyday life. The most interesting and witty of these were pieces were by Antosha Chekhonte[29] and Vlas Doroshevich. These two writers [nourished] my dreams about [producing] cheap (popular) publications. Meeting them was not a simple matter. I was restrained by the inequality of our [respective] positions and by my trade as a dealer in woodcuts. Acquaintance did not seem feasible. I admired them but did not have the audacity to approach them, even though I had first met Doroshevich three years earlier when he, a student expelled from school, had come in and handed me [his work?], but this had been long forgotten and buried in the past. Now he had become a first-rate feature writer. His witty stories, in the competing sheets, those of Pastukhov[30] and Lipskerov,[31] sold like hot cakes while he shifted his favors from the one to the other depending on who was prepared to pay more. He was out of reach by then; although he knew me well yet he never noticed me. Even if I happened to be sitting at a table in the best restaurant next to him and his company, we acted like strangers and did not acknowledge each other. He, a handsome, caustic, witty, and cruel favourite humorist, viewed everything around him with disdain. For this they paid him whatever he asked, just to have the exclusive right to print his witticisms in a newspaper.

The other, a brilliant writer, a pure artist of the written word, [was] gentle and pleasant in the beauty, wit, and elegance of [his] thought, inimitable [yet] modest as an angel. His gentle sensitivity and modesty were such that whenever the slightest contradiction or misunderstanding arose he would do all he could to accommodate the other party. In his youth his excellent articles decorated the above-named publications with his truly artistic work. Brief in form, brilliant, talented, and appreciated for their value, they used to be read with fascination. His modesty was noticed by Suvorin,[32] who appreciated his great and shining talent and took him under his wing in Petersburg as a contributor to the Supplement to *New Times* (*Novoe Vremia*) – [he was] an extraordinarily brilliant talent. Suvorin, always the great master, persuaded A.P. to work with him in publishing the supplement. Chekhov's gentle, modest, and soft personality could not withstand Suvorin's pressure: it won him over and Chekhov disappeared from the pages of the periodicals. Suvorin began to publish all of A.P.'s work and [monopolized] him as a publisher. This period, following Chekhov's work for the Moscow periodicals and for Suvorin, had been lost to me. A few years passed; my petty and confused affairs carried on somehow. My beloved Chekhonte had not written anything long since for *Alarm Clock* or *Light and Shadows* and I had forgotten him. Then, one day, I walked onto the Red Square from the Iverskaia Gate.[33] A young man ran after me and stopped me. I looked around and saw Chekhov. "Good day, Ivan Dmitrievich," he greeted me, taking out some rolled-up papers from under his arm. "Would you like to buy a manuscript from me?"

I thanked A.P. for his kind offer: "Of course I would, happily, and not just one but ten, as many as you wish." I took the manuscript and we walked together. I asked A.P. to drop in at my shop at Old Square, to seal our deal there. And there, at Old Square, we signed the agreement and settled the account. A.P. liked this simplified transaction so much that from that moment he became my dear and close friend. I asked him to come to me with his requirements, [telling him] that if he ever needed anything at all, our cashier Pavlych would take care of everything. This created a bond of friendship between A.P. and myself. I would visit him at Melikhovo where his parents lived. We would go for long walks together. His dreams soared widely and deeply: he loved *Rus'*, the peasants, and showed much concern with [the problem of] universal popular education. The schools were his cherished dream – everything for knowledge. He believed that the peasant ought to be able to do everything for himself at home and at the farm. Give him education and he will do anything. What the school had to do was to teach him rational rural work, followed by applied artisanship [trade], to enable him to understand everything around him and [know] what to do. In this way the peasants would make the country rich. The factories, as they operate now, enserf the labor force; all this must be changed and made perfect. There ought to be more mechanization and less human labor and all the participants [in production] should participate in the profits.

3

THE DEMISE OF THE
ITINERANT PEDDLERS[1]

Sytin soon had his presses going full tilt to fill ever-larger orders for his own books, the Mediator books, calendars, and posters. In the 1890s he had conquered the empire's market for woodcuts (*lubki*) and other publications. His new equipment could print fifty thousand books per day and he employed about two thousand peddlers to sell publications in the countryside. But many priests complained to the Holy Synod, Ministry of Orthodox Affairs, about the Mediator books and the government began to see those of Sytin's publications that were distributed by the peddlers as potentially dangerous propaganda that had to be brought under stricter official control.

I

[The Mediator publications] appeared in pretty artistic covers, on good quality paper, and they were successful beyond belief. Everyone began to talk [about them]. However, the newspapers did not say a word. And took an unfriendly attitude. The little birds talked about an Antichrist [let loose] among the people: the heretic Tolstoy and his apostles. It was necessary to tread very carefully to keep one's head intact.

The books were being published under strict censorship. The Mediator publications were common property. The books could be reproduced by anyone, free of charge, but nevertheless Katkov[2] called me to see him and inquired who was working with me and who were the authors. I explained everything – that this was being done by a publicly minded group led by a general's son, Chertkov. His father used to have a lot of "pull" in Petersburg. He was still alive. I was warned not to become too involved and to carefully observe [the rules as to] what was permitted. The work progressed, the contacts within literary circles broadened. It grew apace. In order to draw any suspicion away from me, the central office, depot, and editorial office of Mediator were up in Petersburg.

My job was to publish and to supply the whole of Russia with books that had never been seen before at such prices, with such contents. Chertkov was triumphant. He was full of joy, was completely devoted to the task, and was like a brother to me. He and I went everywhere together. We visited everybody. He inspired all with love for the undertaking, the writers as well as the artists, beginning with Repin, Savitsky, and others.[3] He prodded everyone else to write for the people. And the project prospered, fast and wide.

When close to sixty diverse books had been – published, the matter came to the attention of Pobedonostsev. Unexpectedly, I received a note to report to K.P. Pobedonostsev at the Synodal office on Nikitskaia Street, after Vespers.[4] I entered the room where the Vespers service was being held. Looking around, I saw Pobedonostsev on his knees. The full choir of the Chudov [Monastery] was singing. I stood there praying. The service ended. Everyone was leaving. The congregation dispersed. Pobedonostsev held an audience there and then and was talking to one of the guests. I came up after him and introduced myself by name: "Sytin." "Ah, so this is Sitov. Yes, your brocades are excellent.[5] I am going to give them wide distribution and will sponsor you."

I corrected Pobedonostsev and said loudly: "Sorry, I am Sytin." "Ah, Sytin!" exclaimed Pobedonostsev, backing away from me. "So this is what Sytin looks like. It is you[6] who have introduced to the people all this devilry led by Count Tolstoy? This whole pleiad of heretics against the Church and the State! Is it your zeal that multiplies all this devilry millions of times amongst the people?"

I replied that I was publishing with the censors' approval. The State authorities had approved and permitted everything. "Look here, don't you talk to me about our stupid censorship officials. You'll fool them all. You yourself ought to be acting as a censor and not publishing harmful pamphlets for the people. I will not allow it. I am warning you: either you stop this evil completely or we will destroy you, but we won't allow this evil heresy against the Church and the Tsar to be spread among the populace."

There was nothing I could say to such peremptory statements. I stood there in silence. Pobedonostsev also became silent. [There was] a pause. Then I said to him: "Your Excellency, what are people to read then? You should give it [reading] to them. Your Synod has no publications accessible to the people. The woodcuts cause no more harm than this heresy."[7]

"Yes, you are right, we'll have to think about it. And you, yourself, what could you do?"

"I am just a system for distribution of books and pictures among the people. The better quality they are, the more my buyer will buy and the more he will sell. Your statesman's wisdom ought to be working towards teaching the people, that is what they [the Tolstoyans] are working for. And I am not at fault. You can see it for yourself: as soon as they were offered a good book they bought it readily. And even those who never read began to read."

"I will send my trusted representative to you. He will discuss it with you and we shall see how you are going to work." "I look forward to it. Please do not delay with your offer."

One week later, I received an invitation from M.N. Katkov. I went to see him and was received. I took with me samples of all the printed Mediator publications. I thought that this had something to do with my conversation with Pobedonostsev. I went into his office. M.N. looked at me and said that I had caused Pobedonostsev much trouble by the harmful books I'd been printing. [The following exchange then took place.]

Sytin: [I've printed] nothing but those editions published by the Committee for Literacy and passed by the censor.

Katkov: "Yes, but Tolstoy's heresy is well known and it cannot be tolerated. Therefore your popular publishing house does both good and harm. You hucksters do not care about these things. But we must view that evil differently. We cannot interfere in matters of censorship. Let K.P. [Pobedonostsev] do it, but we are going to rein in your itinerant peddlers. You go on bringing fashionable goods into your store and I am going to put a bridle on your peddlers and teach them to care about what they are selling."

II

I asked what kind of reading matter was needed and desirable in the countryside then. Katkov replied that they should be reading the Psalter, Church Calendar, and the Lives of the Saints. "The Biblical History is a good book. And your irreplaceable "Bova" ...[8] But why should I be talking, you know better than I do what the people used to live by and what they read. Our people love everything that has to do with the church. That's what you should be giving them."

I left Katkov with a heavy heart. And six months later it was announced to all our peddlers when they applied for permits that they required permission from the governor to sell specified books. They had to submit the catalogue and the actual books in order to receive a trading permit valid for one year. Without it they would be arrested and sent back home under escort. So perished our itinerant peddler throughout the whole of Russia. All within one year. He [the peddler] became extinct as far as the trade in books and pictures was concerned. Tens of thousands of peddlers abandoned their century-long trade.[9]

Pobedonostsev fulfilled his promise. I was visited by V.I. Shemiakin, the minister for Parish Schools in Russia. We met. This former liberal suggested that he and I work together. I told him that it would be very difficult to achieve any serious success in such work in view of the differences between us. "You see things in a broader perspective," said I. "Continue your own work and don't interfere with others. You have destroyed the itinerant peddlers by your extreme measures and now you have decided to create your own publishing house. And who is going to do the selling? A structure built up during centuries should not have been destroyed with one stroke, within one year."

In order not to let matters deteriorate even further, Shemiakin and I devised a series of approved books on religious-moral and historical themes as well as fiction for publication within his program for the people and for the parish schools. Revised by their authors, the books turned out not too badly. Shemiakin was by no means a novice and quite a few of our historians joined in the effort. The books were produced in cheap popular editions, between ten and fifteen printer's signatures each. Of course, the lowest price was applied, a minimum of one kopeck per printer's signature. People as well as the Synodal book-stores began to buy them. Everyone mourned the demise of the peddlers but it was too late to revive them.

Pobedonostsev glowed with pleasure at having made his contribution to the people. He checked all the books himself. He corrected and approved them. He was happy with Sytin. And Sytin did everything: he paid the authors, published and printed on his own account, sold to the Synod as well as on his own. Two years passed in this fashion. At the end of the second year Synodal bureaucrats had figured out that Sytin published books [in editions of] twenty to thirty thousand and the books went at half price.[10] The money was paid to Sytin and on this series Sytin made 15,000 per year according to the accounts [and also] paid 15,000 to the editor Shemiakin. I gave them this account with special satisfaction, so that they might see the profitability. And it was here that something I had long expected happened. V.K. Sablin[11] realized what a nice collection they had created by someone else's efforts. Why give it away? It was their property and their idea. What need was there for Sytin? Surely they could do it all by themselves, making the same 30,000 per year. By themselves and for themselves.

They called me to the Synod and suggested that I hand this series over to them to become their property. I did not protest too much. I said that I had been doing it for them and would now be prepared to hand it over happily to Damansky,[12] the head of the Household, there and then. I signed over all the authors and the publication without charge. I [then] went to Pobedonostsev and told him that I had been "had" – the Synod had taken away my series. They wanted to publish by themselves. He [Pobedonostsev] heartily berated his idiots as well as myself for having done this without asking him first. He said that this wonderful undertaking would now be ruined by them.

I assured him that it would work even better when they were able to see the results of their own efforts. Pobedonostsev said: "But you know only too well what our bureaucrats are capable of! Why don't you say what you really think?" I tried not to let him see that but, apparently, he guessed it. I had done my job and paid my dues. I had held off "the Threat" [Pobedonostsev] for two years, until I consolidated my strength, by which time Pobedonostsev's power could not hurt me. My further service to this enterprise did not make sense. And I withdrew peacefully.[13]

Other than by destroying the peddlers, Pobedonostsev was power-less to harm my publishing business in any way. In the absence of the *ofeni* I began to expand my business by opening branches in all the cities and towns. From there the distribution was carried out by mar-ket merchants in the Districts [*uezdy*] and large village markets. My problem was to find a good location for every seller. After three years he [the merchant] was usually able to find a profitable spot for his shop, if not for good, at least for the winter. The book and the picture had not been seen as profitable goods in Russia in the 70s and 80s. But when Tolstoy appeared, followed by all the Old Guard: Leskov, Saltykov,[14] Chekhov, Ertel', Korolenko, Mamin-Sibiriak,[15] Potapenko,[16] and others, it became possible to step out boldly into the steppes in search of the reader. This reader sat in the wilderness or in hovels. It was hard to move him. And there were also dangerous characters [local authorities] on the road who would set up wolf traps on the way. One had to look sharp and to approach carefully. What has been related above represents such a wolf trap. It was covered with dry sticks which they noticed only a year later.[17]

III

Whether because of Sytin's strong spiritual ties to the Russian peas-antry or his obvious inclination towards the Old Believers' exalted view of the role of religion, he often returned to the question that tor-mented him: why did the government, the educated classes, and the official church fail the Russian people? He was not the only one who believed that the Russian people, other than the Old Believers, were largely indifferent to the Church and only complied unthinkingly with its outward rules and that the Church had failed to provide spiritual teaching to counter the moral decay and stagnation that he saw among the peasants. Sytin, true to his active nature, continued to think of how to remedy this situation – always returning to the idea of a greater production of accessible educational literature. In 1916, when Nicholas II gave him an audience, Sytin spoke to the tsar about these problems. (See chapter 6.)

Holy Scriptures, Synod, Schools

... to sing[18] and no one anywhere gives it a thought. This is a problem with the ritual and I, as a layman, cannot delve deeply into it. This is both a mission and a fault of every single priest. Look for example at the publication and distribution of the Holy Scripture; these are a matter for the Synod and, especially, for its chief administration. After all, it was they who, in the last fifty years, completely lost the principal and faithful reader who appreciated literature. [I recollect] my entry, as a child, into Sharapov's little business. We and everyone else in the book trade considered it our duty to buy books from the Synod for domestic use by the peasants: the Psalter, Calendars of Saints, the Book of Hours, prayer books, and the New Testament. There were over thirty thousand itinerant peddlers in Russia. All of them were banned in the 80s. Now it is already forty-five years since, in any rural home, not a single religious book published by the Synod can be found. Why did the peddlers bring them? They did it in order to explain the significance of and to awaken interest in religious books. To persuade a peasant to buy as the only prayer before God. If there happened to be children in the house, they might learn to serve in church, read the Hours, the Apostle [Epistles],[19] and participate in singing in the choir loft. In order to appreciate the irreparable loss of the wandering peddler in the 60s and 70s up to 75, [imagine] what would have happened had the government not forbidden but encouraged and provided religious books from the Synod, amplifying this with the immense Synodal patristic baggage in Russian translation.[20]

Then the peasant would feel that the Church was his mother and not his step-mother. And he [the peasant] would himself tell the priest how to guard his flock. And the flock would be made of believers knowing what they needed to know about Christ and His teaching. But now all this is done by decree and prescription. All the luminous spirituality has been lost by the Church. The [parish] priest, with his weak babble, cannot teach that which he does not know himself. In rare instances, he might come up with a sound lesson by accident but it is not as if he had read and understood it by himself. Yet the most magnificent sacred sources are rotting in Synodal basements, forgotten by all except the philosophers and the Old Believers.

In Germany, small collections, especially translated for the people, are sold in all bookstores. Their readers are not divided into classes, they are all the people there. There are no blacks, nor reds, everyone is the same colour. They are not ashamed to read the spiritual literature of the common reader. It is sad to see how, in their blind folly, they [the upper classes] have divided Russia into three camps: (1) the crazy gentry, professors, and scholars; (2) the fattened bourgeoisie with its offspring, the liberal youth; and (3) the workers and peasants.[21]

The peasant, less corrupted than the others, has been preserved almost intact. For all of these sixty years he remained untouched by their culture. They, in their struggle to educate the people, failed to make a close contact with him, the [financial] means for that were lacking. Most importantly, there was no vibrant teacher. They had no firm ground under their feet. There were the semi-literate village teachers, poorly supplied with the necessities by the impecunious authorities from two sources: the Church through its Synodal funds and the zemstvo through its social ones. They – the Church and society – were mutually suspicious of and hostile to each other. There was no unity between them. And the fourth and the main tower of strength is the Old Believer, the most genuine Russian peasant. In him, everything is strong, tough, and sound. He has learned everything and knows everything firmly as bequeathed by his ancestors. His base is his strong, firm belief. His essential books are the pre-Nikon patristics.[22] He keeps the traditions of the past, the pre-Nikon books as well as all those that pertain to the duties of a Christian from the post-Nikon era. He knows what the corrections in the books having to do with the prayer ritual consist of and he rejects them. Why, then, not let him be? He does not hurt [anyone], why not give him the right [to dissent]? Yet they [the authorities] have been fighting him for centuries, only because of the letter of the law and have branded him [and his brethren] as schismatics.

Because of the letter of the law the Old Believers died by self-immolation.[23] And now, because of her intolerance, the Church has ended up as a bureaucracy, with ritual show-off piety. It suffers all and forgives all, a servant of all that is permitted by the directives and blessing of the hierarchy taking its orders from Pobedonostsev. The Synod stands at the crossroads [and the churches] are getting emptier by the day. [A believer asks:] "What can one do, say something to console me, you are my father." One [priest] says that "we are going to hold out" but he sympathizes with popular education. Another says: "We need so many Orthodox believers per parish." Is it possible to enforce love through this kind of a church and is it possible to raise, without literacy, a man and a citizen who would centre his life on cooperation within his own family and with society when there are no true and solid foundations in the church itself as well as in the State? These are the words of two high officials.

In Russia one destroys the Church and corrupts the human soul, rendering it a formalistic, executive, ritualistic, bureaucratic servant of human desires. And the other can endure but [cannot] sympathize with the welfare of Russia and the education of the people. And your greatest achievement and duty, Sovereign Lord, is to give Russia a liberated Church and broad popular education [operated by] the government and the society. The masses are ignorant, they have not yet moved out by three-quarters from that dark ignorance where Russia had been before [the abolition of] serfdom. They have been arguing and fighting for all of sixty years about schools, about education, but they have not moved yet. They know not how to approach this sacred task.

IV
School and Knowledge

Sytin did not remain idle while lamenting the lack of government commitment to the enlightenment of its people. He joined forces with well-known Moscow social activists who wanted to start renewing the Russian public instruction system from outside. In 1907 he helped institute and gain official approval for a stock company that was similar to what today is called a joint-stock non-profit philanthropic foundation. He had already acquired a considerable reputation as a successful publisher. Now he ventured into good works that would also let him enter the lucrative market of providing textbooks to schools. The new company was to raise private capital and enlist experts to put

these funds to work. Sytin chose the name School and Knowledge for
the company.

The fiftieth year of emancipation[24]. The constitution of the School and
Knowledge Company. The founders: (1) M.M. Kovalevsky, (2) V.I.
Kovalevsky,[25] (3) A.L. Ertel', (4) V.A. Morozova, (5) I.D. Sytin. The
purpose and significance of the Company was to create a Center for All
Russia in Petrograd that would organize the establishment of schools
where needed: their construction, equipment, and maintenance. To
publish textbooks for the schools, other books, and whatever the
schools might need. To develop private initiative in providing the means
of assistance to schools so as to eliminate illiteracy completely.

What happened in the Duma – member Purishkevich[26] announced
from the rostrum that Sytin was setting up a statute for schools for
the whole of Russia: how could such a responsible undertaking be
entrusted to this kind of an enterprise? And then, my founders, the
two Kovalevskys and Morozova, sent in a letter refusing to participate.
Everything collapsed.

4

HOW *RUSSIAN WORD* WAS BORN

Like all strong men, Sytin had on the whole a very positive attitude toward humanity: he accepted people as they were and did not waste time lamenting their imperfections or cursing them for their bad deeds. He took hostility and nastiness in his stride and appreciated good qualities when he saw them. Certain people evoked in the hard-bitten businessman something close to tenderness: see his allusions to Chertkov and especially his memories of Chekhov, the great Russian writer of the period, acclaimed in Russia and abroad. Chekhov's life was cut short by tuberculosis and Sytin, like all his other acquaintances, cherished the memory of a man who was known for his wit and talent, as well as for his wisdom. For Sytin, the claim that Chekhov had been his inspiration in starting a newspaper meant that he had had the great writer's blessing. It also reveals a practical side to Chekhov that has been either unnoticed or dismissed as "unbecoming" by Chekhov's hagiographers.

I
How I Met with A.P. Chekhov

As I was leaving the chapel of Iberian Mother of God on Red Square, Anton Pavlovich Chekhov came up to me: "Hello, Ivan Dmitrievich!" I was pleased with this lucky encounter: "Good day, Anton Pavlovich!" [I said.] I knew him but we were not acquainted"I have a suggestion for you," A.P. said.

"Glad to be of service."

"I have a request." Here Anton Pavlovich produced a notebook and asked if I would like to publish a book of short stories. I thanked him for the offer. "I should be glad to publish your book. Let us go – our[1] shop at Old Square is close by; we'll go in there and draw up the agreement." We went in and wrote down the conditions. We paid A.P. two thousand for the book of short stories that he offered to us for publication.

This first meeting with Anton Pavlovich created a strong bond between us. I began to visit him frequently whenever he came to Moscow from Melikhovo, where he made his permanent home. I regretted deeply that we had not met earlier. He used to stay at Moscow Hotel No. 5. It was there that the original idea of a newspaper was born. A.P. was a great newspaperman and loved the newspaper business. He said to me: "You are running a large book-publishing business. It can develop only if you own a good newspaper. A newspaper promotes any business, especially a publishing one. A newspaper is an absolute necessity for you. These are difficult times but nothing is impossible. One has only to have the know-how."

"But I am barely literate."

"That's not important. It's a mere trifle. We will find the [right] people, but you need a permit. You know lots of people, so keep thinking every time you meet someone [if this is someone from] whom you can get a license. Once you find such a person, go for the license. And the rest is unimportant, everything will fall into place."

Several months passed. Neither of us had forgotten the idea. A meeting with Suvorin[2] was arranged. Anton Pavlovich brought the old man to me at Piatnitskaia, to see my printing plant. Accompanied by us, Suvorin inspected the whole plant. He grumbled, saying that he envied much of what he saw and cursed his people for not knowing that better printing presses existed. We then went to Arsenich's for tea and lunch. Chekhov said to Suvorin: "I've been after Sytin to publish a newspaper." Suvorin replied: "This is a difficult business. I doubt if he could make it a success. [But] let him try."

"And you, Aleksei Sergeevich, could you not help?"

"How could I help? You know that they [censorship officials] don't like me. I would harm Sytin."

It was clear that he was not pleased. Sometime later this happened in my apartment. We were drinking tea with a small company. There was A.A. Aleksandrov, an employee of mine and a [former] tutor to L.N. Tolstoy's [son] Andriusha, who had been recommended to me by L.N. Tolstoy. [There were also] Ivan Leont'evich Shcheglov, G.P. Georgievsky, and me.[3] We were talking and suddenly I said: "And how would it be, gentlemen, if we started publishing a cheap newspaper accessible to the people? Look what a great editorial board we have here: A.A. as the editor, G.P. – editorial writer, I.L. – feature writer. And there you have a ready newspaper. All we need is the permit to publish. This will be gotten for us by Anatoly Aleks. [Aleksandrov]." I offered him a hundred rubles to go to Petersburg to apply for the permit. All those present were much pleased with this unexpected proposal and accepted their parts in it with satisfaction. Aleksandrov left for Petersburg the following day and a week later came with the permit to publish the newspaper *Russian Word*. 5 rubles per year [was the annual subscription price]. To be published free of censorship.[4] All concerned accepted the offer of employment.

II

Having received the right to publish during that difficult and oppressive time of the governorship of [Grand Duke] Sergei Aleksandrovich,[5] I asked Anton Pavlovich what were we to do with the newspaper. He said, undaunted, that we must let it destroy itself and only then would we be able to make it better. We decided to publish a politically reactionary paper for the time being. I collected capital of one hundred thousand [rubles] and invested it in the first year of publication. We began to publish an extremely reactionary paper in the *Moscow Bulletin (Moskovskie Vedomosti)* plant with the participation of Gringmut, Tikhomirov, Nikon of the Holy Trinity Laura, and others. F.N. Plevako also took part.[6]

Fifteen thousand copies of the newspaper were sold, the loss was over one hundred thousand. There was no more money. Aleksandrov went to the grand duke to ask for money. The latter, much satisfied with the newspaper, gave thirty-five thousand. In two weeks all the money was gone again. Aleksandrov went to the Tsar himself who, like the Grand Duke, gave thirty-five thousand. Back from Petersburg, Aleksandrov came directly to see me and said: "No, I am not going to edit any more. I am going to close the paper. You've dragged me into it and you can either get me out if you wish or I am going to close it but I am not going to waste the Tsar's money. It is such a waste of money." I asked him if a takeover could be arranged.[7] He undertook to arrange it. We went to Petrograd[8] to see Pobedonostsev. He met us in his office. He rose from his desk, shifting his glasses onto his forehead. He had a catalogue of Sytin's books in one hand and a red pencil in the other: "What is this pair I see coming?" he yelled, coming out and approaching the centre table upon which he placed the catalogue and the pencil. We sat down.

At that moment Sabler[9] came running in and asked K.P. to go to the next-door office for a moment on a very important matter. Pobedonostsev left. Aleksandrov picked up the catalogue from the table and put it in his pocket. He told me that he did it to keep us out of harm's way.[10] Pobedonostsev returned and sat down at the table. He had forgotten the catalogue and asked us, "What do you want?"

Aleksandrov said: "We have come to ask for permission for me to hand over the newspaper *Russian Word* to Sytin."

"What? To Sytin?" Pobedonostsev roared, "What in hell does Sytin need it for? Is he going to publish it? How is he going to do that? Surely, this will become just one more yellow-skirted whore on the boulevard.[11] There's enough of them without it. And you yourself are publishing the kind of a paper that has turned my janitor into a boor by reading it!"

"I beg you for help, K.P. I have no means to continue publishing it. I will stay as editor, so things will remain as they are now," [Aleksandrov said].

"Well, Sytin is hardly likely to steer the same course. This is not right. Yes, I regret now that I got mixed up in this business. Well, if the Grand Duke Sergei Aleksandrovich has no objections, you can carry on breeding readers for the gutter press. I won't interfere any more. Out you go."

Following this, we went to Soloviev[12] [at the] Main Administration [of Press Affairs] to transfer the permit. He was surprised that Pobedonostsev would have given his approval, but he gave us a preliminary permit, subject to the Grand Duke's confirmation. Upon return to Moscow I called on Anton Pavlovich Chekhov. I told him the end was near, but that Aleksandrov still remained, albeit only temporarily. We gathered at a large Moscow inn. It was a large group: from *Russian Bulletin, Russian Thought* [*Russkie Vedomosti, Russkaia Mysl'*], all associates and friends of A.P., over twenty people in all. We arranged for a small, merry celebration in a large private room of the Moscow inn. We made plans, talked a lot, drew up projects on how to run a newspaper that would be accessible, varied, and rich in content, truly one for the popular masses.

Everything went on merrily and well and in the morning Pastukhov put in a notice in the *Moscow Newssheet* (*Moskovskii Listok*) to the effect that Sytin had bought the *R.W.* and that an editorial conference had taken place on the previous day about what direction the *R.W.* was to take from now on and who was going to give that direction. This notice alarmed everyone. I was called to the Main Administration [of Press Affairs]. Soloviev told me: "You'll have to sign this paper or you won't get the permission to publish." This piece of paper bound me not to change the editor of the newspaper, otherwise it would be closed. I answered that I would not sign without first checking with K.P.

I went to Pobedonostsev. It was Sunday and he did not want to receive me. I said that the matter was extraordinarily urgent. In the end he received me, fuming angrily: "What do you want again?" I showed him Soloviev's order. He read the condition and burst out laughing, saying: "So what do you want from me?" I asked if I should sign under this condition. "But of course you can. Sign not one but three pieces of paper for him, let him use them for you-know-what. And tell the idiot that I had thought he was a legal expert who knew Russian laws. Surely neither he nor the Grand Duke make the laws, they apply to everyone. Say you have bought a house and the seller tells you: 'I am selling it to you under the condition that should you fire my janitor the house will revert to me and the sale will be null and void.' Surely, you'll just have a good laugh, sign this nonsense and kick out the janitor the next day. Who will own the house then? So, you may sign the paper to make Soloviev and the Grand Duke happy. You can change the editor. And, go, my good fellow, to Soloviev today and tell him what I've just said."

I asked for his permission to see Soloviev the next day. Pobedonostsev retorted angrily: "You are to go right away, you've been so insistent
to see me today, go and see him today as well. I am going to ask him
when you'll be there. If you try to cheat I will never receive you again."

I went back to Soloviev and recounted my conversation with Pobedonostsev, in an abbreviated form. He understood and approved all
that had been proposed, for the sake of peace. But he warned me that
there must be absolutely no changes over the period of one year.

Not one of those I subsequently recommended [for appointment as
editor] was approved by them. So I struggled on for over a year. Finally
I went to see Meshchersky. He was the Tsar's great henchman.[13] I went
to see him at the ladies' fashion show he organized at his house at
Easter time, and bought an expensive dress. I introduced myself and
said: I have a great problem, Prince, it is the newspaper."[14]

"Oh, yes, this has caused much talk. I would like to know what do
you need a newspaper for? My employee is writing for you. Why is this
paper causing so much trouble to you? Pray explain."

"Well, Prince, my business is growing. I need a lot of turnover
money. The business is still young. I don't make much money and it is
hard to work with just pennies. With a large numbers of subscribers I
have a free subscription policy and it is keeping me going.[15] Please give
me support with a leg up. I need an editor who would be sure to be
approved at the Main Administration. And you are the one that can
do it, your candidate would certainly be approved."

"Listen, this is very interesting and I understand your problem. You
are not causing any harm to the realm by your publications. You are
publishing great books. Why shouldn't I help you? I think I will. Take
Aderkas,[16] if later on you find him unsuitable, move him to something
less important."

So Meshchersky and I came to an agreement. The old man went to
the Main Administration and his protégé was confirmed as editor.
Another year passed in this way. Aderkas replaced Aleksandrov, but
then he also had to be replaced by Kiselev.[17] And then it took still
another year before we were able to get our man Blagov.[18] Dear Anton
Pavlovich never saw the newspaper acquiring a human face. It had
struggled for seven years of painful agony. It was Blagov who, as the
editor, brought new life into the *Russian Word*. [However] I had to

strengthen the newspaper and so I went to Odessa to see Doroshevich.

My old friend met me and I said to him: "Well, now I am also publishing a newspaper."[19]

"What, a newspaper? What do you need a newspaper for?"

I told him about A.P. Chekhov's dream. The hardest part was over. [Doroshevich said]:

"You need help, how else can you manage? That is Sytin for you. His own problems are not enough. He's found himself some more."

"It is a tough job, Vlas Mikhailovich. Would you write articles for me from Odessa?"

"Okay, I am ready, but it still won't be the same as working in Moscow."

"You should look at things with greater optimism. It wasn't so long ago that Sytin had published nothing but woodcuts and now almost all the [Moscow] University is working for us, while the middle and primary schools buy our textbooks. Why couldn't we publish a newspaper as well? You yourself, V.M., understand that Sytin has been prompted to go for a newspaper by an imagination other than his own. It was A.P. Chekhov who persuaded me and constantly prodded me about it."

Doroshevich introduced me to V.V. Novrotsky, the publisher of *Odessa Newssheet* (*Odesskii Listok*) who asked:

"What did you come to see me for? It is not to ask V.M. to come to Moscow? Don't hurt us, you mustn't do that."

"Not at all, V.V. I am just a little publisher. I came here to learn from you and from V.M."

"Then go on learning but don't drag our Vlas away from us."

III

Vlas was an exceptionally gifted feuilleton[20] writer. After we had gone through all our reminiscences and good wishes I managed to persuade him to write for us, from Odessa for the time being.

My situation did not improve all that quickly and my editorial office at Old Square was still something of a lame duck. The time was not yet ripe to put it on a large scale, it was necessary to move very gradually and carefully. There was a talented feuilleton writer working for the *Petersburg Gazette* (*Peterburgskaia Gazeta*) and [its] supplement, *Petersburg Newssheet* (*Peterburgskii Listok*), by the name of Dianov. I went to see him and made him an offer: "What would you say if I asked you to work for us? Prince Meshchersky is helping me, lending me his editor – you know him. And your talent is being wasted here."

"This is indeed so and you are right in making me an offer. This is my salvation. I believe that you'll do anything for me. You know, I am paid fifteen thousand a year by the publications I am now working for. How much are you going to offer me?"

"The most important thing for me is not the money but the work you'll perform for me."

"Ivan Dmitrievich, this is a new undertaking for you. You'll have to develop the business. Your newspaper will do something that no one has done before. We are aware of this. Let me work for you. I know that all your employees work in an exceptionally good environment. I'll give you any guarantee you wish to perform whatever function we may agree upon, according to your directives. I shall be a happy man."

We concluded the agreement and the conditions. I gave him money to establish himself in Moscow and we began to work together. After three months with my instruction and his monumental drinking I gave him another twenty thousand for the return trip to Petrograd. In this disastrous manner ended the early career of my new employee who was invited at the same time as Aderkas.

Upon my return from Odessa I was horrified by the need to remove Dianov and Aderkas. This, besides the terrible emotional suffering, cost me forty thousand rubles in extraneous expenses. There is no business as vulnerable to panics and dangerous folly as the newspaper business. One has to have strong nerves and confidence in the undertaking.

I frequently went to Petersburg. A new establishment, the Monarchists' Club [was inaugurated] on Troitskaia Street. I was invited to come and speak at the consecration of the new location. [There I met] my young new priest,[21] an admirer of our new booklets by Leskov and Tolstoy. He distributed them in his parish of St Spiridon during the sermon, by the thousands, at one kopeck each.

He had been invited to assist at a prayer service and asked me to come. I thanked him with gratitude and went. The whole star-studded world [was there?]. Metropolitan Antonii conducted the service, together with our little priest. Another priest made a beautiful speech. After the service I came up to him and said: "Father Grigory, give me a copy of your sermon for the *Russian Word*. He replied that he had already given it away – to Komarov for the newspaper *World* (*Svet*). I insisted, telling him that I was asking him to work for us. I went to see him in the morning with the same offer. I took his article and at that moment began our friendship and collaboration on the newspaper *R.W.* of Grigory Spiridonovich Petrov.

At the same time the *Russia* (*Rossiia*)²² was set up in Petersburg. Amfiteatrov and Doroshevich united in one newspaper, with magnificent success.

I was just a little martyr biding my time. My little paper fed on crumbs from the table. I was not forgotten and no one avoided me. I was accepted by all as one of their own. I visited Piter.²³ I used to dine at Cubat's²⁴ with Doroshevich and Amfiteatrov.²⁵

Before he began to edit the newspaper, Amfiteatrov saw me in Moscow and talked about a great newspaper. I, of course, was only able to wish him great success and did not even dream that I might be able to continue to be part of such a powerful group of men of affairs given Amfiteatrov's appetite. I had known this *Novovremenets*²⁶ for a long time. And then *Russia* came out. [It had required] an outstanding amount of capital. Every worthwhile and important journalist in Petersburg came to work as one big newspaper family. Amfiteatrov cast his net far and wide and ran the show on a grand scale. I did not lose contact with these two stars.

I visited their editorial office and, most of all, their printing presses while they were working. I would go there for supper and, often, at dawn to fish for sturgeon … at the point of St Basil's island. [I enjoyed] merry conversation and [heard] much of what an editor has to know and learn. The future of *Russia* was not always stable. The business grew and with it the appetite [of the editors]. They were making significant progress. [But]the income could not keep pace with the need. [However] it was considered criminal to worry Uncle Amfisha.²⁷ And so everything ended in a monumental collapse of the newspaper.

By dramatic coincidence I arrived in Petersburg on the day the famous feuilletton [appeared]. In the morning I went to the telephone exchange, straight from the train. There I was handed the newspaper *Russia*: "I.D., read today's story."²⁸ I read it and couldn't believe my own eyes. Right away I went to Doroshevich's apartment. When I came in he was running around the room in panic and said to me: "Have you read it?" "Yes I know [already]."

"What am I to do?" he yelled. "What has Amfishka done? The newspaper is finished. Dead in the water. And he will be sent to Eniseiskaia guberniia."[29]

"Yes, most likely, they've dispatched him this morning."

"They've sent his overcoat after him. He didn't have time to put it on."[30]

"Well and how about you?"

"I am going abroad right away. I don't wish to stay here one day longer. Listen, I.D., be a friend, do me a special favour. Give me ten thousand. I'll sell you the full collection of my books. Let's draw up the legal agreement right away."[31]

"Listen to me, Vlas Mikhailovich, what do you want ten thousand for today? You are going abroad for two or three months, or even less, it would require two thousand per month. You need six thousand. I have that much on me. Take it now, without selling the full collection. You were offering Novrotsky your Sakhalin sketches for four thousand. He refused. I will take them off you for these six thousand. And everything will be in order. Now go and come back soonest.[32]

He rushed up to me, embraced and kissed me warmly. "God has sent you to me in such a grave and dangerous moment of peril. I felt so bad that I was ready to end my own life. Well, now let's go for lunch. We'll go to get the passport first and then on to Cubat's."

At Cubat's we continued our conversation about our future work together.

"What has your little paper to offer me, what is it good for?"

"It is gathering its strength. This is not the *Russia*. It cannot go ahead in leaps and bounds. When you come back you and I will slowly make it take off. Even you will lose your pepper sitting in one spot."

"Yes, [but] you should make it a serious newspaper enterprise. Don't sit waiting in one place for the whole year."

"Let us gather a working group of newspaper employees. You are a master at this; help me to do it. And you, yourself, can be away, abroad. We must have a firm skeleton of two or three strong and seri-

ous men. The rest would be working bees. They'll have to gather nec-
tar assiduously and well. I need the main core. In your *Russia* there
was no such core, but a large revolutionary nest of all colours. This has
taught me something. And I think that you have learned something.
Your job is to write, write, and then write."

[I told him:] "In order to do it better you have to be free and illu-
minate and renew your material. To do this you have to be everywhere.
And to know all that is best. This is what we'll do. Whatever you do
and wherever you are, whether in Russia or abroad, the newspaper
R.W. must accompany you in spirit like your own son. And it undertakes to pay you four thousand rubles per month, whether you write
anything or not. It does not matter where you happen to be. It would
not change anything if you were to sit in the editorial office and work
there. Even if you produce one piece in four months it will be more
talked about than if you were to write every day. But then, one cannot
afford to lose the reader. To have too many breaks would present a
danger both to the author and to the newspaper."

And so Doroshevich and I became lifetime friends. But one curious
thing happened. In Petersburg, in 1905, the year of frightful distur-
bances in the printing plants, Propper [33] enticed Doroshevich to come
over to him. He offered him six thousand, promised him a lot, and he
[Doroshevich] agreed. This was the time when *R.W.* flourished. He
stayed with Propper for over a month, did hardly any work, but was
considered employed. But he couldn't take it and came back to *R.W.*
in a friendly and congenial manner. When I recall now all the details
concerning periodical publications, I think of all the worries and
alarms they caused! Such jolts can be recommended as a remedy
against apathy. Like no other, this business teaches one to react and to
have good eye for details and to work at tremendous speed and to do
this every day, better and with more talent than others [the competi-
tors]. This business excites enthusiasm for the passions and excitement
of this work, which becomes even more addicting. The Japanese war
came.[34] I needed a principal war correspondent accompanied by people who would have access to official dispatches of government military information. We went to Testov's tavern[35] to talk about it.
Somebody had to go immediately. We awaited the manifesto,[36] me,

Doroshevich and our permanent collaborator G.S. Petrov. Doroshevich turned to me and said: "This matter requires a lot of money. It is
for Sytin to decide who to hire and how much to pay him."

I said: "Send V.I. Nemirovich,[37] even though he is old – he is well-
remembered from the last war. Provided he is willing to work!" Then
I turned to Petrov: "You are a Petersburg man, be so kind as to go and
see him yourself. You are his friend; ask him to help us and to leave
soonest. We will give him five thousand a month, with one thousand
five hundred advance upon his departure." Doroshevich was so pleased
that he clapped his hands: "Bravo, Sytin! This is wonderful. Grigory
Spiridonovich, this is a wonderful and pleasant mission. What do you
think?" He replied: "I have nothing to add. Nemirovich and I will be
happy to drink to the success and I am leaving for Petersburg tonight
at 11."

And two days later Nemirovich and Petrov were in Moscow and
signed the agreement. And drank here at Testov's to a propitious
departure from Petersburg. Doroshevich said: "V.I., we were sitting
here two days ago. Did G.S. tell you when he came to Petersburg what
Sytin had said?"

· Nemirovich answered: "He said to me: we invite you to be a correspondent of the R.W. We'll pay five thousand rubles per month and a
one thousand five hundred advance. I picked up my hat and came here.
We are a great team, gentlemen."

This gave the initial impetus to the success of R.W. The war was
on. The well-organized [war] correspondence laid the groundwork
for the success. Nemirovich had been instructed not to worry about
money and to send everything by wire. He did his best and bravely
went for broke and also, in addition, organized three more war correspondents with the same duties. And they were all very successful.
The despatches of the R.W. met with great success, both in Russia and
in Europe. Simultaneously expansion of the printing press and further
modifications were taking place. Until now, it had been all dreams,
but now they were coming true.

The dreams dated from Chekhov's time. [I asked him:] "Dear Anton
Pavlovich, where do you think we should place the editorial office of
the future newspaper when fate decrees that it becomes great? What
is the right place for the editorial office?"

[Chekhov said:] "I wish it to be in Moscow, on Tverskaia Street, the best street in Moscow. Put the office in the centre of it. And you'll be in the heart of Moscow, summer and winter, night and day."[38] He blessed this idea of ours.

His other equally serious concern was to open rural schools in Russia – as many as were necessary – and to teach every single person to read and write. [He used to say:] "Textbooks are no less important. [than newspapers]. It will all come. The most important thing is that all children learn to read and write and that there are more, cheap books."

That's how the dream was born to provide schools and teaching resources.

5

ACQUIRING THE COMPLETE
WORKS OF L.N. TOLSTOY

.It is not generally known that Sytin paid the full amount asked by the
Tolstoy family for the rights to the first posthumous edition of the great
writer's works. He also paid the asking price for the unsold copies of
Tolstoy's already published works in the possession of his widow, Sofia
Andreevna. This chapter includes three somewhat different versions
by Sytin of the negotiations leading to his purchase, each of which provides additional details about the negotiations. While he took exception to the tactics of the negotiators from St Petersburg, he parlayed
their actions into a triumph.

Leo Tolstoy had named his daughter Aleksandra Lvovna as nomi-
nal executrix of his will but V.G. Chertkov was to be the actual executor. Both were determined to realize the stipulations that Tolstoy had
included in a last, secret will. He had made fundamental changes in
his bequest: the lands that were part of the estate of Yasnaia Poliana
were to be distributed to the peasants on the estate without charge and
his works were to become common property, meaning that anyone
could publish them without payment of copyright fees. His widow,
Sofia Andreevna, knew that these requirements would impoverish her
four sons, who were already living in penury. The complex negotiations that followed pitted the widow and most of the family against
Chertkov and Aleksandra Lvovna.

Tolstoy's grandson describes the difficulties over the inheritance of
the great writer: "The family atmosphere had become truly unbearable by 1907 when V.G. Chertkov returned from his exile in England."[1]

Chertkov claimed "special status as a close friend and disciple, and obtained a right of access to the writer's study which previously only Sofia Andreevna had had ... he insisted that Tolstoy write a new will in secret from his family. On 22 July 1910 Tolstoy signed a secret will stipulating that his youngest daughter, Alexandra Lvovna, was his only heiress." According to the will, "All Tolstoy's literary output became public property, while Chertkov got the exclusive right to be its publisher and editor." Aleksandra Lvovna (Sasha) also felt it was important to carry out another stipulation in the will: "If any money is left after the first publication of the works, it would be nice to buy out Yasnaia Poliana from mama and the brothers and give it to the peasants." Sasha interpreted the directive as follows: in order to maximize the financial advantages for her mother, she would sell the rights to publish an edition of the collected works and also sell the unsold copies of Tolstoy's already published works that were stored in a warehouse. The task now became to find a publisher who was ready to pay Sasha's prices.

The Tolstoy family invited the well-known attorney N.K. Muraviev to manage the project.[2] He called a meeting of family members and Chertkov to decide how to proceed. This group invited two publishers to consider several options as to how the works might be sold and published in such a way as to yield 300,000 rubles to be used to purchase the Tolstoy lands from the estate for distribution to his peasants. The family group, through Muraviev, asked the two invited publishers, *Niva* from St Petersburg and Sytin from Moscow, to negotiate an agreement that would lead to the participation of both in the publishing project. Only the involvement of two publishers, it was thought, would make it possible to meet the financial requirements. The two were asked to meet, negotiate, and return with a joint proposal. Neither was to contact Muraviev or the others independently. The *Niva* representatives tried to out-fox Sytin. It was at this point that Sytin showed his mastery of negotiation.

First Version

L.N. Tolstoy has died. His family, that is, his children and wife, Sofia Andreevna, wanted to fulfil his wish and to cede the rights to publish the first edition of the complete works of Lev Nikolayevich.[3] The whole family, their close friends, and admirers of Lev Nikolaevich got down to preparing and editing the huge volume of both printed and manuscript materials, without remuneration. The condition was that the publisher wishing to be the first to publish [the collection] edited by the committee, in whatever quantity he might choose, upon conclusion of the agreement would pay the sum of 300,000 rubles for the purchase of land belonging to [the estate of Yasnaia Poliana] to be transferred to the peasants. This preliminary legal task was entrusted to a close friend of L.N. and his family, Nikolai Konstantinovich Muraviev. He then, together with V.G. Chertkov, entered into negotiations with two publishing houses: *Niva* in Saint Petersburg and Sytin in Moscow.[4]

In addition to publishing the collected works, the prospective publisher was obliged to take over all the remainders held by Sofia Andreevna: all of L.N.'s books published by herself that had not been sold. All these stored remainders were valued at 146,000 rubles. This payment was to be made simultaneously with that of the 300,000. Two Rozener brothers [who were sent by the A.F. Marks company[5]] from the periodical *Niva*, I.D. Sytin, V.G. Chertkov, and Alexandra Lvovna gathered for detailed negotiations.

The following was proposed to us, the prospective buyers: the first option: one of us would buy everything and pay the 446,000 or, by mutual agreement, Marks would publish through *Niva* and Sytin would produce a superior quality low-priced edition. The two were to agree among themselves as to who paid how much [as long as] the heirs received the total sum of 446,000 rubles. The allocation between ourselves and Marks began as follows: the *Collected Works of Tolstoy* were to appear as a supplement to *Niva*, free [of] charge. Sytin [was] to publish the *Collected Works* as well, at 10 rubles for fifteen volumes and, in addition, a ten-volume superior quality edition, at 40 rubles, by subscription. We were given one week to negotiate the deal between ourselves under the condition that neither of us enter into [outside?] negotiations that week, before the new, mutually acceptable agreement, was arrived at. "Marks" felt that our initial offer of fifteen volumes for 10 rubles was not advantageous and suggested not less than 25. He would even agree to 40 [rubles]. We were to pay half-and-half, 150,000 each [for the collected works], with Sytin taking the remnants for 146,000 rubles. I could not agree to this. A week later I discovered that "Marks" had submitted his suggestions to Chertkov. I found this strange but indirectly pleasing.

Our scheduled meeting opened with the question: what have you decided? I declared that our gentleman's agreement had been violated. We had not arrived at any agreement and, besides, it had come to my notice that G. Rozener had sent his offer to Chertkov at Teliatniki.[6] I therefore asked those assembled to decide what action to take: which one of us remains as a purchaser and which one is rejected. This was presumably what was implied by Rozener's offer. V.G. [Chertkov] then said that *Niva* preferred to take over the whole deal. I thanked those present, expressing my regrets that such decisions were being made unilaterally, not in a gentlemanly way. I thanked them for their consultation and left. Four days later I heard that all the conditions of the agreement and payment had been drawn up and a date had been fixed for the agreement to be signed in the presence of a notary public. But on the appointed day the purchasers failed to appear at the notary's office – they had both left for St Petersburg and the deal blew up in a matter of a few days.

Sytin's Letters to N.K. Muraviev

The times when you, Nikolai Konstantinovich, and I used to meet so frequently and boisterously are long gone. In cold weather, in a snowstorm, you in a heavy fur coat and I in a lighter one, we would drive to Teliatniki, where Aleksandra Lvovna and V.G. Chertkov lived. After the passing of L.N. we considered the problem: a complete edition of [the works of] Tolstoy had to be produced: this was what the family and Chertkov wanted.[7] Such an undertaking demanded a great deal of serious planning. It was suggested to us that we should raise 300,000 rubles for one edition of the complete collected works, with the stipulation that anyone could have the copyright since the author had renounced it. Lev Nikolaevich had declared his works to be common property, consequently it was necessary to produce the edition as cheaply as possible and to pay 300,000 for the purchase of the lands [that made up the estate of] Yasnaia Poliana and to offer them as a gift to the Yasnaia Poliana peasants. V.G. [Chertkov] had a good,

dependable partner in Marks. *Niva* brought the information [and inti-
mated?] that they definitely wanted to purchase [make the deal], but
there was no copyright. We would hardly be able to carry the deal.
300,000 roubles [were required] for the right to publish and 146,000
rubles for the remainders in storage at Sofia Andreevna's. It was therefore decided to examine the possibilities with Marks and Sytin, offering them both editions and leaving them to divide [the job] between
themselves according to their capabilities.

It was decided to convene a committee in Moscow and to bring in
both publishers, Marks and Sytin. Marks sent in two fine fellows, the
Rozeners, and Sytin came by himself. They told us to decide among
ourselves, within a week, if we wanted to publish jointly, dividing the
job between ourselves, the sum [price] remaining fixed. We decided to
consider uniting [the project] over the course of one week. We met. I
sat and watched my competitors [who appeared to be] competent
and serious businessmen. I asked them to tell me what they wanted.
"We want to produce, as a supplement to *Niva*, the full collection of
L.N. over two years, free of charge, and are prepared to pay for this
150,000 rubles." They asked me what my offer was. I said that I
wanted to publish the full collection of works, in one year, in between
ten and fifteen volumes, [to sell] for 10 rubles. I would also pay
150,000 rubles and take the remainders for 146,000 rubles. [In addi-
tion] I would produce a beautiful superior-quality edition at 40 rubles
for ten volumes.

"No," they said, "we don't agree. We can only allow you to publish
for no less than 25 rubles for the edition, and have nothing against a
40 ruble one." "But this doesn't suit me either, for no one would buy
the expensive edition from me [said I], I am therefore asking you: let's
solve the problem in a simpler way: You take all and pay [for it]. This
would be better and simpler." "No," they said, "we don't want to
solve it this way. Let us negotiate."

"But you don't want to give me a different offer," I said, "and I cannot change mine. With my [proposed] apportioning we are equal and
our interests are covered. I am happy to be working with you for this
makes it easier for me: If I took everything it would not work out for
me unless I produce a supplement, which I do not have."

Second Version

Greetings Nikolai Konstantinovich!

It has been a long time since we've seen each other. How interesting was our encounter yesterday: all of us Tolstoyan followers were in attendance.[8] We marked the fortieth anniversary of the launching of the Mediator. We have worked together well. After Lev Nikolaevich's death, his family and wife, Sofia Andreevna, with his friend V.G. Chertkov were obliged to fulfil the wish of the deceased: to collect all the literary material for a complete edition of all his works, in full. It was then proposed to you, Nikolai Konstantinovich, that, in view of your friendly relations with the whole family of the departed, you would take it upon yourself to execute all the practical and legal work concerning the testament and to sort out the extremely complicated practical [financial] affairs. All the works of L.N. belonged to everyone, there was no problem of property [ownership], but it was necessary to produce the financial means in order to leave all the land of Yasnaia Poliana to the peasants in the memory of the departed. The purpose of publishing the complete works was to obtain the sum of 300,000 rubles to carry out this important transaction. This has cost you much work and dedication. Vladimir Grigorievich and Alexandra Lvovna are dear, good, and warm-hearted people, but [they are] babes in the woods when it comes to practical business. You were the only one who devoted yourself, without a break, to the execution of this important task, which was carried out boldly and successfully under your direction. You were the one who gathered us all at Teliatniki. There we debated what was to be done and how, to get the complete posthumous edition of Lev Nikolaevich produced free of charge [to be sold] cheaply or as a supplement, but it was necessary to raise the 300,000 for the peasants in the memory of the Great Apostle and friend of the people.

A committee was formed of three persons: V.G. Chertkov, A.L. Tolstaia, and N.K. Muraviev. According to the plan worked out by yourself and V.G., you invited us – the Rozeners representing *Niva* and Sytin – and gave us the task of publishing the full collection of L.N. Tolstoy, with all its posthumous supplements, in one edition. We were to pay the 300,000 and, besides, [take over] all that was left stored at Sofia Andreevna's. Her publications were valued at 146,000 rubles, the total sum thus being 446,000 rubles. *Niva* and Sytin were to devise the means to achieve this. We were to give you the answer as to how we were to divide it between us and who was to undertake to publish what. For this we were given one week, at the end of which we were to meet at Loskutnaia Inn. *Niva*'s and Sytin's job was to divide [the project] into parts and [to decide] who was to pay for what. *Niva* offered [to publish] a supplement to *Niva*, free of charge, and to pay 150,000 roubles. Sytin would assume the right to publish the complete collected works in full, in fifteen volumes for the price of 10 rubles, and to publish a superior quality edition in ten volumes, [at] 40 rubles, and to pay 150,000 rubles and would [further] agree to assume the remainders of [at] 146,000. The Rozeners did not want to allow Sytin a 10 ruble edition, but only a 25 ruble [one]. Because of this, our agreement fell through. However, it was suggested that both parties refrain from announcing this before the deadline and not make any offers to the heirs until the meeting. This took place one week later. Nikolai Konstantinovich opened the meeting and asked us to report our decision. I said that it had come to my knowledge that V.G. Rozener had made a written offer, contrary to the agreement, therefore let the committee declare its decision as to its choice of the purchaser. V.G. [Rozener] declared that *Niva* offered to purchase and publish the edition on its own. Chertkov agreed to this. I excused myself with thanks and left the meeting.

Five days later Nikolai Konstantinovich invited me to call on Alexandra Lvovna concerning the edition. I went at the appointed time. There I met everyone: Alexandra Lvovna, and Nikolai Konstantinovich who said to me: "Do you, Ivan Dmitrievich, know that the scheme concerning the sale of the edition of Tolstoy has fallen through? Our buyers have bolted for St Petersburg. The deal is off. The conditions had been written down, all that remained was to sign all the papers at the notary's and to collect the money. Would you like to see all the papers regarding this final deal?"

I picked up the papers and read them, everything had been worked out in such detail, with all the potential legal complications foreseen in such clear detail, that I could not raise any objections. Rozener and Nikolai Konstantinovich had done a perfect job. I then asked what was wanted of me. N.K. said: "You have to tell us whether or not you would agree to purchase and publish under these conditions on your own?" I asked all those present: "Would you allow me to sign these conditions right away and to pay according to the terms established in the contract?"

They were all amazed and overjoyed by this pleasant and easy solution of the deal. They shook my hand in a friendly manner and I was no less pleased to have encountered, at no cost [to myself] those very good men of business who had done all the bargaining for free and had got very good terms and then threw everything away. I signed all the papers there and then and we closed the deal at the notary's office the next day. Everyone was glad of this happy ending.

The immense task of publishing the complete collected works of L.N. has begun. For the family and their close friends, especially Nik. Konst., the execution of this task meant having to systematize and edit the materials for immediate publication, by the time agreed upon, of the collected works, in two editions: the cheapest in fifteen or more volumes, costing no more than 10 rubles and the superior quality one, a luxury, bound, large-size edition, ten or twelve volumes for 40 rubles. All this was admirably carried out in the course of one year. The reading public received a cheap edition of the complete collected works. The sum of 300,000 rubles was paid. The land was given over to the peasants and the remainders held by Sofia Andreevna liquidated against a payment of 146,000 rubles.[9]

6

ENCOUNTERS WITH P.A. STOLYPIN[1]
AND OTHERS

Sytin's meetings with the Tsar's officials were never pleasant occasions, as he clearly indicated, but he needed their support, or at least neutrality, and his 1911 interview with the last truly statesmanlike minister of imperial Russia took place on the publisher's initiative. It happened at the time that Sytin was trying to create a national network of newspapers linked by his own telephone and telegraph lines, provisioned by his own paper and machine factories, and supplied with world news by a syndicated wire service. He was negotiating with the largest western European newspapers and news services over a European wire service. His first step would be to create a new paper in St Petersburg. The support of the all-powerful president of the Council of Ministers, Stolypin, was necessary and Sytin decided to take the bull by the horns, despite his usual and often-mentioned fear and dislike of the arrogant aristocracy.

I

A.A. Makarov,[2] the assistant minister of the Interior and a personal acquaintance, told me that P.A. Stolypin was very dissatisfied with me on account of my publishing activities.

This was unexpected news to me. But, realizing, as so often happens in these matters, how much depends on personal ill-will and tall-tales by persons who do not balk at slander and gossip, I asked Makarov if he would arrange a meeting for me with the minister. I thought that in the course of a personal conversation, I could dispel any misunderstandings and, perhaps, dissipate the slanders, if there were any.

Makarov promised to arrange everything and, actually, I received P.A. Stolypin's telegram very soon in Moscow. He summoned me to a 2 o'clock personal meeting.

I confess that the [forthcoming] meeting somewhat disturbed me. What tales had been told to him and what in particular had displeased him? Experience in life had led me to believe that ministers rarely became dissatisfied on their own: usually someone had been "reporting" to them and only after a "report" did they feel either gracious or dissatisfied.

My ticket for the meeting with P.A. Stolypin was the twelfth, but for some reason they did not summon me when my turn came. "Why was this?" I said to myself. "Numbers fifteen, and twenty, and thirty went into Stolypin's study and still they did not summon me." Finally, when the reception room was completely empty except for me, they called me: "Come in, sir."

Stolypin was receiving in the spacious study of Alexander II. He sat at a small table but even seated he dominated the room by his impressive stature and commanding figure. His black-bearded, pale face looked a little tired.

"Mr Sytin? Please sit down." The minister waved his hand at an armchair and I sat down.

"You, I know, have a very large business in publications for the people."

"Yes, Your Excellency, my business is large and very difficult."

"There have been complaints about you. Your business is large but it is too confused. You play the liberal, but it is precisely because you are a publisher for the people that special caution is required, so that you don't corrupt the Russian soul."

"Your Excellency, your information comes from prejudiced people. I run my business with great prudence and am more than cautious. I understand my task simply and I go about it simply, without any hidden motives. Our people are ignorant, they need knowledge and I am trying to give them inexpensive and useful manuals and textbooks. If Your Excellency would be so kind as to take a look at our catalogue, you will see what our work is like."

"All right, I will look over your catalogue, but you should understand that information for the people ought to be clean and not destructive."

From these words, I understood that he did not feel greatly displeased with me and that whatever report he might have received about our work, it was not too malicious.

"I will be glad to present Your Excellency all the materials and plans of my company."

"Well, this is fine. To tell the truth, I have work for you; I'd like to use your great experience to help in spreading books on village agriculture among the people. Our program of independent farmsteads requires useful books for the people.[3] By the way, in your newspaper, our program has been criticized and rather sharply ... How do you look upon this matter?'

"I, Your Excellency, on this point do not share the opinions of my paper. I view individual farmsteads with the greatest satisfaction. I myself am a peasant and I know what the peasant needs."

"Yes? I am happy to hear it. This means that we share the same opinion? So, let's work together. We will give the peasant a good selection of books: a series of manuals on agriculture, on trades, and on all cottage industries. How about it? How do you look upon it? I find that it is high time we organized specialized reading-rooms in the countryside for peasants; they would have all the required technical manuals and samples of machines and tools. In this respect, we are very far behind."

I admit that I absolutely did not expect to hear these words from the stern minister, who the entire press was describing as the emperor's favourite, put in office to promote the interests of the landed gentry. People who are only concerned about their own group interests do not speak this way. In any event, in Stolypin's tone of voice I felt a love of Russia, of the whole of Russia and not just of his own class.

"Your Excellency, you are speaking of something that for a long time has been our dream. For the last ten years, if not more, we have all been waiting for the government's support, or at least its permission to allow others to do what it was not going to do ... And suddenly you wish to turn attention to the urgent needs of the of the countryside ... This is such a good cause that I would be pleased to give your

Excellency all the assistance within my powers ... And not only by my work but even by material contributions ... I believe in the ultimate success of farmsteads; I know what independence from the commune means to the peasant, and if the peasant's hands are untied, and he becomes his own master, then the entire practice of working the land, the whole rural economy, will change. And the example of a successful farm will be infectious ... I know this business very well; I also am the son of a peasant. If along with this there will be peasant reading rooms, if the book, which has been hidden from the peasant under lock and key, finally, comes to him, the Russian village will be unrecognizable after ten years."

"This means that we are of one opinion? I am very pleased. Let us pull together."

Our conversation ended in a different tone than it began.

And a week later one of Stolypin's officials, P.P. Zubovsky,[4] came to me in Moscow and asked if I would give him my program for future publications for the people.

I showed him a whole series of catalogues and drew his attention to the fact that three-quarters of the books for the proposed reading rooms were already printed and that it was only necessary to add textbooks for adults and to select good sets of books on cottage industries.

Zubovsky, in turn, reminded me about the impending anniversary of the peasant Emancipation and of the War of 1812 and asked me what we were planning to do to mark these anniversaries. We had also been giving thought to this, and we had been working out a program of anniversary [commemorative] editions on a wide and even grand scale (we had fifty professors already working on this project). So it only remained for us to plan a series of very cheap popular brochures and pictures.

From the talk with Zubovsky, I received a general impression that Stolypin had taken to heart our conversation about peasant reading rooms and that his very broad plans were already ripening.

Unfortunately, however, P.A. Stolypin soon undertook his fateful trip to Kiev[5] for the festivities, and there took place something that he had foreseen for a long time and had written in his testament: "I am to be buried in the place where they kill me."

II

A.S. Suvorin

A.S. Suvorin (1834–1912) was a journalist and then editor and publisher of the most important daily newspaper, *Novoe Vremia*. The paper was the voice of Russian conservatism in the final three decades of the nineteenth century. Sytin entered the newspaper world at the time when Suvorin was old and embittered by many tragedies in his family life and a feud with his older son, who had opened a rival newspaper, *Rossiia*. Sytin's dealings were with Suvorin senior. He regarded the old man with a mixture of admiration for his business acumen and compassion because of his loneliness. In Sytin's eyes Suvorin was a living reminder of the old adage about money not being able to buy happiness.

I had no business connections with the elder Suvorin, but we naturally knew one another and frequently saw one another. Aleksei Sergeevich liked it very much when I dropped in to see him and he liked to come see me when he was in Moscow. He used to call me by phone in the morning.

"Come over, Ivan Dmitrievich! I, as usual, am staying at the Slavianskii Bazaar. The weather today is quite marvellous and I would like to go to the Novodevichy Monastery, to visit our friends in the cemetery.[6]

"I am ready to go with you. It has been a long time since I have been there. I will call for my automobile and we will go."

At the Slavianskii Bazaar Suvorin always stayed in a large and comfortable suite, the very same one in which Pobedonostsev always stayed.

"How is it, Aleksei Sergeevich, that you and Pobedonostsev are partial to this suite? There must be something behind this." Suvorin laughed heartily.

"Don't be malicious, Ivan Dmitrievich. It is a matter of habit. A man becomes accustomed to things and rooms."

We got into the automobile and drove to Novodevichy where many acquaintances and close friends were buried, including our mutual friends – A.P. Chekhov and A.I. Ertel'.

The cemetery was a cozy, peaceful, and heart-warming place.[7]

The small but stylish tombstone to Chekhov reminded me of a Roerich picture: the deserted north and "eternal calm" seemed to flow from it.[8]

I fell on my knees and crossed myself three times, thinking of the unforgettable Anton Pavlovich. Being close to his grave reminded me of so many things and I felt moved, as though I was holding his warm, friendly hand.

Suvorin also prayed with tender emotion. He had known and loved Chekhov as no one else and, although Chekhov had turned away from him, now, at his grave, the old man forgot the bitterness of the past difference of opinion and again offered the love that had been rejected.[9] It was clear from Suvorin's old, grey-bearded face what place Chekhov still had in his heart.

We visited other graves. We were melancholy, recalled a lot, and, as always happens in cemeteries, only good memories came to our mind. From the cemetery we went to a restaurant on Sparrow Hills[10] to talk about our good friends; we found a table where the whole Novodevichy Monastery and the cemetery lay before us as in the palm of our hand. But we were still under the influence of the visit to Chekhov's grave and did not feel like talking.

We spoke about the pretty, green unused land that lay along the Moscow River and were surprised that such a huge and lovely place had fallen to kitchen gardens.

"Well, there, Aleksei Sergeevich, let's move Moscow to this side. Look at the beauty that is being lost: here are the Sparrow Hills, and the Moscow river, and the Novodevichy Monastery."

"Yes, Moscow is growing absurdly, it is not expanding on this side ... We are uncivilized people and do not understand the value of beauty ... We do not even see how rich we are. On this picturesque place we have planted cabbages."

We fell silent as we began to eat. I mentioned that not long ago when I had been in Petersburg, Suvorin had not received me, and I asked him why.

"Tell, me, Aleksei Sergeevich, what was happening with you when I dropped in and you did not receive me, were you ill?"

"No, my friend ... I was ill in spirit ... I had attacks of fear and breakdown ... Something was tormenting me. Those days were terrible for me ... I was afraid ... painfully afraid. Everything told me that the subscribers to *New Times* were becoming fewer in number, that they were turning their backs on me and that I stood alone to face the ruin of my business. You cannot imagine these oppressive fears and doubts ..."

These words took me aback.

"Dear God! Is it possible that such a superficial matter as subscriptions could create such icy horror in your spirit?"

"You are still young ... You have not seen anything ... Someday you will understand more ..." I understood, however, that Suvorin was not joking; he was serious about his nightmares. Maybe there was a direct psychological connection between his involuntary confession and our visit to Chekhov's grave. Chekhov did not part with the old man for nothing, on a whim; he left on principle. And it could have been that Suvorin felt terribly alone and unhappy after this break. It could have seemed to him, immediately after his break with Chekhov, that everything was falling away from him, and that each subscription was for him a test and examination of his whole life:

"Will they turn their back on me or won't they? Have they fathomed my fears or haven't they?"

Of course, money played no role in this matter: this was an examination of the spirit, a test of his self-esteem. Prior to the break with Chekhov, Suvorin had never undertaken such an examination.

This is why the old man underwent such torture every year when *New Times* conducted its subscription campaign.

"Will they turn their back on me or won't they?"

This is why he shut himself up in his office alone, received no one and saw no one.

During these days each year the old man awaited his sentence ...

III
Rasputin

Sytin's description of the Moscow attitude toward Rasputin is very eloquent; moreover it shows how effective the opposition campaign against the imperial couple had been. Rasputin's influence on political life was much less than what was attributed to him by those who wanted to discredit the imperial couple. While the St Petersburg press was silent and the court circles limited themselves to gossip, in Moscow the opposition was more vocal – it was a Moscow newspaper that published an account of an orgy at a restaurant during which Rasputin allegedly behaved even worse than usual. Sytin repeated the rumours that were rife in the circles that he frequented. He was shocked and offended, like all other Russians who believed the best of their monarch.

About two years before the outbreak of the Great War there prevailed in Moscow, as everywhere else in Russia, a sort of politically suffocating atmosphere, as if a nightmare had settled upon the Russian hearts and there was no relief in view. The old power was rotting on the vine and lay as if paralyzed. It was no longer able to take even a single step towards a tighter union with the people and it had run its course. The shame of Rasputin and all that he stood for was acutely felt by all and everyone had the feeling that the gates of all Russia were tarred by this dirty name.[11] The sensation of shame, painful and unbearable, was so acutely felt that one picked up a newspaper with a feeling of revulsion and it was hard to look a foreigner in the eye. Rasputin was undoubtedly destroying the whole face of Russian culture. Next to him everything seemed somehow phony, clownish, and contemptible.

IV
The Tsar

With much hue and cry the heroes of the Duma upheaval[12] rise against the government. The case of Rasputin's assassination had exposed a terrible disorder and dislocation in all circles. And the chaos spread like wildfire among all strata [of society]. People lost control of themselves. Every group or faction hated all other factions. Hostility reigned in all circles. Everything collapsed. The disorder and the terrible disasters at the front augmented the chaos but the front still held. Stürmer[13] became minister. He belonged to the extreme right. My publications in Petrograd were silenced. Grigorovich[14] warned me [that] hard times were coming … for the supporters of the publication of the [military] encyclopaedias and other publications. I asked for his advice about seeing the Tsar in these extremely difficult times and having a conversation with him. He listened to me and to my interests and said: "Look, this is a very good idea. Do it, by all means." I asked him for the required letter of recommendation and went to Stürmer with the request that I be granted an audience with the Tsar. Stürmer required two days [to make the arrangements] and let me know, through the ADC [Aide-de-Camp], that the Tsar expected me at the Supreme Headquarters. The date and time were set. They sent me a ticket and an ADC as an escort.

On the way to Mogilëv[15] I had a stroke of luck: I ran into Archpriest Shavelsky,[16] who was also going to the HQ. I decided to travel in the same compartment. He asked me why I was going to see the Tsar. I told him that I had now reached a difficult moment in my life. I wanted to see the Tsar and hear what he had to say. I outlined my proposed conversation with the Tsar to him and he approved. I then asked him to do me a favour as an old acquaintance: to warn the Tsar of my intentions and asked him to prepare the Tsar to hear me out patiently.

Upon my arrival in Mogilëv, to my joy, I found M.K. there.[17] He introduced me to everybody. The life there was quiet and rough. The Russians were few and everyone kept to himself. I waited for the final permission. After two days I was called by Voeikov, the imperial adjutant.[18] The Tsar's ADC asked me to tell him in advance all the issues that I was planning to raise. I replied that Shavelsky had probably already informed the Tsar of the purpose of my visit. That satisfied him and he made the appointment for me the next day, at 2 p. m., after lunch, at the Tsar's office. I came [at the appointed time] and waited for the lunch to end. The Tsar came out and I introduced myself. He stopped in the centre of the room, I came to him and he extended his hand.

I said: "My Sovereign, Your Majesty, I have been a publisher for fifty years and have taken upon myself and dared to see my Tsar so as to hear him in person and to receive direction on that important matter to which I have devoted my whole life. You, My Sovereign, have granted the reform of the liquor monopoly in order to reduce drunkenness, but the sober people must be given literacy, schools, and a wider development of popular education. Witte[19] failed to carry out this most important reform." I suggested to him that he establish a system of education based on wide public involvement with the participation of the Government [to develop] publication of textbooks, Bibles, patristics, and handbooks; to build country schools so that in ten years' time there would not be a single illiterate person left. The supervising and executive ministry was to be in Petrograd. We would have set up a permanent exhibition of sample textbooks from the whole world of everything else that we need.

"This social enterprise of immense importance would not have required a thing from the Treasury, but it would have created a great social university of the people, from the bottom to the top and not from the top to the bottom as is the case now. Witte asked me for the program. I replied that the Government organs, in cooperation with the upper layer of society would fulfill all the needs of the people and the Government."

The Tsar asked me where I proposed to obtain the money. [I replied] "We will not ask a penny from anyone for such a glorious undertaking, but will get everything from [the] Society.[20] I offer my factory for the project. We will pay [off] only the shares that amount to Rb. 180,000, while the property is worth 5 million. And this for long-term repayment. Furthermore, there are the assets of the paper factory and other substantial sums of money. Everything is there.[21] A paltry sum will produce a return of small capital for the Society in one year and the enterprise will yield tens of millions each year. But we will work for the benefit of Russia. The Government cannot view indifferently a situation where millions are made on the sacred business of people's education by those who conduct it not for the benefit of enlightened education but for their personal profit."

The Tsar asked: "And what did Witte tell you?" "He told me that the Government will tolerate education undertaken with the participation of [the] Society everywhere except for government institutions and classical schools, but will never sympathize with it. This was Witte's opinion. My most humble request, my Sovereign, is that you permit me to tell you about the statesman K.P. Pobedonostsev. I worked with him on religious and Synodal publications and saw that that organization is responsible. Our Orthodox Church, up to recent times, has maintained an intolerant attitude toward those who believe in the same Christianity but profess the Old Faith. It is time they were left alone. They [Old Believers] have maintained their stand for a long time but this [attitude] is a great sin on the part of our ruling Orthodox Church. I took the liberty of telling Pobedonostsev that unbelieving beasts (*skoty*) attend church in our country instead of the genuinely faithful. K.P. said: 'What is this? What do you mean?' And I replied: 'I have good reason to say this. What does she offer when people are growing more and more indifferent to the Church? Where is her true teaching role? Could it really be reduced to the ritualistic part, carried out superficially? Surely what is needed is to light a sacred flame in a man's heart that will never die out.'"

V
Why I Published the *Military Encyclopaedia*

A group of very talented, progressive officers published the liberal *Military Voice*. They came to me asking for help with this military undertaking. I told them that I was not going to publish or participate in publishing a paper, but if they were to provide the resources and take it upon themselves to compile a serious work, viz. the *Military Encyclopaedia*, we might get together for that purpose. I warned them that my aim was to utilize all the resources of the appropriate military personnel, not just to publish an encyclopaedia. For me it was important and necessary that the military address themselves to this task with devotion and energy and make it possible [for me] to organize the publication together with them and their whole staff. [I was prepared] to use my available resources and my firm so as to give our great, almost illiterate, peasant army all the knowledge they needed by means of libraries in their barracks [containing] technical, agricultural, and builders' manuals, textbooks, and manuals so that the NCO's, directed by technically literate instructors, would be able to improve their knowledge. [I told them:] "The soldiers serve a three-year term. They waste tremendous amounts of time that could be employed in learning. But the soldier could leave the service as a skilled tradesman, equipped with knowledge acquired at the staff school. If you undertake to include this badly needed program in our project, we would make a sacrifice for this great task."

So our project began. They agreed to my proposal. *But we had yet to carry it out.*

The first project. We began to publish and continued for three years of painstaking labour. It was a rather thankless task: the liberal views of my group did not pass unnoticed in [190]5 when the new stupid and intriguing minister took over.[22] We had to consolidate our strength in order to establish a proper business [venture], but the year 1905 brought with it quite a different, more unfavourable streak – it led us back rather than advancing ... Having published 15,000 [copies of the first edition], we, together with our contributors and editors, decided to present our work to the Tsar so as to be able to proceed more resolutely towards our goal.[23]

We were told that the Tsar did not wish to receive the whole editorial board and that the presentation could be made by just the editor. We then sent the Tsar one sample volume through another minister, Grigorovich. We received no response to that. Even a *Military Encyclopaedia*, edited by very highly educated officers and a general, did not satisfy the chieftains at the Ministry. We reflected sadly that even at home there is no faith and hope for a better future.

So it had been since 1861, the collapse of serfdom. After all these responses I sent a copy to the naval minister, Grigorovich. He took it to the Tsar and took an interest in it himself. He invited me [to see him] and we cleared up the issue. He praised it warmly and I told him of my sacrifices of over one million [rubles] on this undertaking, which was so important and needed in Russia. All this happened too late, just before the war [of 1914]. The project came to [an end]. Thus a fine and worthwhile undertaking was lost. It could have brought results, but all it produced was four years of noise and fruitless efforts, with a loss of one million rubles.

The second project: A full historical collection covering the fifty years of the whole period after emancipation. What kind of reform it was, how was it carried out, and how it ended. A monument to great and awe-inspiring events in the life of Russia.

The third project: The three-hundredth anniversary of the Romanov Dynasty [in 1913]. Life and history. And the more or less favourable conditions of life in Russia.

These two historical [collections of] materials, each published in nearly twenty volumes, were of tremendous importance to all our contemporaries. What have we been through here historically and what heavy trials and tribulations did history bring to us? A reader could see

for himself our progress and our errors. Stolypin asked me if I was
working according to a planned program. I told him that history itself
was my planned program. I employ everything that is best in the academic community around me.

The Military Encyclopaedia [another version]

The year 1905. A military newspaper appears in Petrograd. I go there
and ask my contacts, "what is this *Military Voice?*" They tell me that
the "warriors"[24] are good and talented men. The material is there.
[They are] all young. Their paper came out and lived vigorously for
one month. And then it was closed for not being topical.[25] People advised me to join forces with them. I have a weakness for anything that
is new. We met and became acquainted. They asked me to carry on
with their paper. [I said:] "I cannot do it, especially not a military one.
[The project] is not well grounded and is risky. Let's publish practical
literature: a military encyclopaedia on the German model with positive
and serious contents."

This proposal was enthusiastically accepted. They were educated,
serious people representing all branches of service and military tactics.
They took to it with great enthusiasm and right away they began to
explain the great and important significance this could have for the Army,
the more so since our barrack soldiers have practically no knowledge
of anything:

"The village schools are poor, half of what they teach is in [Church]
Slavonic. Here the soldier will spend two years in service, formerly
three. He needs to learn not only how to read and write but to acquire
a trade. What is needed is to provide him with a good, simple book on
mechanics [*tekhnika*], trades, agriculture. After two years he will have
learned more than he had done at school and about more essential
things."

Certainly I counted mainly on the sales of practical technical literature to the soldiers, but he [the soldier] would take back to his village
both his [acquired] learning and the book, to keep things going. The
journal *The Scout (Razvedchik)* offered the mass of soldiers nothing
but Pogozhsky's old booklets. General literature did not reach them
and used to be forbidden. I counted on an approved compulsory program being confirmed by the Military Council of our General Staff.

Fate decreed that this was not to be. Eighteen volumes of the *Military Encyclopaedia* were published. Two remained unfinished. Three thousand bound volumes were published. The remaining three were in loose sheets [printers' signatures] and were thus left as rejected materials.[26] So the dreams remained unfulfilled.

P.S. The main aim was to combine all the publications in all the branches of popular knowledge and supplement them with manuals on agriculture and domestic crafts specifically for soldiers. The minister of the Navy, Grigorovich, offered sympathetic assistance in all my undertakings in this regard. But all our great efforts ended in a crash.

[At first] my proposal was happily accepted by everyone and received congenial support. We talked. The idea of the newspaper was abandoned completely and we turned to solving the task of how to publish a large encyclopaedia. All the editors were there. They worked out the budget and decided to engage five more editorial assistants. The program [layout] was to be modeled on the one currently being published in Germany. Next day they acquired the premises for the editorial office on the corner of Morskaia and Nevsky Prospect. It was a large, attractive, and bright office. They submitted the announcement and hung out a sign reading: "The Editorial Office of the *Military Encyclopaedia*." One other large space was rented to accommodate the compositors and proofreaders. Two presses were set up and began operating. The ready layout [laid-out page proofs] was sent to Moscow. After ten days the editorial office was ready, attractively furnished. Invitations to the opening were issued to all sympathizers: members of the State Duma, senior military figures, and some representatives of the press. All expressed sympathy and their wishes for success. What was striking was that they were all aware of the great importance of the project, even to the Government.

There was undoubtedly a great need for this important undertaking, but neither the minister nor the highest-ranking officials attended the opening prayer service. I had the feeling that everyone was thinking: "There is the stupid fool! What is he trying to get into? Why is he looking for trouble?" This, like anything that happens in Russia, did not surprise me. On the other hand, I had not done anyone any harm. They [probably] thought: "Let him fool around with it if the enjoys throwing his money out: 8,000 rubles per month for editing, over and above publication costs." I was firmly convinced that, if I had made a useful contribution to our enormous army, then all the intelligent people within the military would come to see and understand what the whole illiterate Russian peasant army needs to learn, using the army's own military resources and knowledge, then they would appreciate the undertaking that we were setting out to accomplish without fanfare and with dedication.

The Military Encyclopaedia (an additional variant)

... to teach the Army to read and write, to take the military ... and all the manuals pertaining to crafts and agriculture, fill the soldiers' libraries, [and] in the time free from other duties, teach them what they will need to know in their villages after they leave the service. So that he [the soldier] would return home with greater understanding and could become a teacher in the village. So that he would bring back with him to the village good and useful reading matter where it would be sold at the cheapest possible price. So far, this not only has not been permitted but there was not one single library in the barracks. It was to remedy this that my circle of officers of the *Golos* [*Military Voice*] agreed to work for, and began to edit, the *Encyclopaedia*.

Even this edition, badly needed by the Government itself, was authorized only with difficulty. For the first two years a great amount of work was conscientiously done by a group of invited officers and generals representing all branches of service. This was a useful literary achievement carried out harmoniously, in friendship with the State Duma. These camps found much that they had in common and what was needed was to cement things more firmly and to develop further. But here, too, some friction existed. The top people, in the persons of the minister and his deputy, did not view the enterprise in a particularly friendly light. To them, the principal figures among the editors appeared more knowledgeable than they were themselves and as having wide connections within the whole of the Armed Forces. Even affection and friendship – all this existed within the Army, in Petersburg and in Russia.

The core was better educated and more sympathetic. There were three hundred participants in the project. They met on Saturdays at the editorial office on the corner of Nevsky. They all gathered for a discussion. Many visitors and sympathizers from among the members of the State Duma. This evoked envy at the top and they attempted to show our enterprise in a liberal light [as having liberal leanings]. The edition of ten t. [volumes] was published. It met with wide approval. We wanted to push the success further. Sukhomlinov [refused to] go and ask the question: can it be submitted for the Tsar's approval? No – it is not sufficiently patriotic. An argument ensued. Allow the editors and myself to submit the published volumes for perusal. After all, this was a guide for the officers of senior ranks and above. And all the reference materials. The cost of this to the publisher was 100,000 rubles per year: maintaining the editorial office and materials, not counting the printing and publication. I am doing this for the benefit and education of the R.S. [Russian society]. No, we will decide on the feasibility of presenting it to the Tsar only after you have completed publishing the whole edition.

This is how sadly things were going even at the very centre of military affairs. Such a nonentity as the Minister Sukhomlinov headed the military department. He was hated by everyone, beginning with the minister for the Navy, and unequivocally despised by the whole ministry and the military sector for his gross incompetence. I was overcome by fear, wondering if everything was to be lost after all, and if my dream of getting through to the soldiers was destined to collapse.[27] I waited for another year. Grigorovich became minister for the Navy. This simplified the situation. I gave him the books, he took them to the Tsar and competently explained everything. I received resounding approval, but by that time the great and ruinous war had arrived. And so my dream of building a bridge to the school through the sacrifice of my book had burst. And everything ended in chaos.

VI

The Most Important Matter

Sytin's account of the desperate attempts of the last imperial favourite, Protopopov, to steer Russia away from revolution and chaos demonstrates how the war brought the publisher's nationalism to the fore, as well as his cautious watchfulness when it came to parting with his money. As heavy losses in the battles and mounting shortages caused despair and criticisms of the government everywhere, Sytin's news-paper muted its criticism. Sytin was thinking of Russia's good as he understood it, and undermining the government, whatever his own reservations, was not his goal. In this he differed from most of Russia's politically involved entrepreneurs, both in Moscow and in Petrograd, as this episode shows. The government's attempts to rally support took place in the face of the sneering indifference of the financiers and indus-trialists who had made millions on wartime contracts by driving out foreign competitors and were now ready to let the imperial govern-ment go to its death. They were preparing to take power.

After 1915 life changed in all respects and the ferment continued. Stormy and noisy sessions of the Duma went on in Petersburg. The right-wingers were more active – because they had friends at the top. The bourgeoisie, who were not indifferent to the press, wanted a red paper[28] supported by the bankers' money. Sytin's acumen did not let them rest. A group of bankers, mindful of the success of *Russia*,[29] asked me to participate in a new Petersburg newspaper. My view was: "Gentlemen, what do you need a new newspaper for; you, in your banking circles, have an old paper that has its [established] readership, take it, strengthen it, shake it up, and it will be better than a new one. You own more than half of the *New Times*. "What we need is a fresh, forceful newspaper, we have already collected the money, we will give you as much as you want." I tried to convince them that it would take much longer to create trust in a new organ than to revamp an old, good newspaper. After a lengthy discussion they were convinced.

They sent for an editor, [but] that "smart aleck" exclaimed, horri-fied: "How could you? This rotten *Times*! Sytin must have been jok-ing when he recommended it, we will create miracles, the best people in Russia and abroad will be working for us, no one will participate in the *New Times*. And you, I.D., will be working for the *New Times*."

"Well, I am not planning to join either the *N.T.* or your new paper."

"But we want you precisely for the new paper."

"What do you need me for?"

"But we need you. We will give you a large share free of charge." This [did not convince] me, although the vice-chairman of the State Duma, the renowned Protopopov, had been trying. He argued a lot [but] I categorically refused.

I became acquainted with Protopopov.[30] He was a minor, excitable industrialist but, tempted by the financiers, he became a member of the Duma, got involved in the newspaper business and in politics, and then left for abroad. When he returned to Moscow there was much talk that he possessed some secret connections with the Court.[31] He became so trusted that he was asked to take over the position of minister of the Interior.

While visiting Moscow, he called on me at my home. A few days later I went to Petrograd and called on the newly appointed minister to return the visit. I thought he might receive me on Sunday at 2 p.m. When I entered the reception hall, fifteen people were just leaving, they were all Petersburg bankers, many of whom I knew. I asked them about the reason why the new minister would want to assemble such a menagerie; "he must have dined and wined you well."

"All that's left for you, dear man, is just the coffee – the lunch is over.[32] But come and see us at the Club tomorrow – we are organizing a meeting, come and listen." I went up to the minister and said: "What is this congenial meeting you are holding here today?"

"Oh, yes, I.D. I invited them on a very important business. Our Government's affairs are in a bad way, in all respects. There is no money in the treasury. I invited them and asked them, 'Gentlemen, come all of you to help Russia. We must unite to save [her]. The times are hard, make your contribution, raise communal capital, the war has brought huge profits to the merchants and to the banks, the Treasury is ruined, I am giving the Government all I have,[33] come and help, all of you, in these difficult times. We must feed the people, set up communal canteens, purchase food and products at the lowest possible price; we must urgently carry out this patriotic undertaking. Disaster is impending; everything must be done to allay the resentment and the high cost of living, raised artificially by speculation. We could easily overcome this acute crisis by our common efforts, provided you are willing to help by arranging for large-scale purchases. Thousands of cooperative workers (*artel'shchiki*) will do the job for you and Moscow and Petersburg will have bread and other foodstuffs.

"I came to the position of minister from the world of business. I now feel the great burden of my responsibility. All of us do nothing but criticize the power [the Government] and here you have the ministerial power on its knees before you, begging – the time of great events is ripe, I am handing over all my power to you, for your disposal. I am your servant, ready to take your orders and accept all your decisions in advance, for the welfare of Russia and of the Russian people [who find themselves] at this moment bearing the oppressive load of this terrible war; are beginning to starve and spend hours lining up for a piece of bread.

"And we, merchants, just stand there and wait. We have sinned grievously in this hour of tribulation.

"They heard me out and said that this was a matter of broad government policy and that they were unable to produce an answer, or even discuss it, before they met with a larger number of their kind for that specific purpose. 'We will discuss the matter in the Club tomorrow and will come back to you with our decision. We understand the situation and will not delay our decision, and tomorrow.' So ended our discussion. And what do you think of it?"

I said: "A.D., we have not seen much of each other. We've known each other for about a year, outside of business matters, for a few months we came closer to each other because of the newspaper where we had some trifling business transactions. Now I am talking to you, a minister of the Great Russia, a position to which you have been elevated just a few days ago. Forgive the manner of my speaking, but I have been listening to your words with deep respect and delight: it is a minister who speaks. A cry for the welfare of Russia and of her people. A minister from the gentry would not have said that. I bow deeply before you, A.D." He embraced me and kissed me warmly and we parted.

I went to our bankers' and merchants' club. About sixty people were gathered there. Among them were noble landowners of hundreds of thousands of *desiatina*.[34] The meeting was chaotic and unusually noisy. First of all, one of them announced the minister's proposal. The actual announcement was phrased in the following form: "Gentlemen, we had been invited to lunch yesterday by the new-fangled minister of the Interior who proposed that we offer our capital for the welfare of Russia. The government has none, but it will add what the state has to our [contribution]. For you have made a lot of money because of the war and so let us feed the people in order not to come to grief and not to see discontent among the hungry people. What do you say, Gentlemen?"

[The response of the membership was:] "No one but a bankrupt merchant [Protopopov] is capable of this sort of talk. Well, good fellow, you've crawled into a nobleman's place and now wriggle [out of it?] any way you like. What we need is to replace this pack from top to bottom."

VII

P.A. Kropotkin

Prince Peter Kropotkin (1842–1921) was one of the best-known geographers of his time as well as an explorer of Siberia. On a visit to Western Europe he joined the anarchist movement. On his return to Russia he began to publish his ideas and was imprisoned. After a brazen escape from prison he lived in Western Europe, where he became one of the leaders of the international anarchist movement. While the movement was known for its terrorist acts, Kropotkin never joined any of the violent forms of political struggle and spent thirty years writing popular works on anarchism. The titles speak for themselves: *A Rebel's Speeches* (1885), *In Russian and French Jails* (1887), *Bread and Freedom* (1892), *Mutual Aid as a Factor of Evolution* (1902), *A Revolutionary's Memoirs* (1902), *The Great French Revolution 1789–1793* (1909), *Contemporary Science and Anarchy* (1913), and others. His books were translated and published worldwide. Sytin's interest in this veteran of the revolutionary movement was mostly businesslike: when Kropotkin returned to Russia after the revolution of 1917, his works, hitherto banned, might well become bestsellers.

When I was in England,[35] I rode past the house where P.A. Kropotkin lived, and ... I could not bring myself to drop in, to become acquainted with him. I don't know why, but for a long time I had wanted to meet this man, and everything that I had heard about him only increased my liking for him and my curiosity.

But to drop in to meet him in this way, without any real reason, seemed to me a great imposition.

"In all likelihood," I said to myself, "our compatriots, visiting England, frequently impose on the hero of the famous escape from Peter and Paul Fortress, and I do not want to join these idle curiosity seekers."[36] But when Kropotkin returned to his native land after the

February Revolution and stayed in the Moscow Kremlin, in the building of the Court, I decided to overcome my reluctance and went to see him in the Kremlin.

When I rang, the writer's wife opened the door.

"Could I for a minute see Petr Alekseevich, in order to welcome him back to his homeland and to ask him: can Sytin do anything to help him out?"

Mrs Kropotkin went to ask him and. after a minute, on the threshold there stood before me the Apostle Peter – the living Apostle Peter: a bald head, two tufts of grey hair on his temple, a small beard, huge forehead, and clear, brilliant eyes.[37] The similarity to the Apostle Peter, as he is represented in church art, was so striking that I was involuntarily taken aback.

"I am pleased to see you. Come in."

We went into a room. I congratulated Petr Alekseevich on his return and asked:

"Can I be at your service in some way in the publishing business? It would give me sincere and deep pleasure."

An idea lit the clear, bright eyes of Kropotkin.

"Would you like to print one of my books? If so, I would be very happy."

He went into an adjoining room and brought back a whole armload of books.

"Here you are, Ivan Dmitrievich, here is everything that I have written. I propose that you take a look at all of them: if you wish to publish everything or only part – print whatever you wish."

"You are very generous, Petr Alekseevich ... But it will be better and easier for me if you yourself sketch a publication plan and indicate what ought to be first."

So began the business side of our acquaintanceship. Kropotkin's books began to appear quickly and, while the printing was going on, I visited him frequently and we became very close.

Besides business questions, we frequently discussed "outside" issues, touching, for the most part, on questions about the Russian and the Russian soul.

And what I heard from Petr Alekseevich seemed to me a true revelation.

"What can one do so as not to be a danger to humanity in this life? Where and how is one able to live a true and reasonable life?"

These fundamental questions P.A. discussed especially willingly and I, from my side, offered him my ideas and my confessions.

"Look, Petr Alekseevich, I have lived a full, long life. I "live by others' wits," as the peasants say, – the wits are yours, from writers, artists, philosophers, great scholars. I understand my role in life very simply: I am only a machine, only a technical device. Others are the makers of a new life and I embody their attainments and I place them among the people in the form of books.

P.A. Kropotkin, it seemed, liked this idea.

"Yes, I understand and I value your business. I have seen that Lev Nikolaevich Tolstoy and other writers worked with you. With pleasure I hand over all my books to you – they are little known in Russia, but in England they have been selling and have gone through many editions."

From books P.A. Kropotkin unwittingly passed to his subject, to his favourite subject, the Russian people.

"Our nation is still young, too young and it receives a poor education, very scant ... What is the Russian given, what does he know? They give him almost nothing and he knows almost nothing. Schooling is weak, written Slavonic, a few basic texts – that is all that has been prepared for the majority, for one hundred million. They have not even learned to work in Russia because people have to be taught work habits ... And what can be said about spiritual self-awareness? How many of our compatriots care about self-perfection through brotherhood, friendship, and mutually loving help? A life, real life, begins only with that. There is no life where there is no love and there is no happiness where there is no brotherhood among people. Have you read, Ivan Dmitrievich, my first book which was published by your house under the title *Land and Factory*?"

"Yes, I read it ... But this idea, Petr Alekseevich, you are preaching – brotherhood and lo ... What you are saying, writing, and printing – these are all Christian truths, but I do not understand one thing."

"What is it you don't understand?" asked Petr Alekseevich and his bright, pure, and clear eyes flashed.

He leaned back in the armchair and his Apostle Peter's face with his two tufts of hair on his bald head became suddenly, strict, almost severe: "Your Christ – There he is." (He showed me the distance between his thumb and index finger.) "But my Christ is like this." (He spread his hands widely as though he wanted to embrace the whole world).

This apostle's face, these clear, brilliant, fiery eyes and this true, active living love, which breathed through his words and his entire being, enormously impressed me. He doesn't believe in Christ, but he has picked up the heavy cross and is carrying it. [He is] the most honest of Christians, but he does not know Christ. Is this it? Then why are his eyes suddenly glistening with tears and why is my soul shaken and reaching out to him?

In tears I fell on the chest of Petr Alekseevich and we both wept.

7

THE NORTH

I

O, my native *Rus'*, you hide within yourself a great power as well as a great impassable morass and stupidity; your mighty strength and wisdom in life and in literary creativity, your fairy-tales, the *Byliny*,[1] songs, and legends – all this sustains your great, legendary, obtuse, and unpolished wisdom.

All that is inherently yours is uniquely primitive and savage; it possesses its own peculiar charm, beauty, and also foolishness. You do not try to improve what you have but you try to postpone the moment when the others will comb your hair, dress you in tidy clothes of an inevitably European cut, and begin to remodel you from head to toe. And they will remodel you so thoroughly that by the age of twelve you will be combination of European appearance with a Russian inner nature. And the longer you live, study, or participate in scholarly or organized manual labor – the further you leave behind your own Russian people with its own unique traits. And the more you tend toward the Western peoples.

[The West] is a strong, attractive, strikingly beautiful cultural world, you assimilate it indiscriminately [it attracts you by] the beauty of its form, language, manners, and attire and you attempt to emulate it in every way possible as long as it is within your reach and depending on your means and conditions of your work. This transformation never stops, from the moment of entering the middle educational institution [high school] and beyond it. And what you left behind seems to you backward and a stupid, simple colourless mass of working cattle.[2] But this working cattle represents the whole great country, the whole of your own grey and black *Rus'*, probably not more than twenty million represent 170 million people, that is just a drop [in the bucket]. And all the remainder of the Great *Rus'* [you see as] grey, dirty, primitive. Everywhere, among the masses, there reigns that coarseness which I myself have witnessed for those twelve years that I lived in the village. We have improved here [in the city] over the [last] fifty years while *Rus'* has remained as it was: black, ossified, and moribund, without books and without faith in life – nothing but moribund, oppressive, coarse superstition. Much remains [to be done]. The new immense and great task lies ahead. The great mass of the strong, young Russian nation is barely literate, nearly illiterate if it comes to action.

You, the modern man, do not know it and it does not know you well, more likely those like you, all advanced and proud, appear to the masses as buffoons, not to be taken seriously. You shout and make a lot of noise about *the welfare* of the people, but you do it in such a way that the people do not know you and your efforts, and you do not know them. You differ from the people in your *spirit* and *way of thinking*, which had been perverted at your modern school and in the Europeanized conditions of your life. But the silliest parties that emerged after ["1905" crossed out], the opening of the zemstvo[3] institutions, the zemstvo liberals and the conservative monarchists, have been fighting continuously over Western ideas in young and immature Russia.

Even before demonstrating their achievements, they opened hostilities between themselves, as worst enemies, while both [pretended to] serve the sacred cause of popular education. The party of the Right united its activities with the Church. This was a grave sin for both, each of them trying to outdo the other in extremism. This split was terribly harmful and corruptive for the people's moral condition and for the students. Two camps were formed and the Church was dragged into their quarrels.

The Russian people are by nature strongly religious, especially the whole of the North. Even though the struggle and the weakening of the Church have gone on almost for *centuries*, the greater part [of the people] still retain their strong religious feeling, especially in the whole of the North. The Far North is strong, it maintains its strength and venerates Sts Zosima and Savvatii and their Solovki [Monastery].

The young novices are supplied by the North to the Solovetsky Monastery:[4] four huge gubernias [provinces] [send] their youth of fourteen years of age and over; from every family they go to the monastery to work there for one year. They go by their own commitment, without pay, the food and board are provided by the monastery. The reputation of this school, indispensable for the young man's and his family's happiness in the North, stands firmly established among the people. [Because of this] you will see, all over the North, striking[ly well maintained] farms and generally friendly, communal well-being. You will find families of fifty and more people living as one family, together with the old people. The patriarchal traditions and the well being of the family, abundance, and hospitality [reign there]. Everyone lives as one family, no one leaves. The "one-year-monk," upon leaving the monastery, is already familiar with the proper organization of a well-run farm and with all the essential handicrafts – blacksmith's skills as applied to the building trade, all the farm machinery, repairs, carpentry and lathe operations, everything that is needed on the farm. He is taught to work and to organize all the production at home and to repair everything. The people go on living, never aspiring to what they don't need, and the cities and factories mean nothing to them. They live and make everything themselves, neither buying nor selling anything and know how to make everything out of their own resources.[5]

II

[This is what a Russian peasant from the North told me:] "I saw beautiful stars and the most important thing, brother – the Northern Lights – back home. This will dispel any doubt in God's holy cause. You, brother, are very wrong in not taking a trip to the Solovki – there you have the genuine God's country. Living in this muddy backwater of Soligalich is not a life.[6] I myself learned and prayed for three years at the holy Solovetsky Monastery, I now do everything myself at home and have taught all my family.

Our household is as good as a workshop, we do not buy anything, we ourselves are tailors, weavers, and cobblers. We tan the hides our- selves. We have carpenters and furniture makers. We have forty people in our family and we make everything at home. Sometimes we might go for a ride to your Galich and Soligalich,[7] to stretch out [exercise] our horses and to see things for ourselves, a pleasure trip of 800 versts. We see a town once a year and that's enough. The mother earth feeds us. And the pious Solovetsky monks are the fathers who teach us to read and write and everything else pertaining to agriculture as well as all trades and animal husbandry. Up to one thousand of us [men] stay there each year.

One comes back after three years and injects new life into the house. There is no family in our region that did not go through this appren- ticeship at the monastery. No man would miss that holy university that leaves an imprint on his life. They teach you everything from how to bake bread to do everything for the home. You work happily for three years, learning and working, everything a joy. Our people have also learned [there] how to observe Church feasts and fasts properly. I bet that you have not seen any taverns in our villages. On feast days we put out monastery-made *kvas*[8] and weak beer made with hops. We don't need any vodka and we live to be 120.

In the village everyone is a relative. The Solovki [Monastery] gave us both knowledge and happiness. We don't need any money in cir- culation. And should you have any books, of course, we will buy them, but the Solovki [Monastery] has its own printing shop. They print books in Slavonic and in Russian that are needed for everyday knowledge and they even have their own paper factory, as well as an icon-painting workshop."

[As he prepared to part from me, he said:] "So, brother, we are here. We have had an interesting conversation to make the journey short. You go your own way and we will go ours. Here is this little house on your way at the end of village. It belongs to a young family. The fam- ily is small, still new, and not yet fully established, you'll find it quieter here. Stay there."[9]

We drove up to the new house with a new farmyard, everything clean and in good order. The farmer's wife is young. She has three chil- dren: the boy is seven and the girls a bit younger. The young, strong farmer, twenty-five (twenty seven) years of age, a sturdy man, is working in the yard. He has an adjoining, fenced-off workshop, as well as a carpenter's annex and a little blacksmith's shack. He is master of all trades and his wife is a weaver. We ask for permission to stay the night and for food. She says: "You can stay, but don't judge us severely and we will gladly share with you what God has sent us."

The atmosphere is warm, hospitable, and merry. Everyone is kind and happy to welcome a visitor. All sit down together to supper. A simple Russian meal: cabbage soup, groats, and bread. The host says: "Don't judge us harshly, we are simple people, glad to share what we have." I ask: " And haven't you got a samovar?" – "No, dear people, we haven't got one and there is no tea here, but have nice *kvas*."

We try the *kvas*: it tastes better than beer or any other beverage, it is pleasant, flavourful, thick, and nourishing. The host says: " That is our best *kvas*, prepared from the monastery recipe."

We drink and praise it highly.

He explains: "This, dear friends, is for us a drink that provides [a remedy for] thirst and hunger, we never drink nor want to drink anything else."

We drank it with joy and asked for some to take with us for the road. They pour *kvas* for us into a pail made from birch-bark, which our host made right in front of us. Our host is also a painter who has trained at Solovki.

"What are your other skills?" we ask.

"Yes, all you see here I have made myself. Only when something is too heavy for me to lift I call on my [brother ? at] ... the big house next door that belongs to our family. I haven't been to the city for two years, everything you see here is the work of our own hands. We have enough to eat, to drink, and to clothe ourselves. This is all thanks to our father the North and our beloved teacher, the Solovetsky Monastery."

What does one need to be happy? – very little is needed: to have no enemies, to serve others, to do for others as you would wish for yourself, to work honestly, to love work as something beneficial, find in it consolation and prayer, in everything that you do avoid offending God. Don't pray ostentatiously but talk constantly to God in your heart.

It is a great fortune to be a Russian, this is the people of the future, young, passionate, and courageous. [The Russian] does not harbour evil in his soul, if he commits a bad deed in a fit of anger he will beg for mercy and forgiveness one hour later. He is extremely receptive and easily loses heart, credulous, very, very kind at times. The intelligentsia has abandoned the rules of serious life, it does not like work, it is wily, it overvalues the powers of education in a self-serving way, but it is torn internally by doubts. It does not know what cause to serve. It is always clamouring for [better] conditions that it [believes it] deserves. It carries on a struggle against the Government, never knowing what it really wants. It preaches to everybody but has no practical skills whatsoever.

The young people leaving the institutions of higher learning are unfit for practical life, with the exception of 10 per cent. They wander idly around without finding an occupation. They criticize everything, hate the Government, fall in with embittered liberals, a large percentage end up in courts, in exile, or emigrate. The fault lies partly with the surfeit of students. Judging by the number of [academic] departments, there are twelve to fourteen thousand, while the actual number of professors able to teach well is only six [thousand]. Two thousand students, financially insecure, survive on charity or by private tutouring, forever thinking of going through university and the race for diplomas goes on. The student does not want to be a rural teacher, as a result more than half the teachers in the primary [people's, rural] schools are young women – school girls who are poorly prepared. The school discipline is bad. The teaching standards are poor and the textbooks themselves are extremely weak. Children leave a three-year school at twelve or thirteen, are barely able to read and write, with no general knowledge whatever.

The strong merchant born after [the abolition of] serfdom is only sixty years old.[10] In this short period he has adapted and has succeeded in developing industry and trade to an astonishing degree. The growth of the textile industry has been especially strong, thanks to assistance from German and English machines.

We have always been poor in spirit. Churches have always been split into a great multitude of sects and doctrines, but our dear gentry has contributed to this in a big way. How much effort, care, and writing L. Tolstoy has poured into it. Christ let him have no peace, Tolstoy wanted to take His place. Kropotkin is like him, look at them, until the moment of death itself they were trying their hardest to explain four words: What is the Truth? They gave up their entire lives and poured out a torrent of reflections and refutations of the most essential questions of [human] life: Where is the Truth? But the answer exists. Most probably, it will be found not by the man who has been arguing about the truth all his life but by the one who keeps it safe in his own heart and lives by it. He does not shout, does not argue, but simply preserves it and keeps it alive in his soul. And the endless debates result in a loss of all certainty.

Maybe it gives fuel to the undying Spirit. This epoch of turmoil inclines me to the following idea; if this Spirit is force then this is its work.

My life's memories ... It's pleasant to recall the past. How nice, that such strong, powerful men tried so hard to enter the human soul and, after all, it is no good wandering in the dark. I have seen it justified in the case of Alexey.[11] Yes, I have seen it. I imagine that you, too, if the light has shone on you, have benefitted from it.

III
Memories of [My] Life

I got mixed up a bit. I spoke about the Church – that is more important. Our Church: Russian, great, of the people, of diverse kinds and branches, she resides in the great popular [one word undecipherable], in the thick of masses, in the remote rustic *skity*,[12] in the tundra, still alive throughout the whole of *Rus'*. There are some priestless ones [*bezpopovtsy*][13] – the original Christians who believe deeply that our [official Orthodox] heresy has deprived us of Divine grace. They perform the rites according to the ancient books, without celebrating the Eucharist. There are Old Believers who observe the original pre-Nikon rule, who have not accepted Nikon's corrections to the rules of Divine service, considering them to be heresy. There are a few more [sects who have made] changes but all of them in essence maintain the old Truth of that literal [...][14] teaching and they firmly follow the regulations of the Truth they believe in. The greater part strictly maintains its stand in the old, still pre-Nikon, ancient faith

Hundreds of thousands of this mass [of Old Believers] living in the remote *skity*, are spread over the huge Russian territory. For example, the estate of Bugrov [called] The Great Testament.[15] A flour miller, he

owns his mill, which employs up to ten [thousand] workers (all of them
Russians, strict Old Believers). He is the sponsor – a father to more
than ten *skity* all over the Volga and the Kama Districts. They all maintain an early Christian commune, keep apart from Orthodoxy, which
they consider a heresy, believe in the ancient Christian Church [as it
was] before Nikon, and keep the [old] customs. Upon examining all
these rites of different Christian variations and sects one is deeply struck
by this profound self-sacrifice in the name of the faith.

Simple Russian people who are predominantly loyal to their faith at
the price of complete self-denial in, decidedly, all respects. And what is
especially striking is that they have been doing this not just for one year
or for a decade but for hundreds of endless years and [all over?] the
great rural [narod-] country. And all this not in some wild forests but
amongst us, so that you can, if you wish, approach more closely and see
it all for yourself. So great and barbarous are our people still, in their
majority. And how about the North with its Solovki? And the whole
Northern part of the provinces of Vologda, Archangel, Kostroma?

Everywhere, among the masses, there reigns that natural coarseness
that I myself have witnessed in those twelve years that I lived there. We
have picked ourselves up [in Russia] over the [last] fifty years while
Rus' has remained as it was: black, backward, and numb, without
books and without faith in life – nothing but the numb, oppressive,
coarse superstition. Much remains [to be done]. The new immense and
important task lies ahead. The great mass of the strong, young Russian people is barely literate, uneducated and one could say function-
ally illiterate.

IV

Upon the expanse of the freest and most wonderful continent of all,
populated by the multi-millions, there stands America, on the other,
opposite, plot of land. A new young nation has grown up – and we are
its brothers. Let us reach out to each other and go and work together
like brothers. You, the elder brother Ross [Rossia], have been dozing
for a long time, you have succumbed to the long-lasting, tedious slum-
ber, you have slumbered heavily and been hypnotized by persons who
have exercised power – they all served clever Evil.

THE ALL-RUSSIAN COUNCIL
OF PEOPLE'S DEPUTIES

Just as he marked fifty years of hard work and could savour his position as a world class publisher, Ivan Sytin had to deal with the uncertainties of 1917. Russia's disastrous war with Germany had shattered its economy and further discredited the autocracy. Sytin celebrated his jubilee anyway and then became a witness to two revolutions. The first, in February, dethroned the Tsar, but the second replaced the Provisional Government with the Bolshevik Party, led by Lenin. This government, by taking over private businesses and eliminating press freedom, forced Sytin to give up, one by one, all his enterprises. Beginning in November 1917, the former moneyed classes of Russia were forced to give up first their bank accounts, then their business enterprises, then their spare houses or apartments as a solution to the housing crisis among the underprivileged classes. They huddled in one or two rooms while the rest of the house was occupied by the former residents of slums and village huts: the kitchen and amenities were shared by all the residents.

Sytin, who showed his considerable survival skills by offering to cooperate with the new rulers, was spared living in a "communal apartment," but he lost everything else, and it was only as a special favour from the Soviet government under Lenin that Sytin and his family were allowed to occupy a spacious apartment in downtown Moscow (their former house was nationalized, as was his printing plant).

Shengerovich [M.O. ?] came to see me on behalf of the All-Russian Council of People's Deputies with the following proposal: "We have been instructed to ask you if you would like to work with us. We would like to establish a trust over syndicates [publishing enterprises] to assume management of the major printing plants and paper factories to supply the needs of Gosizdat[1] and of all the large government institutions." This appealed to me so much that I happily agreed – it was my kind of business: [it was] on a large scale, a grandiose undertaking, a novel and interesting enterprise. The three of us, I, Derbyshev, and Shengerovich got together to discuss the matter.[2]

Sytin's main printing plants, Kushnerev's,[3] plus two or three others, amounted to the near-total of such plants in Moscow. This was beautiful. All that was needed was to distribute the work properly among them to achieve order[ly production] and substantial returns. Our paper factories were weak and not very suitable for large-scale operations. Sytin used to get 80 percent of his paper from Finland. I had a preliminary site and the means for the construction of a large plant at the waterfall.[4] Everything had been worked out. All this could be put into operation in a very short time. This looked so good and clear that both I myself and the others were sure that it would be accepted by all large government institutions. A most convenient and reliable undertaking, especially for the Gosizdat. All they would have to do would be to supply the material to be printed to have the work done responsibly and on time, without having to worry about the paper supply. Everything would be done properly, automatically, with attention paid to minute details. This would greatly safeguard production and make it cheaper so that the market would be supplied on schedule, according to the time of the year. We agreed to go to the Gosizdat together. I suggested to my comrades that we should have [employ] over fifty thousand people. This was great and I felt very happy. It would be five times larger than our old business. But I have one small request – said I – "I stand alone against the rest of you. Do make a small concession: bring into this group two additional people, for the sake of my reputation so that I might avoid being labeled a *money-grubber* who, just by himself, undertakes such a huge project where everyone else is just a worker. Include Sabashnikov[5] and Dumnov.[6] These are two old entrepreneurs. They won't interfere with us, but I will gain a little prestige."[7]

They [the workers] heard me out and said: "Do what you want. But don't let them spoil things for us."

I replied: "But how could they? Their job will be to sit somewhere in an office, in a bookstore. And Sytin will have the prestige. Two old ... They will cost us 300 rubles each."

"Do as you wish, but see that they don't ruin things for us. Make sure of this, for you will have to answer for them."

They [Sabashnikov and Dumnov] agreed and came to the meeting. We explained everything in detail: This was going to be a grandiose undertaking, useful and solidly founded. We ought to support it and work for it with enthusiasm. Sabashnikov kept a discreet silence, but agreed. Dumnov was doubtful. He said that he more or less agreed, but [only] to the extent Schmidt[8] did.

Two days later we went to see O.Yu. Schmidt at Gosizdat. Derbyshev made his report, thoroughly and in detail, to the effect that this would bring Gosizdat great benefits. He explained: "All the raw materials and paper would be prepared in advance. Both the quality and quantity [would be guaranteed]. The printing facilities would give you everything you need and on time. Your enterprise would be beautifully equipped, according to modern standards. It would be easy for the publisher to prepare material, scheduling it according to the season. We would leave this to Sytin. It would be his duty to provide the goods, between you and ourselves, according to the seasonal duties set by you. This would make the business substantially cheaper and would satisfy the customer."

Schmidt heard us out and said: "This does not suit me. I do not wish to be tied to your printing plants. You have the plants – go ahead and print whatever we give you and we'll buy the paper ourselves. But we will not agree to work in union with you. We will just place our orders with you, according to our requirements."

[Sytin:] "Are you not worried about the chaotic operations of such a publishing house as the Gosizdat? With their immense structure they are working without any system, without coordination between the goods [production] and the seasons. Everything is going in all directions, the central office does not know what the lower levels are doing."

[Schmidt:] "This is our business. We don't want to bring outsiders into it."

And so we parted. As we came out the workers said to me: "Why did you let us down so?" This was extremely painful to me. What did it mean? And then, in the evening, I learned that Dumnov and Sabashnikov had their own trusted man in the person of G.I. Chefranov[9] who, at their request, had warned Schmidt that Sytin and the workers had arranged to run the technical operations in a sophisticated manner, on a Sytin-like scale: "Our advice is not make an agreement with them, but rather work on a small scale. You hire us ... [for] 75%, and the three of us [for] 25%." Two days later they offered this deal to me. I realized what a despicable solution this was. This came later and, of course, they all cheated each other and went their own way. Everything was in Chefranov's hands. It rested on one little smart answer, to cover themselves.

It all ended in a preposterously absurd way. I was at fault, in having undermined a great undertaking by co-opting for it people who did not understand and did not wish to understand the significance of this project.

The evening ended in nothing. Ferman[10] left the meeting worried because no one had any opinion concerning the serious business; they did not even know how to discuss [it]. "How is it that you, Sytin, made the proposal and went with it [to Germany], when your bosses found the project to be untimely?"

"Why untimely?" – said I – "when I personally have expended 30 thousand rubles, worked out all the plans, and the banks agreed to share this excellent project with me on a fifty-fifty basis?" I presented our calculations. To produce six million *puds*[11] of paper [newsprint] at the full capacity, with an investment of 3 million rubles. The price of one *pud* on the spot was 60 kopecks. You've seen all the details. Surely Stinnes[12] would not have agreed so readily to participate? The people listening to us had no interest in this business and the others worried about their old junk, fearful of losing it.

After further attempts, Ferman left having achieved nothing, expressing his regrets upon departing, on his own and my behalf.

Why Did I Participate in Mostorg?[13]

What follows seems to be a draft of a letter that Sytin had considered sending to the Soviet government when he learned he was being accused of defrauding the state and threatened with a fine and a prison term.

My close friends, former men of affairs who had been running large enterprises in Russia told me: "We had been invited by Mostorg to set up a large state enterprise on the principles of a stock company where Mostorg would hold the bulk [of the shares] and we, in smaller part, would contribute capital and our personal labour. The Mostorg would be in full control. This project attracted me greatly: no petty profits but a most sensible union on a country-wide scale. To work in cooperation as a team with the leaders of the old commercial Russia, reconstructing everything according to the social principle. [This would involve] all of the Moscow trade world. I dreamed and rejoiced in this brilliant idea. I did not dream of working myself and I would not have been able to at the age of seventy-five. Enough of that for me, my time has passed, but I became absorbed in another task. I believed that I might be able to unite the best forces in Russia and abroad and publish a specialized business-technical-commercial newspaper, with a monthly supplement in the form of a journal, to deal with all the problems of state enterprises [such as] business in general, factories and plants, and broad commercial operations. After all, our country is one huge desert. We are the youngest people on the world scale, a fresh, young material, ready to engage in happy fruitful existence and joyful labour. In the past only one-fifth of our live [dynamic] strength has been utilized, the rest has remained in its primitive state. So also is the continent: immense untouched wealth [reposes] in the bosom of the earth and on its expanse.

I am addressing the highest government organ, the Sovnarkom.[14] I had been invited to participate in the work of the newly organized' Mostorg, as well as that of the Gosbank[15] where I had been elected as an external member of the Committee of Inspection (*Revizionnaia komissia*). My close associates Popov and Rogozhin were the directors of the proposed new corporation the Mostorg- a state enterprise with the participation of private individuals.

I agreed to participate because the whole group, including formerly prominent men of affairs, pressed me to include my name. They knew that I could not become a large shareholder, just for 1,000 rubles at the most. I agreed and left for America. In my absence a catastrophic event took place. I do not know the exact events, but it has turned out that a large group of people who had been invited to participate found themselves under judicial investigation for crimes against the State, something I had not been aware of.

How could they have been asked to work for the Government? Before our work could be organized they were charged and sentenced to many years imprisonment. We, the participants, were sentenced to pay damages [for breach of contract] of 300,000 rubles each. When I came back from America I was horrified. The receipt for my deposit of 1,000 rubles was taken away from me. I turned it over to the Court. All my property was seized. The furniture from my home was sold for 600 rubles. I am appealing for justice to Sovnarkom the highest organ of the government. Be merciful and look into my insignificant case. To me this is all that is left in my life. It is the same as death. I am seventy-five years old, I have been doing what I could to be useful. Absolve me from my great sin in that I, in spite of my seventy-five years, still had the audacity to be alive and to indulge in illegal transactions. From the moment of the revolution, I have met with nothing but a warm friendly attitude towards my activities here and even abroad. Our state organs treated me magnanimously, as a friend. Many of their members had been my co-workers. I have worked all these ten years without a break. For the first two years without pay at Tverskaia, Comrade Iponidze is the witness, and two years at Piatnitskaia – with Comrades Eremeev, Svetchikov and V.V. Vorovsky.[16] I remember him warmly. He and I could have worked together until now, as friends. A lot of work was needed in connection with the paper concession, both abroad and in Russia. It is not my fault that this business fell through because of a misunderstanding. Two and one-half years of hard work at the Taganskaia prison and the Ivanov Correctional Home under the authority of the NKVD[17] and, if even in that latter place everything turned out to be to the mutual satisfaction, it is well and good. This was my test of many years. I gave everything to my people's government, within the country and no less abroad. I am sincerely glad of one thing: that among my old friends, some five thousand workers both in Moscow and in Petrograd, I have found fond memories and good feelings about our work together. I sincerely beg that [my case] be considered mercifully and that I be forgiven the penalty for my grave error. Because why should I suffer the death penalty for having trusted people with my signature, did that cause harm to anyone? The

Government punished me with [by taking from me] 1,000 rubles and with the seizure of my property to the value of 6,000 rubles.[18] I plead guilty ... but [ask that you] forgo the punitive [*karatel'nyi*] measures. Close the case. The bailiff will drive me into my grave. Or give me an order to leave for abroad. I have no strength left to endure the torture of prosecution even in the final years of my life. This is a severe suffering, worse than death, to become a man without a good name, one of the living dead.

II
Paper/Newsprint

Our printing plants, the two in Moscow and one in Petrograd (formerly Marks) required over fifteen thousand *puds* of paper per twenty-five hours. The factories then existing on the territory of Russia could not guarantee us a reliable supply, let alone the price. We could not even think of economizing as long as we were able to meet the deadlines and not halt work at the plants. All the [paper] factories were in the heavy capitalist grip of Kuvshinov, the Riabushinskys, Govard [Howard], the Vargushins, Protas'ev.[19] The factories dated back to the times of serfdom. They did introduce a few improvements, but they were far removed from [satisfying the needs of] the consumer, in whom they had little interest. Suddenly, in 1905, came the explosion of the press and mass literature. Our dawdlers [*tikhokhody*] did not move. However, our salvation came from Finland, which helped us by supplying us with paper and paying the duty of 1–10% [0.1%] per *pud*, charging us less by 10% than our own factories. We, the consumers, felt quite at home with them: free credit and reasonable prices, 10% cheaper. Our firm owes its well being to Finland. The business grew. We had to ensure a reliable supply of paper. Here I was helped by G. Nikol'sky, an official in the Ministry of Government Properties. He was an expert on the North and knew all the waterfalls with which Finland is so well endowed, their types and characteristics. And he found for me a waterfall, the most powerful and the most suitable of the existing seven and, under the conditions, the best in all respects, giving us all the advantages. Better than Finland. On the river Kem', close to town and to the sea. He handed me a prepared plan with an estimate of the power and the total construction of the factory. The man had worked on the plan for six months and [an additional] three on the investigation [of the site], together with two assistants, which cost me 20,000 rubles. I took this plan to the Supreme Council of People Economy (VSNKh.). At that time A.L. [sic – actually L.B.] Krasin,[20] encouraged me [to proceed]. He gave me the assignment to go to Germany to recruit a shareholder for the enterprise. Stinnes had been suggested to him as one, who while alive, was very fond of profitable deals. We kept silent. I, Khinzhe, and Eynem.[21] In Germany it was decided in principle to send Stinnes' representative, Ferman, to Moscow with us and to draw up all the agreements here in Moscow. He offered three million rubles toward the construction of the factory. Half of the site was to be ours at the waterfall, and everything half and half. This was to be the basic principle. We arrived in Moscow. Krasin was not there. There were Svetchikov, A.A. Bel'sky, and Bogdanov.[22] We had three meetings. Bel'sky spoke in a more or less negative vein: "What do we need new factories for, we have several old ones, direct the work to them ... [?] the factory employees. This Sytin scheme is for "everything to be bigger and cheaper." And what are we to do with the old factories? Leave them idle? They ought to be made fully operational first, before new ones are built. The time is not ripe yet. Everything has to be put in order. My position is that this [scheme] is premature."

Everyone remained silent. Only Sytin was for expansion: "We are going to expand after we've put the old ones back in order and then [go for] the new." We went through three meetings in this controversial manner. The point of the argument was that it was too early. It was only the beginning of the revolution. They reasoned: "In a year's time we will build new ones, if needed, and for now we will work with the old ones." I kept telling them that I wasn't in this for myself. I saw that our factories supplied the product four times [more expensively?] while I will have ... [?] here. They would build the factory for us without it costing us anything. I told them: "And we will sell the raw material – lumber – on the spot, at a good price. [It will be] a double benefit. And just one proprietor: the State. The agreement with Stinnes is for three years. We can part at any time." Ferman just listened. Later he told me: "Nothing will come out of it, Sytin. They are simply trying to protect their factories from being discarded; it is a pity that Krasin isn't here." He was in England[23] [at the time]. So the deal was lost. My great pity is that I had lost so much of wonderful priceless time. The waterfall keeps on running and waiting. Ferman sat in Moscow for three months. And the deal came to nothing. The agreement did not materialize and Ferman left.

The waterfall empties its waters into the sea, it is a unique place, all set and ready for a low cost ... By its cheap and true industry of the kind and cheapness with which Finland is so amply endowed. A profusion of timber all around and all the water [sea] links with the whole of Europe.

[Another Version]

My proposal to L.B. Krasin and A.M. Lezhava[24] was to utilize my available plans for a concession for a paper plant on the Kem, right on the railway line, with a large waterfall of over 20,000 [horse-] power. These had been prepared for me by the Engineer Nikol'sky ... Of the waterfalls those in the North are the most powerful and convenient [suitable] – of the type of Finnish waterfalls – for a powerful paper factory. I got the approval. I went to Berlin. I put the proposal to Stinnes in person. He examined all the diagrams and the whole plan. He found my proposal to be quite acceptable and serious. And right away he decided to send back to Moscow with me his representatives Ferman ... [and?] two technicians, specialists in factory matters. We arrived in Moscow. I went with Ferman to the VSNKh to see Peter Alekseevich Bogdanov. We explained everything. We decided that the Committee would meet to consider this deal in the next few days. A week later the meeting of the Committee consisting of K.M. Svetchikov, N.I. Bel'sky and a few professors was called.[25] Bogdanov himself showed no interest in the matter. I made the report, stressing the seriousness and the need for this great project so important to Russia, with the capability of producing up to 10 m[illion] *pud* of paper. All the details and advantages had been well researched. The sea links with overseas, huge forest resources, railways all around, waterways, and free labour force, by agreement. Stinnes offered three million to cover the construction costs and asked for the right to operate on the parity principle. Your half for the waterfall and the site – 1 m[illion] and the forest resources during the first year to be valued at 2 m[illion] in rubles. For the subsequent years the going [market] price for timber to apply and cash accounts for the other items. The operation to be on the principle of parity.

They listened to my submission. Everyone kept silent. [Then] Bel'sky took the floor: "This is a large new project. We do not have enough specialists. We suggest that, to begin with, you expand our old factories and supply them with machinery. And then, in the future, move on to larger projects." [I argued:] "But your factories, to our best knowledge, were set up still in the days of serfdom. The machinery and the steam power have all become obsolete, not one of them can be competitive in the nearest future, whether in the volume of production or its economy.

9

MEETINGS WITH GORKY AND LENIN

A.M. Gorky

The literary pseudonym of Aleksei M. Peshkov (1868–1936), 'gorkii' means "bitter" in Russian. A boy with an original talent and an enormous thirst for knowledge born into a poor working-class family, Gorky may have chosen it to remind his readers, and perhaps himself, that his early life had been one of extreme hardship. His novels and dramas describing the life of social outcasts, rebels, and bourgeoisie brought him worldwide fame and great wealth in the 1900s. His socialist convictions and tuberculosis made it imperative for him to leave Russia and he spent years living in a villa on the Italian island of Capri, which became a place of pilgrimage for many Russian socialist activists and literary figures. As Sytin's reminiscences indicate, Gorky's commercial success made him a figure of great interest to publishers.

Sytin visited Gorky on Capri twice. The first visit was in 1911 and the second in 1913. In these recollections he seems to have elided the two visits and repeats the story about the attack on him on the beach in Naples. His reminiscences are found in typescript in the archive of the Sytin Exhibition Centre, Moscow. In the file, the description of the 1913 visit is archived first and that of the 1911 visit second; they appear in that order here.

Version One

V.G. Korolenko came to see me in Nizhnii [Novgorod]. Others were there during the Fair.[1] "Look, Sytin, you are interested in all talented authors. You should meet Gorky. He gave me his address." The next day I went, but A.M. was out at work. He lived in a poorish little hut at the foot of a mountain. The Fair was over and I left.

[Years passed.] 1913 was an awful year, difficult and wearisome.[2] I didn't know where to turn, I was seeking a way out. I wanted to run away from people and from life. In spring everything is enlivened and flourishes, and yet my melancholy and boredom were also growing. I went to Berlin and was wondering what I could do to escape. Suddenly a bright idea hit me – I must visit our recluse, A.M. Gorky in Capri.[3] He is sunning in the southern sun, far away from automobile noise. I asked the newspaperman from the *R.W.* [*Russian Word*][4] to accompany me to the world of bright sun. Naples, Capri. We soon made up our minds to go. The journey itself was a delight. Italy and Rome, the ruins of the great past. Especially Rome. It is a majestic temple, everything in the past. Naples has more life. The wonderful southern sea gives it joy, beauty, and glory. There are marvellous hotels on the seashore, everything is luxurious, bright, light: streets, shops. I go for a walk to the seacoast; everything is peaceful. Suddenly a whole horde of desperados, about ten boys, all in rags, encircle me and demand tips "for macaroni." It's frightening. First, I give them some small change. "No," they say, "that's the small change, you should give us everything you have – your wallet and money." Without delay I give them my purse and try to run away. One of them runs behind me and grabs me by the feet. I fall down, and before I can jump to my feet, the one who is closest to me grabs my wallet and runs away. All the rest follow him. I remain, alone.

Well, nature granted glory and beauty to this place. But a dark evil force dominates the society here. There's sun, warmth, and beauty here, but attacks of the "macaroni" type mean that people do not have enough to eat and there is no happiness and comfort. First, "give us some money for macaroni," and then "give us your wallet." When I return to the hotel my friends tell me they are surprised that those boys haven't taken away my coat. I realize that things happen, even in places where the nature is gorgeous; someone will still force you to give them money "for macaroni."

The next morning we went to Capri on board a wonderful ship. One immediately felt that the life here was very simple, no splendour and grandeur. Everything's in the past, just the life of our average provincial town. But the nature is rich and beautiful. The road from the docks leads to the mountains. And on the top there's a market, a few hotels, and two temples. The dacha[5] of Aleksei Maksimovich is right here, the path from it slopes down the other side of this huge rock of Capri. There's a good footpath towards the sea that affords a gorgeous view and a wonderful swim.

I stayed at the hotel, but most of the time I lived at Aleksei Maksimovich's villa. The wonderful view from his villa gave me joy. "You're sitting pretty here, Yekaterina Pavlovna[6] – this dacha is a wonder. I really appreciate that you've shown me, what beautiful nature there is on earth."

Great patricians used to live on this rock. The Monastery of Capuchins is here, the famous ancient monument of past centuries. A walk along this huge rock of Capri is marvellous. Here's the famous historic place – a cliff over the sea, where the old sovereigns threw slaves into the water, using their bodies to feed the sea fish they had for their meals. While walking I observed everything. But we were still occupied with thoughts about Russia.

"Everything's fine, Aleksei Maksimovich, but what about Russia? She's expecting you. We came for you. Let's go back to Russia. She needs you. It is dark, severe, cold, but it is dear still and close to us because it is our own."

"Yes, I love Russia as it is." [Sytin:] "And do you remember Nizhnii? And the affection that V. Korolenko and I. Petrov had for you.[7] You are very dear to them." After many talks A.M. decided to come to Russia. And he did come at the beginning of fall, 1913. He stayed at our dacha in Bersenevka, an estate in a Moscow suburb. He lived there for three months, till spring. And in spring he moved to Finland, where we started to publish a monthly magazine, which had a middling success. Days and months went by. The revolution was approaching. We had to prepare a monthly newspaper that later was organized without my participation.

Version Two

Aleksei Maksimovich Gorky gave me a lot of joy in my life. It was just before the war. And it was a hard and gloomy time.

Everything was falling apart; I wanted to run away from it. The ruins of Russian were suffused with a nightmare, and there was no gleam of hope visible. I remember, everybody was expecting a catastrophe in those hard years. That gloom was torturing me too. I was seeking a way out, trying to run away from myself. I went to Warsaw. My young [grandson] Mitya[8] was with me. There was gloom and boredom everywhere. In Warsaw I remembered that I had wanted to meet A.M. Gorky. It would be nice to go and see him in Capri. The next day everything was ready and we left for Italy.

The long trip, the Italian sun, and the blue sea enlivened my soul. Oh, God! What a joyful, happy, heavenly world. In Naples it seemed to me that I had got to a country of luxury and richness; the palaces and hotels were sparkling so brightly in the sun, the windows of expensive shops were dazzlingly inviting. But when we went to the sun-lit Naples bay later that night, I was encircled by several men, who at first asked and then demanded money "for macaroni." I gave them all the money I had about me and was very happy that I managed to escape. No, not everything is fine there.

The sea, the sun, Vesuvius don't solve the problem of "macaroni." After the night in Naples we headed for Capri, the renowned toy island; where Roman emperors had sought oblivion, where Garibaldi lived his last days, and where now our disgraced Russian writer had found shelter.

Aleksei Maksimovich gave me a kind and friendly welcome. He lived high up in the mountain. The view from his place was brilliant. The beauty and unbounded distance of the azure sea.

I went directly to his house from the harbour. It was a small modest summer cottage.

"Where can I stay?"

"Why, you can stay with us, we'll host you."

I thanked A.M. and was glad to be with him all the time during my short visit.

Here I am, at the docks. I'm saying to him: "It's my dream. I'm not quite normal, A.M., I've flown to you to seek comfort: it's turbulent in our country, awkward and turbulent, and the main thing is that it's silly."

"Yes, old chap, you're doing the devil knows what, you may turn the whole of life upside down. Just wash your hands [of it] and we'll go to the terrace for tea and a chat."

"My shelter is a total comfort, an earthly paradise. Fresh air and spiritual joy heal my soul and add more power to it. I've become younger in body and soul. Let's go to the terrace and have tea and appetizers."

"Well, now we'll take care of your health after the trip."

"Yes, A.M., only now do I understand what insanity means. I've come to you for healing, you know what medicine to use."

"How should I treat you?" A.M. is laughing. "When you diagnose the case, you'll know what the disease is."

"I hope for and look forward to being healed or I wouldn't have come to you."

"Capri will heal you."

"That's true, but besides what Capri can give, I need your spiritual and cheering sympathy. I trust in you like in magic."

"Well, I'll be happy to see that this magic works for you. And you are right: it is miraculous that our motherland *Velikaia* [Great] *Rus* [the Russian people] has remained alive, and miraculously surviving," says A.M.

"So, I'm right that I need a miracle from you."

"You may want to have a rest?"

"Oh, no, A.M. I've been resting during the whole trip. And now I'm glad to have a chat with you and I'll be glad to go for a walk with you if you wish to do it."

"Let's go to the sea-coast and look at the nature around."

The walk lasted less than an hour. After the walk we went home and talked shop. The next day we surveyed the island of Capri. What beauty and prehistoric life everywhere! A.M. showed me a huge island about a *verst*[9] down. One could see from there what was going on: the sea surf down. They threw Caesars' unfaithful wives and slaves who got in trouble from there. A terrible historic place.

And here is a huge old monastery of the Capuchins. A cardinal from Naples used to live here once. And now everything is deserted, dead, covered by the grass of oblivion.

But even among those wonderful ruins, where all centuries and all epochs had left a trace, we still remembered about Russia.

"Well, A.M., how about going back to Russia? You need Russia, don't you? And she needs you. Let's go home."

We returned to this topic several times, and I could see he relished the prospect of returning to Russia. The problem was to get permission. It was possible to get it, and it was finally received without much problem.

I said good-bye to A.M., hoping he would soon return to Russia. Several months later A.M. returned to Russia. I offered to let him stay at my estate in a Moscow suburb. He willingly accepted my offer and lived there till spring, and then he moved to Kokalla in Finland, where we started to publish a magazine called *Chronicle* (*Letopis'*). Soon the publication had to be halted: we were in for a turbulent period in our history.

Gorky went to Petrograd, where he started the publication of the newspaper *New Life* (*Novaya Zhizn'*) and simultaneously began publishing books. I sympathized with him in that business and helped him indirectly, but couldn't take part in it personally.[10]

Meetings with V.I. Lenin

Sytin wrote three versions of his meeting with V.I. Lenin in Petrograd in February 1918. In characteristic fashion, seeking to talk to the top man when he had a major problem, following the nationalization of his properties in Moscow, including his daily paper *Russian Word*, he had headed to the capital to talk with the Soviet leader. His purpose was to find out what the future would hold for him under the new regime. Sytin's eldest daughter, Anna Ivanovna, held on to her father's notes about the meeting for many years and then placed them in the Sytin archive at the Sytin Exhibition Centre in Moscow. Sytin's tone changes by the third account, as though he senses the perils that are closing in on him and wants to make sure of Lenin's protection for his family.

Version One

Sytin's company was the first to be subjected to nationalization. On the very first day the new government took office, the newspaper and the printing plant where *Russian Word* was published were subjected to nationalization. I didn't object and didn't take any steps, but I went to Petrograd, Smolny [Palace], to see Vladimir Ilyich Lenin in order to avoid any misunderstanding during nationalization. He received me in his office, and sent an aide-de-camp to meet me. I was surprised to see my friend Gorbunov's son.[11] "Hallo, Nikolenka, where's your dad?" "Dad is in the Caucasus." "Well, take me to Vladimir Ilyich." We enter a modest office, I bow and ask Vladimir Ilyich to spare me a minute. [He says:] "Please, have a chair." "What's the matter?" – [I explain:] "My newspaper *Russian Word* has been nationalized in Moscow." He says: "That's right, it's just the beginning, all your businesses are subject to nationalization, that's the common lot."

I answer: "It doesn't scare or frustrate me, but there is one problem that worries me: what are you going to do with this old guy?" I point to myself. "Is he liable for nationalization?" Lenin replied: "We will not nationalize him and will give him a chance to live freely as he used to live if he has nothing against us," I thanked him and declared that I would assist them in using all my equipment. And we parted friends. Nikolenka took me back, he had been in the room with us during our talk. I told him: "Well, that's fine, I'll find something to do for myself in the construction of a new life." I came back to Moscow in a cheerful mood.

Version Two

[When] the revolution came, my companies were the first to be nationalized (the newspaper *Russian Word* and others). I gave the new government the right to do what it wanted with my companies but wanted to understand completely, I myself went to Petrograd. I came to Smolny and asked where I could see V.I. Lenin. They directed me to the middle floor. I followed the directions and asked who could show me Vladimir Ilyich's office. I gave my business card and waited a little. A young man came out; I looked at him and recognized the son of my old friend

P.M.[12] Gorbunov. Nikolai Petrovich asked me: "Would you like to see Vladimir Ilyich?" "Yes." "Vladimir Ilyich is waiting for you." We walk towards the office. It is marked off by a wooden partition. We enter. Vladimir Ilyich is sitting. He asks me to sit down. "What's the matter?" asks Vladimir Ilyich. I say: "Vladimir Ilyich, can you spare me a minute? My newspaper *Russian Word* has been nationalized in Moscow." Vladimir Ilyich says: "Yes, and your other companies are subject to nationalization." "I won't object, I myself will help willingly. But my question is, what will you do with this piece of goods, will you nationalize it?"

Vladimir Ilyich laughs and says: "We will not nationalize this old guy, we'll leave him alone; if he is not against us we are not against him. Let him live as he used to live, and if he is not against us, we won't do him any harm." I stood up, thanked Vladimir Ilyich and left the office.

Version Three

On the first day of nationalization of my company I went to see Vladimir Ilyich in Petrograd, Smolny, and asked for an appointment with him. Vladimir Ilyich received me.

"Why are you here, Sytin?"

"Please, let me state my request in five minutes."

"Please, sit down and tell me your problem."

"Today my companies are being nationalized in Moscow."

"Yes, that's the common lot, we are nationalizing everybody," Vladimir Ilyich says.

"I personally will assist in the process of nationalizing my companies. But my request to you is personal, about my big family, fourteen people, youngsters and adults, and I myself am an old man. I've come to you to ask for my family. I personally will pass on to you my offices and companies and will assist so that there will be no delay, and will help, wherever it is possible.

But I've come to ask you for my family. Let us keep the apartment in which I'm living now, and let my family stay where we are."[13]

Vladimir Ilyich says: "Stay where you've been living, we won't move you. I give my word, if you are not against us."

I rose, shook his hand with my both hands and bowed with gratitude.

"You'll see, Vladimir Ilyich, I'll prove myself in future."

After this talk I handed over all my companies to them, and there wasn't the least bit of trouble

PART II

RECOLLECTIONS ABOUT SYTIN BY OTHERS

10

EVDOKIA IVANOVNA SYTINA
AND BERSENEVKA

Sergei Sokolov

Sergei Sokolov, who wrote these memoirs, was Sytin's wife's nephew. It is clear from what he chose to describe that in his subsequent life he never enjoyed as much material comfort and affluence as in the days of his childhood under the wing of his severe but protective aunt. In this memoir Sytin appears mostly as the companion of his wife, Evdokia Ivanovna, indicating that the business and family spheres were strictly delimited in the Sytin marriage: Ivan Dmitrievich was the absolute ruler of his enterprises, while at home it was his wife who ruled over the children and the household and who organized assistance to the needy relatives – whom the Sytins, like all the newly rich – seemed to have in large numbers on both sides of the family and for whom they assumed full responsibility when necessary.

Evdokia Ivanovna Sytina

Evdokia Ivanovna Sytina was the elder sister of my father, Ivan Ivanovich Sokolov. Their parents – Ivan Ilarionovich, their father, and Maria Grigorievna, their mother, Sokolov – had two children, daughter Evdokia and son Ivan. Their father, Ivan Ilarionovich, was a strict and severe man, very demanding, and so the children got a morally strict education. When they reached adulthood they themselves were strict, severe, and demanding. They had never been indulged by their father. But their mother, Maria Grigorievna, was a tender, kind, and fair woman and she took great care of them and gave them warm affection, as though she were nurturing them with warm sunlight. If it had not been for her love, they would have been severe and angry people. My father, Ivan Ivanovich, often mentioned his mother Maria Grigorievna as a kind and gentle woman and always spoke about her with love.

Maria Grigorievna died when her children were still young and their father Ivan Ilarionovich brought into his home a young stepmother. In their early years my father and our Aunt Dunya (this is what we called her when we were young, later we called her simply "Aunt") helped their father. My father was an assistant cook to my grandfather and Aunt kept house for grandfather until he remarried. Besides, she was a dishwasher, she washed dishes when grandfather was hired to cater receptions. In general, Ivan Ilarionovich did not give his children a chance to play and fool around. Both father and Aunt got only an elementary education. Aunt completed four grades and father fewer. Both of them were unlettered, but thanks to their natural intelligence they were cultured people. My father respected Aunt and was even a little afraid of her. He called her "Dear Sister Evdokia Ivanovna" and addressed her as "you" rather than "thee" and always carried out all of her instructions. Aunt Dunya married Ivan Dmitrievich [Sytin] through an intermediary marriage broker, and that took place before Ivan Ilarionovich's second marriage. Ivan Dmitrievich liked her because she was an efficient, quick, and neat housekeeper, was cute, and one can even say good-looking. My father, after his sister's marriage, also married by brokerage the daughter of a man who owned a small sausage factory, Konstantin Efimovich Generalov. Generalov had a workshop and sales shop on Tverskaia Street in Moscow next to the store of the Eliseev Brothers. My dear mother Anna Konstantinovna was a complete opposite of Aunt Dunya. She liked to laugh and have a good time and was very kind and loving. My dear mother's family life was quite different from that of Aunt Dunya. In her family life Aunt Dunya was in accord with Ivan Dmitrievich, because she always had the upper hand over Ivan Dmitrievich. She had much common sense. (Ivan Dmitrievich respected and loved her.) He always sought her advice, not only in family affairs but in his publishing business. Later, when Ivan Dmitrievich's business expanded, she had talks with important people such as Lev Nikolaevich Tolstoy, Anton Pavlovich Chekhov, V.M. Doroshevich, and Aleksei Maksimovich Gorky, who presented her with a copy of his book *Mother*. (Aunt Dunya enjoyed reading and read a lot and liked the theatre, especially the Malyi Theatre.) My dear mother was very unhappy in her family life with my father. She loved him very much but because of his faults – he was hot-tempered and despotic, he liked to drink a lot with his friends and to show himself off in their company, and the like – because of his character, life with him was very hard; as a result, at the young age of thirty-four my dear mother looked like an elderly woman and she passed away leaving eight children for father to take care of. My youngest brother Ivan was eight months old. On the day of her death, my mother was fully conscious and her mind was clear. In the presence of almost all her close relations, she asked the closest relative on father's side, Evdokia Ivanovna, to take care of the children and Aunt completely agreed. So after my mother's death Evdokia Ivanovna protected and took care of us, although we lived in a separate apartment and had a cook and baby-sitter. Aunt Dunya often visited us just to see how we were getting along, what we were eating, and helped the older sisters and my brother Konstantin to get into the *gymnazium* where they studied. And as we younger children grew up, she arranged schooling for us. I remember, for example, that thanks to Aunt Dunya, Uncle Vanya (that's what we called Ivan Dmitrievich) took me to a commercial school, which had just opened on Stremiannyi Pereulok [Groom's Lane]. He held me, a young boy, by the hand and introduced me to the director of the school, Alexander Nikolaevich Glagolev (a man who loved children). At that time I certainly didn't understand much and certainly did not realize that such an important person as the publisher Ivan Dmitrievich Sytin was taking his nephew by the hand and asking for his admission to school. Besides this incident, I also remember when we lived in Tverskaia Street, no. 48, the Sytin Company, where the printing plant of the paper, *Russian Word*, was located. When we lived there Ivan Dmitrievich dropped in on us at Dunya's in early spring to see how we were getting on because Aunt had gone with her family to the estate at Bersenevka and hadn't managed to send us there yet.

Aunt Dunya showed so much attention to our family that she bathed us small children in her bedroom in the bathtub that was separated from the sleeping room by opaque glass. After the bath, she wrapped us in a fuzzy bath sheet, put us on her double bed, and rubbed us down, after which she gave us an apple or a caramel. (I remember in her wardrobe that had a mirror in it, there was always transparent candy from Eynem's candy factory.) If Aunt couldn't bathe us herself, the nanny of her children – Petya, Mitya, Olya, Anya – did it. The nanny didn't like to bathe us very much, and was always grumbling. And when she washed our legs and feet with a soapy washcloth, she pushed back my knees so hard that it was painful. I remember putting my legs straight in response, but I could not bring myself to protest out loud because I knew she would look at me angrily, open her mouth, showing two yellow fangs, and hiss something. I don't know why, but she always called me "Twister." In general, I have a warm, affectionate memory of Aunt Dunya.

Very often, she put us all at a round table to serve us dinner, supper, or tea and the like. Of course, not everyone. (I frequently stayed with them at Mitya's request because we were great friends.) The table was set in the small dining room next to the big dining room, which was used only for special occasions. In the small dining room the whole family sat at the round table – the whole family plus some of us Sokolovs or Logachevs, especially Ivan. Aunt Dunya sat in the middle of the table and Ivan Dmitrievich sat next to her at her right, and next to him his older sons, Kolya, Vasya, Volodya, Vanya, then Petya, Mitya, me, and/or somebody else. Then Dusha, and when Olya and Anya grew up, they sat to the left of Aunt Dunya.[1] The maid (I remember only Natasha), a stout, quiet, and neat woman, brings out boiled meat sliced into pieces in a small dish and Aunt gives everybody a piece, starting, of course, with Ivan Dmitrievich. (He sits at the table with a white napkin tucked into his shirt collar and hanging down his chest to his knees [in order] not to stain his business suit.) Sometimes he reaches out, selects a piece of meat for himself by stabbing it with a fork and I remember that at that time he put on his pince nez, which he took out of his pocket. The table is fully laid on a white tablecloth. At each place, there is a big plate, a little plate for bread, a fork, a knife, and a little crystal or silver dish, on which the knife and fork rested, a silver table spoon, a napkin in a ring or without it – in a ring for members of the family, without it for a guest. And again, in the middle of the table there was a large crystal bowl for salt, then mustard, horseradish, salted cucumbers, and pickles in a salad bowl. All these dinners or teas were ceremonial, and the older children could talk to Aunt and Uncle, calling them "Mamochka" or "Papochka." The younger children had to eat in silence, but sometimes they whispered among themselves while looking in awe at Mamochka and Papochka. So there was order and neatness in Aunt Dunya's house. She taught all her children and Ivan Dmitrievich himself to be neat and to value order, except the oldest son Vasya, who was at that time a student in the medical faculty of Moscow University. He was always late for dinner, supper, or tea. He didn't like to dress up, was often unshaved, and later on even grew a moustache and beard, always wore glasses in a metal frame, liked to smoke. He had beautiful teeth, was very handsome, never wore shirts with ties, always wore a sateen blue *kasavorotka* with a belt.[2]

On Ivan Dmitrievich saint's days, especially when the family lived on Valovaia Street next to the printing company, he, his son Vanya, Evdokia Ivanovna, and their daughter Dunya received guests – not only relatives but different business people. From early morning various cakes were brought to the house accompanied by greeting cards from their friends. The dinners on those days were very ceremonial, chefs and waiters were specially hired, a big dinner was prepared with wines, appetizers, hot dishes, hot meat, ice creams, sponge cake, and fruit. After the dinner, all the guests danced, especially the quadrille; even Aunt and Uncle took part. They took each other by the hand, made a chain, and skipped through all the rooms of the house to the music, starting in the reception room, into the big dining room, small dining room, along the corridors, past the staircase leading upstairs, where there were three rooms for the girls and Petya and Mitya. Then they passed Aunt and Uncle's bedroom and returned to the reception room. And all were merry and flushed.

After such days, our Aunt Dunya always sent two or three cakes to us, the Sokolov children, with delicious buttercream topping. And also some hot roast meat and cold steamed fish. The chambermaid Natasha, the senior chambermaid, said that it had all been sent by Evdokia Ivanovna herself for us to eat in good health and she said it respectfully and with a smile.

Our Aunt Dunya hated to be called "Madame [*barina*]." She preferred to be called by her name and patronymic. This chambermaid, Natasha, was a middle-aged woman, completely illiterate, but she was a direct, good woman, respected everybody and never said a rude word to anyone. She was stout, always neatly dressed, and her hair was smoothly arranged. She wore a white, starched apron, embroidered, and had earrings shaped like small gold balls. She had served in the house of my aunt for many years and stayed with them until her death; she died at the beginning of the revolution [in 1917].

I don't remember very well on which day exactly Aunt put up a Christmas tree in her house on Valovaia Street – at the New Year or on the first day of Christmas. Each year she herself decorated a very big fir tree that reached to the ceiling in her big, white reception room decorated in imitation marble, with two pillars at the entrance to the room. She didn't let anyone into the room but Natasha while she was decorating the Christmas tree. The tree was always decorated not only with toys, beads, silver and golden ribbons, and flags but also with candied fruit jelly in the shape of berries on twigs, and *mont-pensier*,[3] crackers, and party noisemakers to break open, from which there came different fancy paper costumes that we put on. The candles were of different colours in candlesticks with different intricate designs that were clipped onto the branches of the tree. When there was a Christmas party all the children of the relatives came to look at the tree. The children of the older daughter, Maria Ivanovna Blagova – Vanya, Valya, Lida, Kolya – their father Fedor Ivanovich, and his mother, Agrafiena Egorovna, and we Sokolov children – Vera, Anya, Kostya, Seriozha, Zhenya, Lena, Manya, and Vanichka. The Logachevs came rarely. These were the children of Ivan Dmitrievich's sister, Alexandra Dmitrievna, – Maria and Pavel – except Ivan Logachev, who lived in Sytin's family with the older sons on the ground floor of the house. We always had a great time with different dishes to eat, fruit and sweets, and returned home from the Christmas tree with various presents.

In summer Aunt took us all to the estate at Bersenevka, for the whole summer, where each family had a separate dacha. The Blagovs stayed in a wooden house, the Logachevs and we Sokolovs in a stone dacha, divided by a stone wall into two parts. We had four well-lighted rooms and a terrace and a kitchen. And the Logachevs had two rooms, a kitchen, and a terrace. When Vasya Sytin married our teacher Liudmilla Vladimirovna, their family also lived at Bersenevka in a house very close to the village, and Vasya in a small house with his own apiary. It was a pleasant time and lots of children got together. Aunt arranged different entertainments for children: "giant strides," swings for one and big swings for six–eight people and gymnastic equipment for different exercises. If a child had a saint's day, there were tea parties with bilberry cheesecakes, sweet pies with raspberry or apple jam filling, or with fresh berries, depending on the season. The Kliazma River ran by the estate and by three ponds, and Aunt arranged swimming in the ponds and in the river. There were bathhouses, a closed one on the pond and an open one on the river. All the children went swimming in a crowd and had a good time. Those who could swam and the others just splashed in the water. There was a lot of noise, shouting and screaming, and we boys liked to splash one another by smacking the water with our hands. There was a pond between the Sokolov dacha and the Blagov dacha, and a boat with two pairs of oars and a chain with a lock. With Aunt's permission, we went boating in the daytime, and our older brothers and sisters used the boats in the evening. They took guitars and balalaikas and sang songs and accompanied themselves.

We also played soccer, and rode bicycles and a small horse whose name was Bulanchik. The horse was yellow with a black tail and a black mane. We rode the horse into the forest to pick berries and mushrooms.

Vasya Sytin liked to go fishing and he took almost all of us children with him, especially the boys and the older sisters. They went in a *tarantass*[4] pulled by a horse, took a load of delicious food, a big cast iron tea kettle, metal mugs, spoons, knives or they walked 10 versts or 3 versts and stayed overnight in Maidorovo or some other village where Vasya picked a spot to camp on the river bank so that we could make a fire at night. He himself took buckets for crucians and went to the river to fish with a trap. During the night he would catch quite few pike. And we all gathered firewood and kept the fire going until morning. We made tea, baked potatoes on the coals, and so on. Certainly all of those trips were arranged with the permission of Aunt Dunya and so she herself supplied us with food from her own pantry.

On Shrove Tuesday, Aunt arranged wagon rides for the children. At the printing plant there were cart horses called *bitiugi*, and two horses pulled one *rozvalny*,[5] and on the sledge there was hay or straw covered with carpets, and the children sat on top and rode from Valovaia Street along Tverskaia Street to the gate of Petrovsky Park. For all of us children, that was great fun. On Christmas vacations, Aunt rented boxes at the theatre. I remember the Korsh Theatre and the children's matinees. I remember *Aladdin's Lamp* or going to the Bolshoi Theatre to see the *The Humpbacked Horse* or other plays.

When at the Bersenevka estate in summer, our Aunt took great care of us. She wanted us not only to have fun but she wanted us to look neat and clean, so she arranged regular visits to the bath for us. The bathhouse was at the edge of the forest park next to the big pond. The older brothers ran right out of the bathhouse to swim in the pond. The little ones were taken to the bath by their baby-sitters.

Besides arranging our entertainments, Aunt looked after our education, too. In summer, we had lessons with a male or female teacher who stayed at the estate. for the whole summer. We had two or three hours of lessons every morning – writing, reading, arithmetic problems, and preparing for re-taking examinations in the fall. When we grew up and became adults, our Aunt did not forget to look after us. We often went to the theatre with [Aunt's] grown children and went to balls that were arranged by our *gymnasia* and schools, especially at the Hunting Club or the Nobles' Club.

Aunt Dunya lived to her sixty-fourth year and in 1924 all her close relatives who happened to be in Moscow at that time were at her graveside in the church on Malaia Dmitrovka. It was called Christmas on Putinka, near Strastnoi Monastery. We were all in bitter tears because we had lost the person who was most dear to us. We knew that we were parting from her forever and that we would never see her again. After the funeral service, the priest said good words about her at the end of the funeral service, that she had been a wonderful person with a beautiful soul.

These are my memories from childhood.

The Village of "Bersenevka"

In some ways this second part of Sokolov's memoirs seems to belong before the section about Evdokia Ivanovna. It is clear from its content, however, that it was written later. It was the second of two note books by Sokolov that Anna Ivanovna Sytina gave to the Sytin Exhibition Centre.

The business affairs at I.D. Sytin's company went so well that the share-holders received good dividends for their shares at the end of the year. Ivan Dmitrievich had more shares than the others, so his dividend was high, too, and he was well off financially, and much money was left after all the family expenses had been paid. So he and Evdokia Ivanovna decided to buy a house and a plot of land. At that time, some noblemen sold their estates and moved to towns. Prince Nesvizhsky was selling his estate that was situated at the small Nesvizhskaia station (Povyarova) along the Nikolaevskii railway ... 45 versts from Moscow, the same distance – 45 versts – along the highway to Lenin-grad [St Petersburg]. Prince Nesvizhsky owned a big forest, arable fields, and an estate house with a number of out-buildings. Ivan Dmitrievich bought the whole estate with the help of his manager, Evgeny Antonovich Butorev, i.e., the land, the forest, the house with all the furniture, etc. Around the two-storied wooden main house there were two brick buildings, a stable, a carriage house, a hay-barn on stone pillars, a horse-drawn carriage, a threshing machine. Prince Nesvizhsky also sold two horses, one for driving carriages, black, called "Voronoi." He was an angry old stallion who always wanted to lead the way and as soon as he saw any horse ahead of him on the road, he started to overtake it and the coachman couldn't hold him back. The other horse was white, called "Pegashka," an old, blind mare used only for trans-porting drinking water in a barrel from the well.

In buying a big estate Ivan Dmitrievich was thinking not only of a summer holiday home for his family and children. His main intention was to establish a model agricultural estate with sown crops, dairy, and poultry farms. He also had in mind setting up a boarding school for training students in drawing and printing and a home for the eld-erly workers of his printing plant.

Meanwhile, every summer almost all his relatives came to stay at the estate: the Blagovs, Sokolovs, Logachevs, and his son Vasily Ivanovich with his wife and children, who had beehives and enjoyed beekeeping. Each family, i.e., Blagovs, Sokolovs, Logachevs, had its own separate dacha, e.g., we, Sokolovs, had four rooms, a kitchen, and a terrace in a brick house with a garden and flowers. The house was situated next to a big pond in a big overgrown park. Our family consisted of eight children, father, and two servants: a nanny and a cook. Our family lived at that dacha the whole summer. The other families – Blagovs, Logachevs, and Vasily Ivanovich – lived almost in the same way. I.D. Sytin hired a manager from the agricultural academy. They sowed rye, oats, clover, fodder grass called "timofeevka," planted potatoes, cabbage, and other vegetables. The gardener cultivated berries: garden and wild strawberries. "Russian strawberries" were especially good, long, sweet, and fragrant. Besides, there were "Usanka" raspberries, black currants, gooseberries. The gardener grew flower seedlings in the greenhouse, then planted flowers in the flower beds at the beginning of the summer. The flower garden was especially nice near the big house in which Ivan Dmitrievich and his family lived. There was a corner with fragrant flowers in it.

When Ivan Dmitrievich came to the dacha in the evening from Moscow he went to bathe in the Kliazma River that was flowing behind their garden. He liked to take a thick bath towel, wear a jacket made of tussore (*chesucha*), use a walking stick, and he certainly preferred to take us, boys with him rather than bathe alone. He couldn't swim, but would walk into the water, soap his head and body, then splash in the water with a chuckle. He would screw up his eyes and would always have some comment, he never bathed in silence. He would say, for example, how good, clean, fresh, and transparent the water was, how pleasant it was to stand on the sandy bottom of the river. At the opposite bank there were stones but some alder shrubs were hanging low over the water and nobody went to bathe there. He often bathed with Fedor Ivanovich Blagov, his older daughter Maria Ivanovna's husband. Certainly, we always bathed with him. Ivan Dmitrievich often talked with Fedor Ivanovich about the newspaper business, as F.I. was the editor of the paper, *Russian Word*. Sometimes he laughed, sometimes he got angry and immediately gave all sorts of instructions to F.I.

After the bath, Ivan Dmitrievich went home where supper was ready for him; in warm weather the table was laid on the open terrace, which was covered with vines, and in chilly weather supper was served in the closed terrace. After supper, Ivan Dmitrievich liked to walk in the garden. He always paced along the path with his hands behind his back, looking around and whispering something to himself. There were old apple trees with wide-spreading branches in the garden; there also grew two big cedar trees that had cones with nuts on them. And there were bushes of white and purple lilac everywhere.

In general, the garden was small, but it was a pleasant, quiet corner in the full sense of the word, even low behind the garden one could hear nightingales singing and the calls of the land rails. On Sunday, after a very simple breakfast – one or two cups of coffee or tea with a sandwich with butter or a slice of sausage – Ivan Dmitrievich went to inspect his fields toward the big forest behind which the village of Loshki was situated. He usually walked alone or with the manager; a small grey cap with a button on top always on his head, wearing a tussore silk jacket and holding a walking stick. The country road that led to the big forest was rarely used because there was a big highway leading to Leningrad [St Petersburg at the time] behind the forest parallel to the country road. So Ivan Dmitrievich walked alone or with the manager and nobody disturbed him; it was very quiet in good sunny weather, insects and beetles were flying in the air, grasshoppers were chirring in the grass, and swallows were flying over the fields and the road, there were shining blue swallows with white breasts, and skylarks were singing high up in the sky. Frightened birds, yellow buntings and wagtails were rising over the road.

In general, such walks, although business-connected were pleasant and nice, especially thanks to the quietness. And certainly Ivan Dmitrievich was in a very good mood, contemplating everything around, especially if the crops or rye, oats, and clover were good. And new plans and projects were developing in his head, not only about running the estate but also about his printing, newspaper, and other businesses.

He returned home from his walk usually by lunchtime, but before lunch he always took a dip in the pond or the river with us boys or with somebody else. There was a specially arranged bathing pool enclosed by walls of battens and inside the pool were two boxes for us kids, where we could jump, holding the sides of the box. In the big box one could even swim.

There were five ponds on the estate, one big pond near the cattle yard and the village of Bersenevka. In the big pond, the horses and cows bathed and drank water. There was another big pond near our dacha and the old park where big, old birch trees, planted in rows, grew. Part of the pond closer to the park was overgrown with sedge and there were yellow waterlilies around and a big boat, which all of us rowed. On the same bank near our dacha was a wooden bathhouse where everyone went for a bath. After the bath, the adults jumped into the pond to swim from a small raft.

Behind the Blagovs' dacha and a young birch forest and on the other side of the path lined with nut grove bushes was the third pond through which a stream flowed and there the pond had been created. Below it was the fourth small pond. Near the big forest was the fifth pond; the water was transparent and white lilies grew on the surface. On Ivan Dmitrievich's estate next to the big house and behind the brick dachas there had been planted young apple trees. Dairy farming had been well established on the estate and milk, cream, and butter were sold in Moscow to the dairy firm Chichkin & Blandoff.

In later times, the gardener grew a lot of strawberries and one could sell strawberries, mainly to acquaintances.

[In Moscow] the house in which Ivan Dmitrievich's family lived was large and there were many rooms in it. There was a mezzanine floor upstairs for the youngest children and their nanny, who was later replaced by a governess. The rooms for the all the sons were downstairs in a semi-basement. The windows were at the ground level and looked out to the front garden and the lilac bushes. The brother of Ivan Dmitrievich's wife, Evdokia Ivanovna Sytina, Ivan Ivanovich Sokolov, as I mentioned before, had a family that was left without a mother, who died at the young age of thirty-four. So Evdokia Ivanovna became the guardian of the children at the request of their dying mother, who was fully conscious.[6] All the children were sent to different schools. The oldest sister, Vera, finished the *gymnasia* with a gold medal and came to Aunt and Uncle to tell them about her successful graduation (by the way, Ivan Dmitrievich was also her god-father). They both congratulated her and put a gold chain around her neck with a finely crafted pendant mounted with jewels. In spite of being busy with printing and editing affairs, Ivan Dmitrievich always found time for such things as presents for his god-daughter's academic accomplishments. This is not the whole story. She wanted to take a teaching job and Ivan Dmitrievich gave her two letters of recommendation, one to the well-known Morozova and the other to the Department of Education of the City Council.

Ivan Dmitrievich's affairs were going on very well despite the fact that his printing plant had been set on fire by the Black Hundreds and the police.[7] Ivan Dmitrievich kept expanding his share-holding companies; that is why his business was bringing large dividends.

In 1918, approximately at the end of July, I, Serezha, the son of Ivan Ivanovich Sokolov, was invited by Aunt Evdokia Ivanovna and Uncle Ivan Dmitrievich to come to them in the evening. I went immediately and their chambermaid Natasha had just left. (She was the senior chamber maid, obese but a fast and very neat worker. She had worked in their house for many years. She was a very good person.) My aunt and uncle were sitting in the big dining room (the room was filled with mahogany furniture encrusted with bronze fittings and the wainscoting and the ceiling were mahogany). There were beautiful pillars by the walls and in the middle of the room a big, long table that filled the room. There were chairs made of mahogany; they were huge and were covered with green plush. The table was covered with a beautiful oilcloth. They were sitting at the table, just the two of them. The samovar in the shape of a globe was boiling. They were waiting for me to have tea with them. There were sweets, jam, candy, cookies on the table for tea. And on the cupboard there was always a crystal vase with fresh fruit. First, I greeted them. The tradition was to kiss Aunt Dunya and Uncle Vanya on the cheeks. I then sat down on the chair opposite Ivan Dmitrievich and aunt poured tea for me and for Ivan Dmitrievich in glasses and for herself in a cup. Aunt started to talk, and she said that they had asked me to come because father, as she called Ivan Dmitrievich, needed an assistant in church affairs and he had decided to ask me to take this position because I was very modest and quiet by nature, didn't smoke, didn't drink wine, and spent a lot of time among women. By the way, I have never smoked and hate wine. Ivan Dmitrievich did not smoke either and I never saw him tipsy. He always looked like a very busy businessman. After the conversation was started by Aunt, Ivan Dmitrievich said, "I don't think you will refuse my request to help me in my work in the church, Nikola na Putinka, next to the monastery Our Lady's Passions (Strastnoi Bozhei Materi). Moreover, he considered me religious because Aunt knew that I went to church with my older sister Vera for vespers and also at mid-day. He said that he was very busy and couldn't devote much time to church affairs and, of course, it was necessary to go to church at mid-day service and on holidays to go both to mid-day service and to vespers. I would have to take care of all the financial affairs. He said that he had no other person but me in mind to do this work. Certainly I did not feel that I could refuse the request because I was well aware of Aunt's care of our family, and I felt I was obliged to help them. But deep in my heart I was very reluctant to take the assignment. I would have to run financial affairs and buy candles and lamp oil and collect money from the parishioners with a collection plate and I hated that. It made me very embarrassed. I prayed to God that this work would not last very long.

Then my father's death set me free from this work. My father had lived in the village, passed away there, and I had to go to arrange his funeral. I went and stayed in the village because I couldn't leave the house and farm. Uncle Vanya had been the warden of the church Nikola na Pustinka near the Passions Nonastery since approximately the end of July 1918. Before him, the warden had been one Sakharov, a big landlord, whose family lived near the church. I was in his house, and he passed on his duties to me in his study, taking from the safe books and the money. Besides, Uncle and I were one evening with the chief priest in the cathedral, a Fr Vinogradov, who received us in the drawing room in his apartment next to the cathedral with comfortable furniture and a half-round table. Tea with lemon was served to us in glasses on a tray. We had a chat with Fr Vinogradov. He gave us some ledgers and, from that moment, I had to start my work in the cathedral. When Ivan Dmitrievich came to the cathedral, he had started a choir and the choir was conducted by I.I. Yukhov, and the choir was well-known and thanks to that the cathedral was always crowded with people. Nobody disrupted Uncle and me behind the counter where candles were sold in spite of the crowds of people in the cathedral. But I had to work hard. I worked with both hands, handing out candles, taking the money, and returning the change. In general, I could not understand how I managed to figure out this selling of candles.[8] Besides, Ivan Dmitrievich was standing behind me in a way others did not notice, pulling on my jacket, and he whispered, "Hurry up, hurry up, hurry up" so that no people would crowd around the candle box. From all this work, I was as red as a boiled crayfish. He just stood behind my back and behind the candle box. Besides I had double work, with the caretaker and the custodian and had to walk around the cathedral collecting money when I was not selling candles. In general, this work was very hectic for me and I could not wait for it to end.

For my work (I worked only two months) he gave me an envelope with 250 rubles and the money in it was "*kerenky*"⁹ and they promised to make me a shareholder in the publishing company, by giving me one share every year.

Ivan Dmitrievich's business went well, even despite the fact that in 1905 his printing plant was set on fire by the Black Hundreds, together with the police. He expanded his business and the shares brought good profits and very often these profits were distributed among shareholders, but the main part of the profits went to expand and improve the printing business. The time came for Ivan Dmitrievich and his family to move again from the mansion on Valovaia Street to Tverskaia (Gorky Street today) where his company acquired a building and some stone residences in the courtyard that were enlarged and redecorated. The new apartment of Ivan Dmitrievich on Tverskaia was in a re-decorated building and in the yard was the printing plant of the newspaper, *Russian Word*. The apartment was on the third floor and it looked like a castle. The windows faced the street and covered the entire wall. The rooms were large, the entrance hall was huge, the rooms were furnished in the decadent style, and the floors everywhere except the study and the dining room were covered with carpets. The living room was large. Two windows as large as the wall gave a lot of light. There were a lot of flowers and potted palms in the rooms. In the corners and near the windows were small sofas and, above them, shelves with different green plants. A special gardener came to care for the flowers and sometimes he brought blooming plants, such as fragrant hyacinths and lilies of the valley. There were heavy, plush brown drapes over the windows. The living room was furnished with rose-coloured furniture covered with yellowish damask and there was a pianola, which played itself by means of electricity, playing different works by classical composers such as Liszt, Paganini, and others when you put them in. The music was rented from a special shop on Kuznetsky Bridge. All the decorations of the apartment require a lot of description, but I would only like to say that all this was a wonderful acquisition by Vanyushka, who first came to Moscow maybe even in bark shoes and patched trousers. This transformation was not life, but a miracle, that could be compared to Pushkin's fairy tale about the fisherman and golden fish.

Only a man with an outstanding intelligence could accomplish so much in life.

For his contribution to the publishing business, Ivan Dmitrievich was granted by the Tsar a title of honorary citizen and was given some orders [medals][10] and at the time of the changes in government at the time of the Bolsheviks he didn't give up his work at the publishing house as many others did. The others sabotaged the new government and refused to work for the new government. From Lenin he received a special reward, received an apartment for himself and his family and a pension.

I can give another example of Ivan Dmitrievich's finding time to do good works for people. The relations between my parents and Uncle and Aunt were not very friendly, and it was all my father's fault. My father liked to drink a lot and to carouse with his friends and did not behave like a man of substance. It was all very unpleasant for Aunt and Uncle and we seldom exchanged visits. By the way, my father was at first appointed director of the publishing business when it expanded and he was really a business-like man but wine spoiled him. He often neglected his work and he ended up working as a cashier in a whole-sale bookshop on the former Nikolskii Street, in spite of the fact that he was a big share-holder in the publishing company. On the day of my mother's death, of course, nobody thought that she would die. The holy icon of the Mother of God was brought to our house. In those days, by request, icons were brought to a house in a carriage with a priest, a deacon, and the priest would say the prayers to the Mother of God or some other saint. My mother felt very bad, and first her right hand went numb and all the relatives, her sisters who were all married with many children, including Evdokia Ivanovna and Ivan Dmitrievich, came to our house for the prayer. But because my mother felt worse, the icon was not accepted and mother even said to father that she was dying and she asked that all her children be brought to her bedside. At the same time, she asked father to take two icons, "Saviour" and "Mother of God," and an iconostasis for blessing the boys, my brothers and myself, and the girls, my sisters. Before saying farewell to all of us, she had spoken for a long time, at first with great fear that some black figures were approaching her from the wardrobe that was standing at the foot of the bed. Then her sisters, Ganya and Grusha, put the small icon on the wardrobe. After that, she calmed down and replied to her sisters' questions that all the black figures had disappeared but two figures in white had come from the wall and told her to say farewell to her relatives. They were sent to take her with them. Then she begged them tearfully to leave her alone. She said she would live now only for her children, and she had many children, eight of them, and the youngest was eight months old. How would they get along without her? Her sisters again asked her what those white figures were telling her, and she said they were implacable and said "we are sent to take you with us and can't violate the will of the one who sent us." Mother was sobbing and all the people and her relatives started to cry. Then mother took the icon of the saviour with both hands and blessed us boys with it and then blessed all the sisters with the icon of the Mother of God and kissed everybody. After that, all the adults said farewell to her and she peacefully closed her eyes, sighed, and passed away. A doctor was called immediately. He brought a mirror to her face. We hoped that there would be steam from her breath on the mirror. And father opened her eyelids, but she was lying completely breathless and her eyes became opaque. The doctor diagnosed it as shifting rheumatism that had reached her heart and paralysed it. When she felt that she was going to die, she asked her sisters Ganya, Grushinka, and Lisa to take care of the children, but they replied that, after her death, the closest relatives to Ivan Ivanovich – her husband and our father – were not they but Evdokia Ivanovna and Ivan Dmitrievich. So ask them to take care of your children. Mother turned her eyes to Aunt Dunya and started to ask her to take care of us; and certainly Aunt, with tears in her eyes, promised her that she would take care of the children, which she did until her very death. With all this, I wanted to show that Aunt and Uncle have done a great deal for us. Without their attention and care we would have become bandits or worse than that.

On the birthdays of Evdokia Ivanovna and Ivan Dmitrievich and in general on special days when dinners for guests were held, to which relatives and many well-known business people were invited, dinner was cooked by chefs, dishes were served by waiters in white gloves, tables were covered by white table cloths, the table was set with crystal wine, water, and vodka glasses and, in general, there were plenty of different foods, wines, fruit, and flowers. Many toasts were offered to the occasion and on other subjects, and Ivan Dmitrievich always responded to the point with a clear and polite toast and with a sweet smile. He stood at his chair and, looking at him, one could not imagine that an uneducated man was talking. He always wore a black frock coat, white, starched shirt. He was tall, stately, with pink cheeks – even a handsome face, especially attractive were his expressive black eyes. He was an amazing person. I am thinking about all of this only at an advanced age, in my seventies. Earlier it had never occurred to me to think about it, and I never had time to think about it. First, it was study, then study and work, then work, and then different concerns and personal troubles and the like. And now that I am not working any more, and especially upon reading the book *A Life for the Book*, these different thoughts about Aunt and Uncle come into my head. I ponder this question, why was it that this young boy came to Moscow and not his brother, Uncle Seriozha. In Moscow, he wound up with some old man who looked like an Old Believer. That was Sharapov, who engaged in minor trading in books and woodcuts. And from this Sharapov, as from a spark, he started his publishing company, which was like a huge fire that spread even beyond its frontiers. First, the boy, Vanyusha, simply worked in a shed of Old Believer Sharapov, helping him with things that he could do at his age without experience and training. He kept the shed clean, put out the garbage pail, chopped wood, carried water, and did other work about the house. (He used to mention this often to us boys that already at our age he was doing this work and not idling away his time. "And you live like little lords." He was saying this in order to teach us to work.) Then his master helped Vanyushka to get married and when he passed away he left his book business to this Vanyusha. After that Vanyusha gained power and became a real Russian hero, because of his natural intelligence. At first, he traded out of a small dwelling because he could not afford a better one. Then he had the idea of expanding his business and he needed more space, and for that he needed capital, and he managed to find a way to do this. He started a book-printing business and created a stock company [*tovarishchestvo na paiiakh*]. Many people rushed to invest their capital – small and large – into that business because it was profitable and promising. When his business grew deeply respected, revered Ivan Dmitrievich – no longer Vanysha – became a rich man.

11

LETTERS FROM VLAS DOROSHEVICH TO SYTIN ABOUT EDITING *RUSSIAN WORD*

The success of *Russian Word* depended on the ideas and work of V.M. Doroshevich. The first letter was written shortly after Doroshevich signed on as editor of *Russian Word* and shows that he is determined to take command of the paper immediately. Sytin describes the events leading up to Doroshevich's departure for France in chapter 4.

[Letterhead:] GRAND HOTEL DE RUSSIE

Paris, 9 March, 1902

Dear Ivan Dmitrievich:

We agreed that you will not interfere with the [running of] the paper. But this once, as an exception, I am asking you to interfere. I am [also] asking Fedor Ivanovich [Blagov] to help you in this regard. This is necessary because Mr Rozenstein, as is becoming clear, turned out to be an extraordinarily unscrupulous man.[1]

The only man we didn't make an error in choosing and who is burning with the desire to be of use is our Paris correspondent, E.K. Brut (E. Belov). Mr Rozenstein, by systematically playing dirty tricks on him, by persecuting him as my protégé, and by withholding his reports from the editors has brought M. Brut to the point where he sent me a letter to my Moscow address asking to be relieved of his duties. [Added between the lines: "this letter and I crossed on the way."] What Mr Rozenstein had done to him is despicable both as far as Mr Brut and the newspaper are concerned.

As you will remember, we agreed that Mr Brut's work would be published for not less than 125 rubles per month. Out of this total, 25 rubles, would go toward the repayment of the advance while not less than 100 rubles each month would be paid to him. Over and above that, 100 francs per month, and with less than this a lively, responsive and mobile correspondence cannot exist.

In actual fact, this is how Mr Brut's earnings have been reduced by Mr Rozenstein: His January earnings amounted to 50 rubles. For February he earned 34 rubles. Out of his 25 rubles were deducted for repayment of the advance – 9 rubles was the amount of his pay for the whole month. What's that? A joke? A mockery? For the two months, January and February, about twenty-five correspondent's reports disappeared. They varied between 40 and 200 lines in length. All this was written at the appropriate time, on topical subjects, so that we would have published it before all other papers.

Mr Rozenstein lied when he told me: "There were no correspondent's reports." I asked him: "Why was there no report about the performance in Paris of the Russian play *Krechinsky's Weddings*? All the Russian papers talk about it." He replied, "Brut did not write it for us." This is a brazen lie. The report on this event, of interest to every Russian reader, was sent off right away, after the performance. Mr.Brut had worked on it overnight. [Inserted: "And there were many such cases."]

I could write at length – but I have become convinced, on the basis of facts, of Mr Rozenstein's notorious lies and his dirty tricks. To what end? This is clear: to squeeze out Brut and to replace him, probably with one of "his own men." Surely you will agree that a man cannot live on nine rubles a month.

We publish the dullest and most detestable articles by scoundrels who have the support of the editorial office but we do not publish pieces that are interesting and needed by the newspaper. In view of this all, the reports submitted by Mr Brut will henceforth be addressed directly to you, Ivan Dmitrievich. Mr Rozenstein dare not even touch them. Please ask Fëdor Ivanovich to take them to the printers himself and to see that they are published the day they are received, without fail. In this way we shall put a good distance between us and the other papers. Fëdor Ivanovich must not be afraid of their literary quality. There have been many instructions as to what to write and what to write about. Should there be anything a tiniest bit doubtful – regarding censorship – it should be given special attention. Such pieces will always be marked by Mr Brut with a request to Fëdor Ivanovich to pay special attention to it. As far as the volume is concerned, Mr Brut will be sending us as much as is needed, taking care not to step out of bounds. I therefore ask that Fëdor Ivanovich alone edit Mr Brut's correspondent's reports. Rozenstein must not be allowed to touch them.

I remember you saying to me, Ivan Dmitrievich: "I am putting all my hopes in you." I am burning with the desire to save *Russian Word*. And unless you cool off this, my desire, I will, with God's help, do it. But if you want me to devote all my powers to that end and truly to do all I can to achieve it, then my basic condition is: all my directions must be carried out to the letter. I know what I want, what I am aiming at and what I need for the newspaper. And, if my instructions are not exactly carried out, I will wash off my hands and say: "Well, Ivan Dmitrievich, you and I cannot work together.[2]

I trust that you wouldn't want this to happen and will give me the chance to do what I can and what I want for the newspaper. I am going to address my further instructions directly to Fëdor Ivanovich. I send him my warm greetings.

With a friendly handshake, Vlas Doroshevich.

12 March [1902]

Dear [Much-esteemed] Ivan Dmitrievich,

I simply have no idea what am I to do with this poor Brut. He himself just grins and bears it and does not say anything. But it is clear to me that his situation and that of his family is desperate. Simply desperate.

What have we done to him! By the grace of Rozenstein, of course. He left some other job because of us. We promised him 100 rubles net per month. Mr Rozenstein, as I have found out here, had worked from the very beginning to bring Levenberg, the Paris correspondent of *Odessa News*, over to us. This is why he is trying to smoke out Brut. Everything that he (B.) wrote would be secretly consigned to the wastepaper basket or, as you have said, would be left on the desk, unopened. Not for one month did Brut receive the 100 rubles contracted for. Not for one! Finally now! His net income is 9 rubles. The man who told me that had tears in his eyes from this injustice. The man labours, he works hard. For this he ought to be rewarded. It is absolutely necessary for us, for the paper, to put this useful man back on his feet so that he can produce for us. According to my plans he is irreplaceable for the paper. I think that you should send him 200 rubles as a reward for his work that had been lost through no fault of his own. Let him get back on his feet and see that, from now on, he will be treated as a human being. Another expense grace of Mr Rozenstein. But it will be the last one. It is better to give a conscientious man what we are morally obliged to give him than to throw money that they have never earned away to such drones as Mikhailovsky or Frenkel.

And this scoundrel Rozenstein had the audacity to say: "What is Mikhailovsky going to do, with a wife and a child on his hands?" How about Brut and his family – that Brut whom he had reduced to 9 rubles per month through his intrigues in favour of his man Levenberg, trying to get him to resign his job. I can see that the man has pawned or sold everything. There is calamity in his household. Better let us make up on something else, Ivan Dmitrievich, but let us give this man the opportunity to be useful to us. Be so kind and write him a friendly letter, to raise his spirits, asking him to work according to my directives. And send him 200 rubles. Let him extricate himself from this unhappy situation which we have brought him into. Should you refuse to do so, I shall consider it my duty to do it myself. I am ashamed to look into the eyes of man who is working for us, who has refused another job for our sake, and who has been brought to dire straits because we've messed things up.

With a handshake, yours, V. Doroshevich.

P.S. Please forward all my mail to Mr Brut's address. Your office has his address and he will know where I am. He will forward the letters to me.

13 March [1902]

Much esteemed Ivan Dmitrievich!

It seems to me that I wrote to you incoherently. I am leaving for Nice and then on to Spain. Therefore, to avoid delays, I ask you to address all my mail to:

Paris, 5 arr[ondissement], rue Claude Bernard 17.

A Monsieur Brout Jefime pour M-r Dorochevitch. He will always know where I am and will forward each letter to me immediately. Please tell this also to Fëdor Ivanovich in case he decides to write me.

I fear that something [bad] might happen. I really feel a great desire to write, to work, and I have great faith in the *R. Word*. We will be successful, we will achieve success. I feel this and I believe it. For God's sake, do not destroy this feeling within me somehow! In such case nothing will be achieved. Carry out my editorial directives exactly and publish my articles *immediately upon receipt*. Except the Sunday features, of course. There will be not one second's delay. I follow the *R. W.* It will be forwarded to me every day, no matter where I happen to be [remaining two or three words at the bottom of the page unreadable].

[Letterhead]: GRAN HOTEL ALAMEDA
Francisco Zurita
Granada Espana

14 April [1902]

Dear deeply est. Ivan Dmitrievich,

Well, it seems that you have no reason to complain that I've forgotten you. The only time I didn't write was when I was sitting in a railway car.

In a week's time I shall be in Paris, now I am living on the last bit of money and therefore ask you, my dear friend, to prepare yourself.

From Paris, I will send you a telegram with my address. This will mean: I request for my salary and honorarium for the period from 1 March to the 1st of April to be transmitted to me *by wire* via Credit Lyonnais, without any deductions of course, as we have agreed between us. (The transfer to [be charged] to my account.)

How are you doing? How is the paper doing?

Please ask Fëdor Ivanovich to write to me in detail, to Brut's address. I shake your hand firmly, yours, V. Doroshevich.

SAVOY PALACE
Chamonix, France

27/14 August [1902]

My dear and deeply esteemed Ivan Dmitrievich,

I received your letter only today: it caught up with me here. A newspaper in Petersburg is conceivable only under one condition: that we rent a direct wire connection with Moscow.

Without it:

1) We would be deprived of the ability to utilize our rich (store of) information.

2) By focusing exclusively on the Petersburg editorial office we would neglect and kill the Moscow business.

With the wire facility we would be able to work on the information, articles, features (feuilletons) with Petersburg for both papers at the same time and transmit them to Moscow ready for printing. All Moscow would have to do would be to produce the Moscow [variant]. Without the wire we would be unable to do this and this would produce the result indicated at 2) above.

For Petersburg buying two newspapers costing 5 rubles would not be much of a bargain. In order to put a newspaper on a really firm footing, it must rely *on itself* and not on the supplement. I've had the whole plan for the newspaper ready for quite a while, I will be back soon, please wait and do not begin anything without me.

I am sending you my most cordial greetings and ask you to convey my respects to the deeply esteemed Evdokia Ivanovna and to give her my cordial greetings and best wishes.

Your very devoted,

V. Doroshevich

[Letterhead:] HOTEL DE LUXEMBOURG, PROMENADE DES ANGLAIS, NICE

3/16-V, 1905

Deeply esteemed and dear Ivan Dmitrievich:

First of all my deep and sincere thanks for the telegram and for your charming letter. Please convey my thanks and warm greetings to Andrei Vasil'evich [Rumanov] and to Makarevsky.

Unfortunately, the beginning of [our] new life is accompanied by distress and fear. My wife became ill with typhoid fever. Two doctors are looking after her, they come several times in a day and maintain that all will end well. But I am terribly alarmed: she is very weak.

Do not despair [I.D.], for Christ's sake! Nothing bad is going to

happen to us. We are not rolling anywhere downhill. 145 thousand is
not a bad figure.³ God willing, there will be more. As far as I am concerned, I will give it all my powers. Now I will write almost every day.
Let me catch my breath. After all, you know very well how I view the
R.W. It is as much my child as it is yours, you know it very well.
Besides all the material concerns, you know my moral ties to the newspaper. Only get away from your habit of throwing yourself every
minute into the depths of despair. What kind of a publisher is it who
falls into despair every day? Brave with books, but cowardly in newspapers. By God, this is not right and it doesn't befit you. Listening to
you would discourage anybody. Try to remember when you didn't
despair – but look at things: are they really in bad shape? Be of optimistic spirit and believe my sincere affection and positive attitude, both
where you yourself and the newspaper are concerned.

   With a warm handshake, Yours with all my soul,
   V. Doroshevich
P.S. To be pacified, you have to be told everything twice. So I repeat
again: I will write almost every day.

                                                 21 June [1905]
Much esteemed Ivan Dmitrievich,
   I badly need to see you. But I am busy all day, working on an article (feuilleton). Could you be so kind and gracious, taking into con-
sideration my ailments (I can barely walk) as to drop in at my place
today after 7.
Sincerely,
                                          Yours V. Doroshevich

unreadable – India/Ceylon?
                                                 5 May [190x?]
   Do not be angry, my dear and deeply esteemed Ivan Dmitrievich,
that I have not written for such a long time. Every day I learn about
and discover such a lot of new and interesting things that it is not possible to grasp everything at once. It often seems to me that I have taken
leave of my senses and everything I see around me is a nightmare.
That's how strange and beautiful everything is. This is the most inter-

esting of all my trips. There is a tremendous amount of material. God willing, I'll manage to write it all up reasonably well and then I shall square accounts, both in the moral and in the material sense: I'll be doing India every day [one word unreadable] than the current one, on topical subjects. To write in a hurry, without checking things over and thinking about them would amount to driving oneself into a dead-end and causing the [readers'] interests to drop.

My hearty greetings to you. My warm greetings to all, especially to Fedor Ivanovich. I see our paper – it is forwarded to me from Colombo. That's how far *R.W.* is received. Not bad. Ross[4] is often quite good.

Please give instructions for the paper to be forwarded to me at: Port-Said, Poste-restante, Mr V. Doroshevich. This is for the return voyage. The journey is terribly hard. The heat is stifling – 40 to 45 degrees. Bubonic plague all around. But I am well. I've only caught [reading of one word uncertain] tropical fever and, for a second consecutive week have not eaten anything: two plates of chicken broth a day [two words] without anything. But I feel strong and in good spirits: everything around here is so interesting. I wander around places where there are no hotels and no shelter. I spend the night either in empty railway cars or at some [railway] station. It is hard, but the excellent material makes up for it. Once more, I shake your hand. Yours, V. Doroshevich.

P.S. Should Kl. Vas.[5] approach you for some money, be so kind and don't refuse. Give her 1,000 out of my account. We'll sort it out when I get back, I won't be your debtor.

2/15 November [1905]

Deeply esteemed and dear Ivan Dmitrievich:

I received your letter yesterday, thought about it for twenty-four hours, and now reply. I am *decidedly against* raising the price. The *commercial* considerations justifying this are the following:

1 The price of 7 rubles is our best trump card in competing with other papers. And it is precisely at this time that we should not deprive ourselves of it. We do not fear all sorts of *Mornings (Utra)* and their ilk, no matter how many of them might be appearing now. They are doomed to short-lived existence. In their desire to be successful they have to try to "shout more loudly" and this will result in their closure.

For a time they take a few retail sales away from us. But their appearance is even good for us. The public, seeing their quick demise, loses faith in these "flash-in-the-pan" papers and will believe only in "the old established firms." But all this is just for now. The laws on publishing will not be long in coming.[6] Then, when survival will become more secure for a newspaper, serious people will enter the newspaper business. Inevitably a few new and more solid newspapers will appear. Serious competitors will emerge against us. And it will be then that we play our trump card: the cheap rate of subscription. Were we to raise the rate now we would be unable to do so then against our competitors: this would amount to losing the prestige of the newspaper.

2 *Russian Word* costs 7 rubles. *Sparks* (*Iskry*) which serves as an illustrated supplement – 2 rubles. The total for the newspaper including the supplement is 9 rubles. If we add one ruble to the price of the newspaper we will already have a "newspaper with supplement for 10 rubles," which makes it more expensive by one ruble than the other – since their paper costs 9 rubles with the supplement.

3 The most remunerative section of the newspaper, i.e., the classified advertisements, has done well for us. Thanks to the wide circulation of the paper. This circulation must not be reduced or even allowed to drop so that the people won't say: "the paper has shrunk." This could undercut the classified section.

4 There will be no extra expense of 50,000 rubles in connection with the "long Duma."[7] The Duma will be of tremendous interest to the public at first, and we'll have to give as much [information] about it as possible during that period. Later they'll get used to it, the novelty will wear off[8] and there will be no need to give such a lot of stuff. Of course, we will have to produce articles, well-prepared reports with excerpts from the speeches. This is how it is done in all countries where parliaments exist and so it will be done here. After three months the reading public will itself complain if it is fed endless columns about the Duma. It will get tired of reading speeches, speeches and more speeches. This section will have to be set up very well: it *must be excellent*. We will think about how to achieve this. But a concise section, containing excerpts from speeches, will not demand so much money! So that your fear that 50,000 rubles will have to be spent on it is groundless.

5 The business [the *R.W.*] has been set up and it is doing well.

Thank God! Why then break it and break it again. No point in trying to improve what is good already. It is easy to ruin something, but hard to put it right again. These are commercial considerations that you should strongly emphasize before the board.

Now follow the *ideological* considerations.

1 In creating the newspaper we aimed at giving the reader, at the lowest possible price, a genuine newspaper, with sound information and with good editorial staff. We want to raise the public's expectations for the newspaper. To draw him away from all the rubbish he is being given just because it happens to be cheap.

2 We aimed at the propagation of ideas that would be healthy, good [positive], devoid of revolutionary extremism and superfluousness, but eschewing all that is dark and gloomy. We wanted to create for our writers (and we have Grigory Spiridonovich [Petrov], Boborykin, Nemirovich, Ozerov, Rozanov[9] a huge, colossal audience. All these, dear Ivan Dmitrievich, will sign up for your team. I urge you not to destroy your undertaking. We've passed through difficult and bitter years – why break up and tarnish a good job now when we can breathe more easily?

These are my points.

I am working on the plan and the advertisement.[10]

I shall be most grateful for some money – for I have encountered great expenses with more yet to come, and I am sitting here without any money.

You will be receiving articles daily.

My warm greetings to all.

I wish to convey my deep respects to Evdokia Ivanovna.

To you a firm and friendly handshake,

Yours, V. Doroshevich

P.S. Once again I beg you not to raise the price. Instead, let us put our shoulders to it with all our might and everything will turn out, God willing, to be super-excellent.

Paris, 10/23 February, 1906

Dear much est. Ivan Dmitrievich,

It is only now – after you have explained and proved by quoting figures the situation of the Company in its capacity of publisher of

R.W. after the fire in the plant and how, after the railway and postal strikes,[11] the income from subscriptions did not, by far, provide even approximately sufficient means for continued operations – I am able to answer the following questions:

What terms can our newspaper offer to V.I. Nemirovich-Danchenko?

350 rubles per printer's signature for a novel, assuming that the novel will around to twenty printer's signatures.

35 kopecks per line for individual articles.

These are really the best terms we can come up with this year considering our budget and the current conditions. V.I.'s novel, *The Faraway Graves*, amounts to a truthful portrayal of the origins and the course of this unfortunate war and it promises to be very explicit. The current censorship and administrative conditions with regard to publishing are such that, were we to start publishing the novel immediately, we would either put to risk the newspaper's survival or be forced to stop the publication of the novel as happened with my *Whirlwind*. Or we would be forced to ask the author for such excessive "softening" that the work would be deprived of all its impact and significance. Judging by the direction things are developing, one should expect significant softening of administrative conditions in the nearest future. Choosing a suitable moment when the administrative situation becomes more favourable – albeit temporarily – we should exploit it and publish the novel, in consecutive issues, without a break.[12] But to achieve this, it would be absolutely necessary for the editors to have in their hands the whole novel, in its entirety. Any interruption under these conditions would be unthinkable. I think that if you were to submit these conditions to V.I. he would find them acceptable.

The novel is of major interest, but this interest is already historical. It will not diminish if the novel's publication is held up for two or three months. And, thanks to the changes in the legislation concerning publishing, it will have even greater impact.

The newspaper is going through a difficult period. In difficult times one does not discard one's co-workers of the happier days. And you know the importance I attach to V.I.'s participation in the newspaper and how much I would like to work with him. I don't think that I, his old and fervent admirer, would need to say any more on this subject.

I would have written all this for Vasily Ivanovich, but unfortunately, he appears to be dissatisfied with me for some reason, even though I have not given him any grounds for dissatisfaction, at least not intentionally, and I don't know how I came to deserve it.

Sincerely ["I shake your hand"],

V. Doroshevich

12

REMINISCENCES ABOUT I.D. SYTIN

What follows is a collection of reminiscences of Sytin by people who had business dealings with him before and after the revolution. They confirm what we see in Sytin's own writings. In contrast to his energy and enthusiasm before the revolution, the descriptions of those who met him after 1917 convey the image of a depressed man who was also trying to prevent the advance of old age – whether by taking suspicious remedies or by undertaking any task that came his way.

The recollections of Sytin by Altaev, Motylkov, and Utevsky were all written and published at a time when Soviet press controls were still in existence and some of their descriptions of the publisher seem to be the result of this situation: for instance, negative comments about Sytin as a capitalist. Iablonovsky's recollection was published in Paris in an emigrant newspaper.

A. Altaev (M.V. Yamshchikova)[1]

I had wanted to work in Sytin's publishing house for a long time. It attracted me because of the wide scope of its distribution of cheap books among the people. I think it was in 1907 that I heard about Sytin's work after I returned home from being out.

"A man came to see you," my maid told me. She was a country girl." "He was important looking, giving instructions on the phone all the time. But his manner of talking and his behaviour were childlike. It's hard to understand. He left a message for you." And she gave me a piece of paper. Much was written on it, but it was all ungrammatical. My books are mentioned but all the titles started with small letters. I cite here a paragraph from memory: "agree to publish your rooned nest cum to talk pushkin street paliroal."[2]

Then followed the day and the hour. "Palais Royal" are famous furnished rooms in Pushkin street, mostly rented by actors. Sytin used to stay there when he came to Petersburg from Moscow. "Rooned nest," I understood, was the title of my historical novel recently published in the magazine *Young Reader* (*Yunii Chitatel*). The next day I was in "Palais Royal" and the same day I signed an agreement for the book in the Petersburg department of Sytin's publishing house. Later I had many books published by Ivan Dmitrievich. And at his request I transferred to him from O.N. Popova the rights to my old *Beacons of Truth* (*Svetochi Pravdy*).

Sytin's books came out very quickly without any delay and sold really very cheaply. But all my works that he published according to his design left much to be desired.

I met Ivan Dmitrievich more frequently after the revolution, in 1918, when I moved to Moscow with my newspapers. He found out about my move from Elena Nikolaevna Tikhomirova[3] and visited me at the Metropol.[4] The hotel had been well known to him since its opening: his favourite table was in the dining room of the Metropol restaurant, in the left-hand corner, near the entrance. He liked to sit there for an hour every day. There he had appointments with authors, discussed the conditions of publication with them, signed agreements. Upon entering my room, Sytin started to talk about my books, giving an account of the copies sold of some books and talking about preparing other books for re-edition. Having received my agreement for publication, he started to select material for a two-volume collection, *Childhoods of Famous People* (*Detstva Znamenitykh Liudei*). He was cheerful, as if things were going their usual old way, and offered me payment in advance.

At parting he presented to me his jubilee edition of the book *Half Century for the Book* (*Polveka dlia Knigi*), a huge volume, richly illustrated, with a lot of portraits and autographs. Unfortunately, I had no contacts with Sytin's publishing house when that book was being compiled. That was why I hadn't commemorated, with the others, my admiration for Ivan Dmitrievich's mighty talent, this real Russian hero.

I immediately remembered stories of how this uneducated man selected the right books for publication out of those offered to him through his exceptional intuition alone. One of the editors said: "This is the way Ivan Dmitrievich solved the problem. He would take a manuscript or a book, turn over the pages, hold it in his hand as if weighing it and would say calmly: "This should be accepted, it will work out." Or he would put it on his desk and say: "We'd better refuse. Nothing good will come out of it." And, just imagine, he never made a mistake. I can't guess what his secret was.

The book *Half a Century* (*Polveka*) tells the story of this remarkable man. A country boy from Galich district, who started as an errand boy in a bookshop, he saved a small sum of money and started his own "business," a minor business selling cheap books with the help of peddlers. In this way he initiated the very noble idea of spreading secular books in villages. And before he could blink an eye, he was the owner of a huge business that dominated the book market.

Sytin often visited me, when he had a good reason or without any special reason. How could it happen that this remarkable representative of the top bourgeoisie, this capitalist, had a longing for the small world of "Metropol"? He would spend hours sitting there and talking to somebody from a different world, who [like myself] had come to Moscow as one of those who came to destroy his customary world?[5] Sometimes it seemed to me he was looking for some moral support from me. Obviously, age and confusion caused by the events that came so unexpectedly started to tell on him.

Days, months, years passed and Sytin looked old and run down. Where was his cheerfulness and his interest in everything that was going on around him, his interest in the Moscow of old days? Now he seldom visits me, and when he comes, he likes to say the same bitter phrase: "An old invalid has dropped in on you. A pensioner. Unemployed. Totally unwanted."

Idleness was torturing him and draining his last strength. Later I learned from his second son, Dmitri Ivanovich, that he wanted to keep fit and started to take a treatment with lysates,[6] which was in vogue at the time. But lysates didn't help, and Sytin's lucid and sober mind started to fade. He began to mix names, dates, events.

On learning about my fortieth anniversary in 1929, he came to see me early in the morning and apologized that he would not be able to come that night to the literary club (House of Herzen).

"I've decided to be the first to say Happy Birthday and I've brought you the book *Half-Century* and also a volume of *The Great Reform* (*Velikaya Reforma*), we can find the whole collection later." He drank coffee and rose to leave. How exhausted his face was!

Sytin went out, leaving behind him the impression of a fallen colossus. My housekeeper was returning from shopping and met him in the hotel building and told me sadly: "As I was coming and he was leaning over the stair rail, looking down the stairwell toward the lower floor, holding on to the rail, and asking me loudly: 'How shall I get downstairs? There is no staircase!' I was scared. Such an important man and behaving as unreasonably as a child. I showed him the staircase and watched him walk. He walked downstairs quickly, not like an old man. Yet he was not himself."

Born in Vladimir province, she had looked upon the famous Sytin as a superior human being who had sowed the printed word in the world of peasants. And suddenly: "Such a man – and like a little baby … Like a little baby … Is this Sytin? The one my daughter referred to as the most interesting conversationalist? She happened to be in the same compartment with him on the train from Moscow to Leningrad. Sytin? 'King of Books,' known to the whole educated world? Hard to believe."

Some time later we got the sad news about Ivan Dmitrievich's death.

My Work with I.D. Sytin
From the Reminiscences of a Second-hand Bookseller
A.M. Motylkov

I would occasionally watch the "chief boss" of the company, I.D. Sytin, at work during his visits to Petrograd.

During the world war of 1914–18 books didn't sell well and the boss would often come to check on the state of things. In general, I.D. Sytin was a very mobile man and, as I was later told by the people who were close to him, he would spend more nights on a train than at home. He preferred watching his huge business personally to managing it from his office, and that was why the organizing role of the owner was a very tangible part of all his undertakings. We also felt it.

He would come to the shop straight from the railway station with a small case in hand, and would have his morning tea with a flaky pastry in the manager's office. It was my duty to serve tea.

My curiosity about this man was natural. According to rumours he had also started as an "errand boy" and had become a "big boss" (I certainly didn't realize his great cultural importance in the book publishing business in Russia at that time).

Ivan Dmitrievich was a stout man with a clever, expressive face and shrewd eyes. He said little and his speech was curt. He was severe looking. He was dressed modestly but exceptionally neatly. His suit was always spick and span.

He would spend most of the time in the manager's office in absolute solitude. He was so absorbed in his thoughts that he didn't see or notice anyone. I had never seen him smiling and had never heard a single joke from him.

But all the clerks knew that behind this severe appearance there was a very kind and cordially sympathetic man.

An author from Moscow, who used to live in the same house in Old Square where the central wholesale warehouse of I.D. Sytin's company was situated, told me a typical story.

"Once," he said, "When I was a kid, I got a five-kopeck coin from my father and together with my sister went to Sytin's warehouse to buy a book. There was no retail sale at the warehouse, but the salesman who knew me decided to give me a *Robinson Crusoe* worth five kopecks.[7] At that time the manager dropped in and started scolding the salesman, saying that he was not doing his business correctly, and he yelled at us too. We went to the door, whimpering. A man in a fur coat was walking towards us. Seeing tears in our eyes, he began to question the salesman and the manager, and then lectured them that they should not offend kids. Then he went to the counter, chose five books for each of us, and gave them to me and my sister. That was I.D. Sytin."

Knowing how kind the boss was, the employees at our shop often took advantage of his kindness. If somebody needed money, he would come up to I.D. and ask him to help, saying that his barn had burnt down with hay in it, or his horse had died. I.D. never checked if it was true.

"How much do you need?" he would ask abruptly.

"Whatever you give," the usual reply would be.

I.D. would call the manager and would give the instruction:

"Give him 200 rubles and deduct 10 rubles from his wage every month."

The deduction would go on for a couple of months and then I.D. would order the debt forgiven. That was the routine and the employees adored I.D. Sytin for that.

He discussed business problems only with the manager and gave orders and instructions only to him. There were moments when he would give the manager a severe scolding, addressing him as "thee," but again everybody knew that he would only reprimand those toward whom he was well disposed. And, on the contrary, if the boss was speaking in an even, official tone, stressing "you," everybody knew he was in trouble.

His visits to Petrograd in 1916 were connected with the purchase of the big publishing business from A.F. Marks.[8] Sytin bought this as a functioning publishing company, having retained all the staff of editors and publishers and even having left the name of the company unchanged. Obviously, questions of entrepreneurial prestige didn't matter to him. He considered it more important for business to preserve the name of this old company, which had earned a good reputation with subscribers.

I watched I.D. Sytin closely a dozen times, when I worked in his shop as an errand boy.

But only much later, after I had studied the book publishing business very thoroughly, and had also read many books, could I really appreciate his personality, the wide scale and significance of his personality, and of his book publishing and bookselling business.

And it was not for nothing that he was called the "Napoleon of the book business." In 1916, when I came to know I.D. Sytin intimately, the fiftieth anniversary of his book publishing work was celebrated in Russia. And you should have seen how unanimous various

representatives of Russian intelligentsia were in greeting the hero of
the day, praising his merits before the people.

A.M. Gorky wrote with respect about I.D. Sytin's work at that time,
which, according to his words "would be appreciated correctly by the
country in future."

The son of a volost scribe from a remote Kostroma village, who had
learned to read and write from a book of psalms and a book of hours,
who had started his career as an errand boy, this genuinely self-made
man later became the greatest book publisher, the organizer of huge
book-printing businesses in Russia, who played a great part in the education of the popular masses.

It was certainly impossible to avoid mistakes in that enormous half-
century work on publication of books that I.D. Sytin had carried out,
but one shouldn't ignore the fact that the general cultural standard in
Russia at that time was not high, and those mistakes were the reflection of the real state of things.

During the Russian-Japanese war and the world war of 1914–18
I.D. Sytin's company published a great number of chromolithographic
pictures of a jingo-patriotic nature for people. Though this was the
reflection of the general tone, supported by the official press, one
couldn't approve of the publication of these "pictures," which poi-
soned people's consciousness with false, chauvinistic propaganda. This
was, certainly, one of I.D. Sytin and his advisers greatest mistakes.

Anyway, it's necessary to acknowledge that I.D. Sytin, who was
good at selecting assistants and staff members, was never guided by
purely commercial interests but sought advisers among the best representatives of the intelligentsia of those days and his closest and most
influential inspirers in all his undertakings were such people as L.N.
Tolstoy, A.P. Chekhov, V.G. Chertkov, I.I. Gorbunov-Posadov, and
others. Very often I.D. Sytin's "mistakes" were the "mistakes" of those
people who sincerely strove to become "mediators" between the intelligentsia and the people in the process of educating the latter and
wanted to rely in that work on the rich experience and the entrepreneurial energy of I.D. Sytin.

Eventually, it was not a matter of separate mistakes but of a general
appreciation of the significance of I.D. Sytin's work.

I.D. Sytin was not the only publisher in Russia at that time. We read in S.F. Librovich's reminiscences *On Guard for Books (Na Knizhnom Postu)*: "Two names were popular in Russia: Yeliseev – for drinking Russia – and Wolff[9] for reading Russia." Yeliseev was the supplier of expensive wines for the bourgeoisie, aristocracy, and advanced intelligentsia. Wolff, the publisher, supplied them with "luxury" literary volumes at high prices.

At the same time common people had to be satisfied with cheap popular prints. Nekrasov,[10] the poet, dreamed about the time when "the peasants would bring from the market Belinsky and Gogol instead of Bliukher and silly Mylord." That had not yet come true. There was not a single man who dared to take up the risk in that matter. The tsarist government and its officials in charge of education were certainly those least interested in it.

And here came I.D. Sytin. Having risen from the very bottom, he clearly realized people's thirst for good books. But a peasant certainly couldn't afford to pay three rubles for a Gogol, published by Wolff. Three rubles was a whole year's poll-tax. Common people needed good books at accessible prices.

The practical ability of the future publisher was channelled in this direction. Having married the daughter of a Moscow confectioner, and having received a 4,000 rubles dowry for his wife, I.D. Sytin started his business by publishing cheap popular prints.

I remember these pictures being sold in the small shop where my father was the manager. One could see such pictures stuck to the walls next to icons in any well-to-do peasant family. It was the most accessible visual art for common people. Our famous painters certainly didn't participate in doing them. Unknown graphic artists from among the common people created these pictures, and country women, guided by their own taste, spread "colours" on them with a hare's pad, making 25 kopecks for a thousand prints. No wonder faces were sometimes painted with bright green, and the sky was painted in poisonous raspberry red. The ordinary consumer was not choosy, the pictures sold like hot cakes.

Later I was looking through those sheets, which were already being sold as rare antiques at high prices for amateur collectors. It is certainly easy to criticize much of that stuff from the point of view of a modern Soviet man and even categorically label it as "ideologically harmful." But if you looked at it from the point of view of a peasant buyer of that time, for whom the printing press did not create anything else, you would be grateful for what you could get.

The generals on horseback, leading troops of soldiers with bayonets atilt to attack in the face of case-shot, that were portrayed in those numerous prints were for common people the embodiment of their own views. You could see the rows of soldiers.

All these illustrations of the Sevastopol campaign, conquests of the "disastrous" Caucasus and the Turkish[11] wars reminded common people of the events in which they had taken part or remembered from the stories of old people. That was why these prints found a place of honour on the walls of peasant huts.

And the songs! "Hello, brother soldier" ["Zdorovo, brat, sluzhivyi"], "Cossacks are setting out" ["Zasvistali kazachenki"], "Our warriors rode" ["Ekhali rebyata"], "In the fields" ["Vo luzyakh"], "One Autumn Evening" ["Pod vecher oseniu"], "A fair maiden, one evening" ["Vecherkom krasna-devitsa"], and many others. The lyrics were sometimes ungrammatically written, but the pictures were amusing, and they met the requirements of the folk poetic consciousness, as they had been created by common people and now were given back to them.

And fairy tales about Bova ["Bova Korolevich"], Eruslan, and many others, which were told by common people in an old oral tradition! They captivated the imagination by amazing adventures and extraordinary heroism.

And finally, a large series of satires of everyday life, beginning with the old "Cock-and-bull story told as a drama" ["Nebylitsa v litsakh"]! I can assert with confidence that many of those prints corresponded to the people's mentality, their need for humour, and, not being limited by censorship, they certainly contributed to the development of a critical approach toward the existing reality.

The question of the significance of cheap popular prints, which were published in huge numbers and, thanks to their low cost and to peddlers, penetrated into the most remote areas of the country where the printed word could not reach, has not yet been properly studied.

Our great poet Pushkin's[12] appreciation of cheap popular prints that he once saw on the wall of a hut at the railway station is typical and worth mentioning: "These pictures are worthy of the attention of an educated man for both their moral and artistic aspects."

In the "infant" age of their development, common people were pleased with these cheap popular prints, found satisfaction in them, and decorated their houses with them. I.D. Sytin realized that and satisfied popular demand.

Later he took up the publication of folk literature, starting with the republication of old, popular and well-known stories about "Mylord Angliiski," "Matros Kariotski," "Frol Skobeyev," about Bova, Eruslan,[13] and others that were well known to and popular with people. He also published sacred books, calendars, books of songs, books on "how to" write letters, interpretative dream-books, oracular books, etc.

A lot of such stuff published by Sytin passed through my hands as a second-hand bookseller. We surely cannot be of two opinions today about dream-books, books of prophesy, and other such trash, which fostered superstitions and prejudices in people. I'm not going to defend these books, although I know that in the major literature at that time (not published in cheap popular prints) many books that ignited the same superstitions were published and circulated. All that, I repeat, was the reflection of a general cultural consciousness of society in those days.

And again, many of those books, as the only reading material for common people, were useful, because they gave the common reader some basic knowledge about the surrounding world.

For a long time Sytin's folk calendars had been almost the only reference book on all issues in our village.

But when I.D. Sytin's publishing business had gotten firmly established and had gained a vast peasant market through a wide network of book peddlers, I.D. Sytin got down to the most important stage of his activity: publication of books by classical writers for people at incredibly low prices. And he managed to publish the works of Pushkin and Gogol[14] in one volume each, charging 60 kopecks instead of three rubles.

Many books were printed in this way:[15] "The Minor" ["Nedorosl"] by Fonvizin,[16] "Woe from Wit" ["Gore ot Uma"] by Griboyedov,[17]

The Captain's Daughter [*Kapitanskaya dochka*], *Dubrovsky* [*Dubrov-ski*] and *Tales of Belkin* [*Povesti Belkina*] by Pushkin,[18] fables by Krylov,[19] "The Chant of the Merchant Kalashnikov" ["Pesnya o kuptse Kalashnikove"] by Lermontov,[20] a number of "folk" stories by L.N. Tolstoy and others.

I.D. Sytin published a ten-volume, illustrated collection and two complete collections of the works of L.N. Tolstoy. He also published a complete collection of works of Victor Hugo, Henryk Senkiewicz,[21] and such valuable publications for that time as the *Military Ency-clopaedia*, *Children's Encyclopaedia* and *People's Encyclopaedia*.

As a second-hand bookseller, I must mention here that the *Military* and *Children's* encyclopaedias have been very popular with readers until recent years (thirty years after the revolution [1947]) and haven't been replaced by any adequate new publications yet.[22]

And, finally, Ivan Dmitrievich Sytin published a huge number of text-books, compiled by the best, progressively minded educationalists. I.D. was the first among all the publishers to manage to bring the cost of a popular brochure-booklet down to 80 kopecks per one hundred.

Much can be said about Sytin's merits. We, booksellers, through whose hands hundreds of thousands of books pass, deal directly with various kinds of book users and can confirm that the old publications by Sytin had been for a long time in great demand by average buyers, attracting their attention with bright cover-pictures and low prices, until they finally disappeared from the market.

I had a chance to see I.D. Sytin again after the revolution in his apartment in Moscow. I was working at that time as a buyer in the bookshop for writers with I.I. Sytin, who introduced me to his father:

"Here's our Petersburg boy."

I.D. Sytin, who was looking much older but as severely focused as before, was sitting silently, listening to my, conversation with I.I., as if searching me out with his clever eyes.

By the end of the talk I.D. stood up, banged his fist on the table and said: "I cannot forgive myself that I did not understand that you were so promising."

I laughed and said: "But I was only a 'boy' then!"

I.D. repeated: "No, I can't forgive myself!"

Probably he, who had been able to notice and promote a capable person when the time came, felt jealous that a man had been promoted without him.

"I could have entrusted any department to you," he said, as if somewhat mortified.

Alas, he is "at rest" now. His colossal practical mind, huge energy, over a half-century of working experience – all these features, which had made him the greatest "American type" entrepreneur under the capitalist economy, were inapplicable in the new post-revolution conditions.

During the first post-revolution years he was still finishing his publications that hadn't been completed yet.

Some attempts were made to involve Ivan Dmitrievich in business but they had no results.

It is known that V.I. Lenin invited him into his office and said during the conversation that there would be no constraints either on him or on his family as former representatives of big capital and that I.D. would even receive a life pension of 250 rubles. In addition, he would be allowed to complete and publish those books that had been printed and kept unbound in his printing house.

When later the new economic policy (NEP) was proclaimed and the question was raised about inviting private capital, including foreign capital (concessions), into industry, which was being brought back to life after the civil war and destruction, I.D. Sytin approached VSNH [All-Soviet Economic Council] with a proposal to organize the papermaking and printing and publishing businesses. At that time one of the German entrepreneurs[23] offered to invest part of his capital in the printing business in our country. I.D. went to Germany at the request of VSNH to have talks with him. But the entrepreneur fell ill, and his son didn't support his father's idea and the talks were cancelled.

It is necessary to point out that when Finnish entrepreneurs offered to let I.D. Sytin start a book publishing business based on the paper industry in Finland, he flatly turned down that advantageous proposal. In his understanding it was equal to treason.[24]

Later I.D. was invited to work in the state publishing house but couldn't come to terms with its manager, O.Iu. Schmidt. The differences were fundamental: I.D. was offered a part in the collective leadership, and he put forward his conditions – individual management and complete independence. The talks didn't bring any results.

In addition, a project was put forth, "Tovarishchestvo [The Company] 1922," in which the ex-book publishers Sytin, Sabashnikov, and Dumnov were supposed to participate in as shareholders together with Gosizdat [The State Publishing House]. But the business fell apart because Gosizdat refused to supply the shop of this *tovarishchestvo* with material to be produced.

I.D. happened to go on a trip to America (obviously, as a prestigious person [to impress] American business circles). It was a business trip that had nothing to do with his specialty: he had to sell works of art.

All attempts to involve I.D. Sytin in the nationalized printing business are confined to those mentioned above.

One can say that there were two factors involved: a lack of absolute trust in I.D. Sytin, ex-capitalist (though progressively minded), and on the other hand, the inability of Sytin himself to adjust to the new conditions. All his skills had been acquired at a different time and in totally different conditions. He didn't fit in here. Life was victoriously following a completely different course, and new people were running the state publishing business for everyone, using new principles that were totally strange and alien to him.

The rapid changes of this new life forced into the background the once enormous personality of I.D. Sytin. He remained forgotten till his very death. In the last years of his life. they say, he began to lose his reason. His death was unnoticed.

A small group of us, former "Sytins," walked his coffin to the Lutheran cemetery. The final ceremony was very modest, there were no speeches.

This probably corresponded to his personal wishes. I.D. had been an extremely humble man in his private life. It is known that in his lifetime he had been closely connected with many remarkable people, had corresponded with them, and had helped many of them. But no archive was found after his death. And he had never mentioned these facts in his memoirs.

It is characteristic that before the revolution, during I.D. Sytin's lifetime, a legend had been created that he was finishing all his "earthly" affairs in order to withdraw from everyday concerns in the manner of mysterious Fedor Kuzmich.²⁵ I heard about this from several people who had known I.D. Sytin. They recounted that in 1916 he bought a health resort in Kislovodsk for the employees and workers of his companies, having paid half a million rubles for it. He made a mysterious remark at the "celebration" of this purchase: "I started from nothing and will pass away with nothing."

It is hard to say what he wanted to express with that, but his last years and his "passing away" from life justified this prediction.

Sytin
On the Occasion of the Funeral of the Great Russian Publisher
Sergei Iablonovsky²⁶

People say that when Krylov passed away, somebody asked actor Karatygin²⁷ who was following the hearse in the funeral procession, whose funeral it was. Karatygin replied, it was the Minister's of Public Education funeral. "Did Uvarov²⁸ pass away?" "It's not Uvarov's, it's Krylov's funeral." "But Krylov is a fable writer." "No, it's Uvarov who was a fable writer,²⁹ Krylov was the Minister of Public Education."

Krylov was a gifted writer, perhaps a genius, no wonder Karatygin called him the minister. But the man who had just passed away in Moscow used to write his letters as ungrammatically and with the same scrawl as cooks do, yet he had more right to be called the minister of Public Education than Krylov. This man was Ivan Dmitrievich Sytin. The contribution of this man to public education and culture in Russia is second to none.

He published the newspaper *Russian Word*, whose circulation was a million and two hundred thousand copies. It would have expanded enormously had the Bolsheviks not destroyed it together with all the Russian press.

The circulation figure speaks for itself; there are a few publications with similar circulation in Paris but they can in no way be compared to the quality of *Russian Word*. Here in Paris it is the yellow press: sensations, murders, scandals, sometimes pornography, it has nothing to do with public education. The newspaper published by Sytin attracted the greatest Russian writers and journalists. Leo Tolstoy was the leader among the writers and Doroshevich among journalists.

Russian Word cost only three kopecks but provided a lot of valuable information in literature, science, newspaper satire.

And *Russian Word* was only a small part of Sytin's activities.

He had a huge publishing business, a bookmaking factory with several thousand staff in Zamoskvorechie,[30] Piatnitskaia St. There Sytin published wonderful books in all spheres of science and also fiction by great Russian writers.

There were a number of different departments headed by great experts. And all those accomplished experts were subordinate to Sytin, a half-illiterate, uneducated man.

His way of running the business was miraculous. He got along well with all his staff. He didn't infringe on their dignity and self-respect, yet he was in control of the whole business. All the books were in his hands, the decisive voice belonged to Sytin; he controlled everybody and everything.

A friend of mine, S.S.A., at that time a young professor of bacteriology and pathologic anatomy, wrote a textbook for students, *Pathogenic Microorganisms*, and wanted to get it published by Sytin. He took his manuscript to F.I. Blagov, editor of *Russian Word*, who was a doctor by education and Sytin's son-in-law. Blagov asked him: "Why don't you take it straight to Ivan Dmitrievich?" – "Well, you are a doctor. Ivan Dmitrievich doesn't understand it." Blagov opened his eyes wide: "Ivan Dmitrievich doesn't understand?!"

When A. went to Sytin, the latter asked him a few irrelevant questions in a carefree manner. But through them he determined the importance of the author and the significance of his book, and a few minutes later he declared that the book would be published. But he kept referring to it not as *Pathogenic Microorganisms* but as *Pathetic Microorganisms*.

I met Sytin for the first time in the summer of 1901. At that time Sytin had a small and rather conservative newspaper, *Russian Word*, which he wanted to develop into a big progressive newspaper, on the advice of Chekhov, Korolenko,[31] and perhaps Tolstoy.

A new editorial staff was being set up, headed by V.M. Doroshevich, G.S. Petrov the priest, N.I. Rozenstein, V.I. Nemirovich-Danchenko.

They invited me to come from Kharkov, where I was living and writing, to join them.

I reached agreement with the editorial staff immediately, now I had to talk with the publisher.

I was sitting in front of a proverbial merchant from Zamoskvorechie with a peasant face and very small eyes. The eyes were sly, suspicious, and very unkind. Yet they were smart, clever, and, with great shrewdness, they looked deep inside you and it seems that they saw a lot. He was not telling things, he was asking questions as if willing to be taught something. Now and again he would stand up, walk around the room. He was limping and it was obvious that it was painful for him to walk.

In the middle of our talk I saw such deep suffering on his face that I asked him: "Is your leg hurting you, Ivan Dmitrievich?" He made a face and said: "Well, I gave my shoes to the shoemaker to re-sole and he, the scoundrel, made them so narrow, that I've been suffering for three days trying to break them in."

At that time he was already a big millionaire. And later, when he became still richer, he led a Spartan way of life.

When I referred to him as a typical merchant from Zamoskvorechie, that wasn't exactly true. It would be more correct to call him a peasant, rather than a merchant, who became rich, but didn't want to abandon a simple way of life and rejected comfort; he just didn't need it.

He had a huge house in the Zamoskvorechie merchant district but the spacious and nicely furnished rooms were kept locked and were opened only for special honorary guests and for big holidays. The living rooms were very simple, even miserable. He didn't accept any luxury for himself, but he would scrupulously see to it that his staff had self-respect and dignity. If he met a member of his staff riding in a squalid cab, he would say: "Dear S.V., isn't it a disgrace for you and for *Russian Word* to ride in such a shabby cab?"

Yet he himself used a much shabbier cab. I don't think that I ever saw him riding in his own coach.

Or if he saw his staff members at the theatre but not sitting in the first rows, he would immediately say: "S.V., why are you disgracing *Russian Word*? Your position doesn't allow you to sit in the sixth row." The tickets were bought at the company's expense.

And he himself would sit far behind.

The printing plant in Zamoskvorechie was very well equipped, the plant of *Russian Word* on Tverskaia was up-to-date. The offices of the staff members of the publishing house were as good as ministers' offices. His business required that; Sytin personally didn't need it. He never had time to enjoy comfort, he worked from morning to night, going into all the details, controlling the whole process.

He didn't get into the editing business at all. There were competent, experienced journalists there, the departments were headed by experts who had their own people on staff and a lot of reporters working for them in different parts of the world.

Sytin's interference in their work was reflected only in meetings from time to time with the newspaper leaders in order to discuss questions of improvement, expansion, changes that involved big financial expenses. Sytin was very generous with this.

The staff members were much better paid than anywhere else, advance payments were simply fabulous. It was typically Moscow merchant-like.

A modest and shy man would have a hard time getting a small sum of money from him, but there were those who knew how to do it

I remember, one of his new staff members, whose wife was expecting a baby, came to Sytin to ask for a small sum of money, 200 rubles to be paid in advance. He explained his need to Sytin and Sytin started to complain about his business in return. The petitioner felt like lending Sytin the little money he had about him. He thought: "I still have a couple of rubles and he will go out into the street tomorrow to beg for money."

He finally got 100 rubles instead of 200, and when he came back to the editorial office and told his colleagues the whole story, they were angry.

"You are spoiling the whole thing for us. First: when you need 200 rubles, you should ask for 400. You shouldn't stress that you need it badly, just mention nonchalantly: "By the way, I need 400 rubles."

And the best thing would be for him to think that you had gambled or frittered away the money. Then you will get all 400 rubles without objection. The more you ask for the more you will get."

What I've told you isn't a very complimentary portrait of Sytin, but there was something larger than life, out of the ordinary, about that man and I know for sure that Tolstoy, Chekhov, Korolenko, and many other outstanding people of Russia felt a true and sincere liking for him.

Sytin was always natural. He never put on airs, never bragged, was equally simple and unaffected with high officials, with great writers, and with workers. Yet he was strict, severe, and demanding in business.

He didn't educate himself till his last days (he died in his eighty-fifth year[32]) but he did not put on airs and, despite the fact that his writing was a clumsy scribble, he was never made fun of and was never the object for anecdotes.

Moscow liked to laugh at "gentlemen,"[33] at Kit Kitichi,[34] yet in Sytin there was something so mighty and outstanding that it didn't occur to anyone to make fun of him and he didn't give any grounds for it. During all sixteen years of my work with the newspaper I cannot remember any occasion when he was ridiculous and I cannot even imagine one.

He was advancing his business, huge in significance and in size, quietly and persistently.

He started with publishing dream books and oracles, Bova the Prince [Korolevich] and cheap popular print pictures; he didn't totally give up their publication later, yet at the same time he was gathering more and more people around himself, and he had a gift for selecting proper people, so that gradually he moved from books of dream interpretations to the publication of fiction, scholarly and scientific books, textbooks, books on history. His editions were marvellous in quality and very cheap. One wouldn't find lower prices on books anywhere. And what he had done for public education and public teachers alone was sufficient to give him an unforgettable and honourable reputation.

He had celebrated his fiftieth anniversary in publishing just before the Bolsheviks seized power, and the volume that was published for that day was a symbolic monument to Sytin's glory. In it Sytin's glory was shown by figures, facts, documents, and it describes a kind of commercial activity previously unheard of in Russia.

Then the Bolsheviks came. At first they seized Sytin's factory and the building where the publishing house and the printing house of *Russian Word* were situated. They started publishing their own newspaper, *Izvestiia*, there, they took a loan of two million rubles from the bank on the huge warehouses with paper supplies and wasted that money on their newspaper.

Then they involved Sytin in the printing business. Sytin could do a lot, besides he couldn't live without Moscow and without work. But I can't imagine Sytin working according to anyone's instruction, especially if it was unprofessional and silly. That collaboration didn't work out.

I don't know anything about his last years, I think they were hard for him.

Bibliophile [Knizhnik]

This short article follows the Iablonovsky memoir and was probably written by him.

I.D. Sytin died having drained the bitter cup of sufferings under the Bolsheviks' yoke. He had devoted his last years to religion and church, trying to escape the nightmares of reality.

His destiny didn't give him a chance to complete his publishing activity of universal education for Russia, which he thought to be the objective of his life. He had waited for the end of the war in order to develop public education on a large scale. He had worked out the plan and had done all preparatory work.

He had attracted the best educationalists for that work and found material resources.

For that purpose he, together with his close collaborators, had bought the publishing house *Niva* from A.F. Marks, which had the rights for publication of the majority of Russian classical writers.

The other share-holders of the *Niva* publishing house with Sytin, whose share was the largest, were A.I. Putilov,[35] B.A. Gordon, N.A. Gordon,[36] B.A. Katlama,[37] A.V. Rumanov.[38] But I.D. Sytin alone had total control of the business.

I.D. Sytin's idea was to publish classical writers at a very accessible price and flood the country with millions of copies. He liked to repeat Nekrasov's words about the time when a peasant (*muzhik*) "would bring a book by Belinsky and Gogol from the market"...

The Bolshevik revolution struck a severe, lethal blow to those dreams of his.

I.D.Sytin had to face the destruction of his hopes, bankruptcy of *Niva*, and destruction of all the plans of his life with the advent of the new people.

Reminiscences of a Lawyer[39]
B.S. Utevsky

I met I.D. Sytin at the Main Department of Prisons. When he came in, I thought that this tall, sturdy, white-haired man was either a former convict or had come to ask me to help some prisoner. He said he would like to see the head of the Main Department, and he entered Shirvindt's office. Half an hour later it was clear to me that he was neither an ex-prisoner nor a petitioner. In another half an hour, Shirvindt asked me to drop in his office and said: "This is Ivan Dmitrievich Sytin. You certainly know who he is."

I had heard a lot about Sytin. He was a prominent personality, outstanding and original. I had heard about him from Muscovites; I knew that he had started his career as an errand boy in a small bookshop, and that he had received no education. Thanks to his exceptional abilities as an organizer, his special grasp of commercial matters, and his understanding of the book market, he became the owner of one of the largest publishing companies; he published the *Russian Word*. It was a bourgeois newspaper but a progressive one. People talked a great deal about his unusual ability to decide whether a manuscript was suitable for publishing by looking through it for a few minutes and having a short talk with the author.

And it didn't matter if it was a book on history, mathematics, geography, medicine, and the like. He replied to the author who had brought the manuscript straightforwardly: "The book will not sell," or "How much do you want for it?" They started to negotiate. Sytin hated to pay much, but was generous to needy authors. When they negotiated the price, Sytin said to the author: "Wait, I can't make the final decision myself. I have a board. I'll go and discuss it with them."

He went to a neighbouring room where there was no board, sat down in a chair, smoked a cigarette, came back, and approached the author with the words: "I've talked the board into buying your book."[40]

He didn't recognize any agreements, neither did he recognize copyright. To be more precise, he didn't know anything about them.[41] The whole procedure of buying a book consisted of writing a note to his accountant on a piece of paper: "Please, give so much money to this man and take a receipt."

The author received the whole sum of money in cash and Sytin never saw him again.

This was the only information I had had about Sytin when I first met him in 1925 or 1926 (I don't remember exactly). Later I learned more about him from the articles and the published letters of M. Gorky. Gorky's judgments about Sytin were contradictory. For instance, in 1901 he wrote about "book-selling crocodiles like Sytin and Co." In 1914 Gorky wrote a letter to Sytin that testified to their friendly relations. The letter opened with the words "Dear Ivan Dmitrievich." The comments on the letter, dated 30 July 1911, show that Sytin travelled to Capri in March 1911 at the invitation of M. Gorky to conduct talks on the publication of a magazine. The talks concerned a magazine under the editorship of Potresov and Martov[42] that Gorky described as "united-Marxist."

I.D. Sytin, great entrepreneur and millionaire, accepted the revolution calmly, though he had lost all his capital in the revolution (he was a patriot and never kept his capital in foreign banks), as well as his huge publishing enterprise. He didn't sabotage the new power. Instead he assisted it from the very first days in setting up the publishing business, helped the government to take stock of all the paper, even the supplies that were stored in his own warehouses. He told me that his son was a good friend and schoolmate of N.P. Gorbunov, who was a secretary and later a supervisor at the Council of People's Commissars in the Russian Federation during V.I. Lenin's life. Sytin called him "Nikolenka Gorbunov" and said that Nikolenka had often been his guest and they had often chatted with him.

Sytin came to the Main Department of Prisons in the Russian Federation when he was already seventy-five years old. He was a tall, sturdy, vigorous man with lively eyes, dressed simply but elegantly.

He made the following offer: the majority of prisoners in Taganka prison were without jobs, and those who had jobs were occupied with primitive handicrafts that didn't teach them any skills. There was a printing plant there, too. Sytin had set it up long before. About five hundred people used to work there. But now it was neglected. Probably the Main Department had no money to organize actual production. Sytin offered to repair the printing plant with his own money and organize the training of prisoners there. He expected that the Main Department would pay him a certain share of profits. This share would be small, for he didn't need much.

Sytin's offer was accepted. He started production and the training of prisoners at the printing plant skillfully and quickly. And it soon started to make a profit. When the leadership saw that he had kept his promise, they suggested that he should start up another neglected printing plant – at the Ivanovo correctional institution.

The Soviet government trusted I.D. Sytin. He was assigned to travel abroad to purchase equipment. He was a consultant for the government on questions of developing a printing industry in the USSR. When he decided to retire at a very old age, he was granted an individual pension.[43] I.D. Sytin died at the age of eighty-four [sic].

NOTES

INTRODUCTION

1 Three preliminary notes: some of the references in this introduction have been drawn from a biography of Sytin, by Charles A. Ruud, *Russian Entrepreneur: Publisher Ivan Sytin of Moscow, 1851–1934.* Natalya Alëshina and her colleagues at the Sytin Exhibition Centre transcribed Sytin's handwriting into easily readable Russian. The translation into English was the work of the late Prof. K.A. Papmehl, Valentina Vinokurova, Marina Soroka, and Charles Ruud. Finally, our endnotes are copious especially because Sytin makes reference to so many persons and customs unknown today.

2 Throughout the manuscripts, Sytin describes important people as addressing him with the pronoun "ty," that is, the familiar form of "you." Pobedonostsev, Katkov, Meshchersky, Protopopov, all are shown as speaking to Sytin in this form. Chertkov and Chekhov, however, address him initially as "vy," the formal version of "you." Only later, as they become friends do both employ "ty" in speaking to Sytin and he responds in the same way.

  The connotations of "ty" depend on the context in which it is used. Among family members and friends it conveys familiarity and affection. It is also used for children and for pets. But when someone like Pobedonostsev uses it, the implications are demeaning. When he wrote years later, Sytin had not forgotten that the gentry were insulting him – he would have noticed and expected this treatment. He was, after all, a peasant, as he repeatedly reminds his reader (although he was probably being ironic) and peasants knew their place in Russia. Sytin does not appear to take the slights personally and instead concentrates on doing business and making money.

3 *Zhizn' dlia Knigi* (*My Life for the Book*).

4 His critics, however, have suggested that Sytin's faith was polluted by his drive for business success. One of the most critical, the journalist Kolyshko who worked for Sytin's *Russian Word*, writes: "Sytin was … a typical Russian doppelganger: he endlessly swung between two poles and two ideals. Politics did not exist for him (or existed superficially), but he had a specifically Russian nature that pulled him in two opposite directions. He was fascinated by the idea of sanctity, but he was also lured by sin. His ideas were floating in the elevated realms of social good and humanity, while his business instinct was drawing him to the cash register… His vigils in churches were followed by wild orgies and Sytin was as frequent a visitor of Moscow taverns as he was of the St Basil's cathedral." Kolyshko's prose is trenchant but also vitriolic. He writes, "The cunning, greed, and cruelty of a street tomcat combined in his [Sytin's] nature with the God knows where acquired sensitivity of a Russian intellectual, a pioneer's boldness, and the daring of a great gambler" (I.I. Kolyshko, *Velikii raspad i vospominaniia*, 211–15). A similar assessment of Sytin comes from the poet Zinaida Gippius, a religious and philosophical idealist: "I believe nothing I hear from Sytin. He is a Russian 'man of business': it is soul this and soul that, but not a [firm or clear?] word of commitment" (Zinaida Gippius, *Zhivye litsa* [Tbilisi, 1991], 1:315).

5 The service of the Russian Orthodox Church appeals to the senses of the worshiper rather than stressing written creeds. The icons, the iconostasis, the rich vestments of the priest, the incense, and the sonorous choir all contribute to the experience of worship. The high-domed ceiling of the Russian church serves to cause the worshiper to raise his eyes to God. Russian worshipers do not sit in serried ranks listening to a preacher: they stand throughout the service and move around, depending on their personal reactions to the religious experience, visiting icons, lighting candles. The foremost lay theologion of the Russian Orthodox Church, Aleksei Khomiakov, stressed *sobornost'* as the central tenet of worship. *Sorbornost* is an Orthodox idea of the unity of believers in their love of God and of one another that is based on their joint participation in the liturgy of the Church.

The Old Believers and the Russian Orthodox Church separated in the famous Schism of the seventeenth century. The Old Believers insisted that the officially supported Church had abandoned ancient forms and ancient truths. The official Church made similar claims about the Old Believers.

6 Boris Uspensky, *Raskol i kulturnyi konflikt XVII veka*, 329–31.

7 Tsvetayeva's comment is found in *Polnoe Sobranie Sochinenii* 5, 360.

8 There is a very good English translation of Avvakum's difficult Russian in *The Life of the Archpriest Avvakum by Himself*, tr. Jane Harrison and Hope Mirrlees, intro. Prince D.S. Mirsky (London: Hogarth, 1924).

9 Sometime after 1924 he wrote his own fairy tale about "Little Ivan the Fool." It was published in 1994 as "An Autobiographical Parable" in *Rossiiskii Arkhiv* (Moscow, 1994), 184–5. N.D. Teleshov, "Drug knigi," *Zapiski pisatelia: Vospominaniia i rasskazy o proshlom* (Moscow, 1980), 197. Sytin spent his last days in Moscow, not a monastery. Earlier, however, he visited monasteries.

10 A.S. Prugavin, *Knigonoshi i ofeni (Vstretchi, nabliudeniia i issledovania)*, 2 vols. n.p., n.d., 1:96. As Sytin says, Mediator launched him into a world of publishing that had theretofore been closed to him as he had been unable to attract outstanding writers to his book lists. Publishing had expanded enormously in Russia following the liberalization of the laws on censorship in 1865. Advances in printing technology had improved the attractiveness of books and the speed and volume of production. A few publishers were issuing titles for larger audiences of readers, and Sytin quickly grasped the publishing opportunities offered by his contact with the great names of Russian literature.

11 P. Biriukov, "I.D. Sytin i delo 'Posrednika,'" *Polveka dlia knigi*, 115.

12 Sytin, *Zhizn' dlia knigi*, 78.

13 V.K. Lebedev ascribes the words to Paul Biriukov in "Iz istorii sotrudnichestva knigoizdatel'stva 'Posrednik' i izdatel'skoi firmy 'I.D. Sytina i ko'," *Russkaia Literatura*, 2 (1969): 210.

14 Quoted in Lebedev, "Iz istorii sotrudnichestva," 210.

15 Quoted in Dinershtein, "Vo imia blagogo," 81.

16 Chekhov to Pavlovsky, 22 May 1899, Chekhov, *Polnoe Sobranie Sochineii i Pisem v tridtsati tomakh* (Moscow, 1974–78), 8:190. Chekhov's comment about Sytin's "characterlessness"; the word is

perhaps translated too literally and is best rendered as "lack of firmness," "weakness," or "wishy-washyness." Chekhov describes a classic conflict between a writer devoted to high principles and a businessman who must make money in order to meet his payrolls and pay numerous other bills. At this time, Chekhov saw Sytin as displaying a justifiable wavering as he embarked upon the risky business of owning a newspaper.

17 Chekhov to S.S. Suvorin, 8 December 1893, *Sobranie Sochinenii v 12-ti tomakh* (Moscow, 1957), 12:39–40.

18 Sytin, *Zhizn' dlia knigi*, 120.

19 The system of preliminary censorship developed in tsarist Russia with the beginning of privately owned printing plants late in the eighteenth century. It required that all material to be printed must first be read and approved by an official censor. Later, in the mid-nineteenth century, the government installed an additional system of post-publication censorship for some publications. Under this system, a book or newspaper would first appear in print and then be subject to penalties imposed either by a censor or by the courts. At different times, such penalties might fall on writers, editors, publishers, and booksellers.

20 Sytin, *Zhizn' dlia knigi*, 125–6

21 Ibid., 130–1.

22 *Russkoe Slovo* 41, 19 February/4 March 1917.

23 The *feuilleton*, adapted from the French, was a long article on cultural or political subjects printed on the bottom half of the front page of a newspaper. The writer affected a lighter tone than in other sections of the newspaper and sought to amuse the reader. Doroshevich became the master of this genre.

24 The paper was sometimes left in Blagov's hands when Doroshevich was on the road. But Sytin had to watch him closely because his editorial and, more importantly, political – skills were weak. Blagov was by profession a medical doctor, although he did not practice. A later editor, Valentinov, claims that Blagov "could not write a simple sentence." Sytin, while visiting St Petersburg, heard from officials that *Word* had become "pro-Jewish" and in a panicked state he implored Blagov to "change course" and "save the paper." He continues, "Here I was struck [by the opinion] that the whole newspaper is Jewish and tabloid ... I do not know what to do ... I am horrified by the thought that the newspaper will be closed ... I am so crushed by horror that I

truly do not know what to do. I think I will go straight from here to Ledniki [a priest?] in Solovetsky Monastery. For God's sake do the best you can. I am dying in flesh and spirit" (Sytin, telegram to Blagov 15 June 1906, Manuscript Division, Russian State Library, 259/21/73a, 1–2 ob.) Sytin seems to have been very tolerant of Blagov because he had married Sytin's daughter Maria.

25 Amfiteatrov, who knew Doroshevich well, writes that he "described colourfully the financial situation of his youth: 'My worst enemy was the sole of my right boot. Because as I used to walk from a private lesson near St Daniel's convent to a lesson in Sokolniki (that is, across Moscow), this damned sole did not want to land straight but now wriggled to the right of the boot, now to the left ...'" (Amfiteatrov, *Zhizn' cheloveka neudobnogo dlia sebia i dlia mnogikh*, 1:156–57).

26 Doroshevich to N.V. Turkin, 26 February [1903], Central State Archive for Literature and Art (hereafter TsGALI); Moscow, 891-1-4.

27 Quoted in S.V. Bukchin, *Sud'ba fel'etonista: zhizn' i tvorchestvo Vlasa Doroshevicha*, 196.

28 Doroshevich to Turkin, 26 February [1903], TsGALI, 891-1-1.

29 As explained by Anne Edwards in *Sonya: The Life of Countess Tolstoy* (New York: Simon and Schuster, 1981), 441.

30 Gorky to Andreev, 26–31 January 1901, *Literaturnoe Nasledstvo* 72 (1965), 82. Gorky used the adjective "syt," a play on Sytin's name.

31 Gorky to Andreev, 2–4 December 1901, *Literaturnoe Nasledstvo* 72 (1965), 113.

32 M. Gorky, Untitled, *Polveka dlia knigi*, 29–30.

33 Sytin to Blagov [June 1910], TsGALI, 595-1-50, sheets 1–8.

34 Gorky to E.P. Peshkova, 12 March, 1911, A.M. Gorky, *Pis'ma E.P. Peshkovoi, 1906–1932, Arkhiv A.M. Gor'kogo* (Moscow, 1966), 9:114.

35 Ibid.

36 Gorky to Ladyzhnikov, 14 May 1913, *Arkhiv M. Gor'kogo*, 7:223.

37 Gorky to Ladyzhnikov, end of May, prior to 10 June 1914, *Letopis' zhizni i tvorchestva A.M. Gor'kogo* (Moscow, 1958), 2:438.

38 Gorky to E.P. Peshkova, 30 November 1916, *Arkhiv A.M. Gor'kogo*, 9:19.

39 Sytin's account of his trip to America can be found as an appendix to Ruud, *Russian Entrepreneur*, 196–200.

CHAPTER ONE

1 By "companion" Sytin very likely means the continuing influence of Sharapov, which had remained with him since his apprenticeship in Moscow. This passage is not entirely clear but elsewhere Sytin writes of the three stages of his life as his boyhood with his family, his apprenticeship in Moscow under Sharapov, and the third or final stage of his life when he was guided by the Russian people.

2 Volost' – the smallest administrative and territorial unit in the provinces of old Russia, which is composed of several villages.

3 Economic or crown peasants were state serfs. Sytin's distinction is between peasants who worked on land owned by private landowners and those who worked lands owned by the state. State peasants were ordinarily not subject to the same onerous controls as other peasants and, although they were occasionally subject to even stricter domination and higher payments, had personal freedom.

4 Roughly, grades five to eight.

5 The Manifesto proclaimed the liberation of the Russian serfs. It was read from the pulpits because the government reasoned that this would be the best means to reach the people of Russia with the news. The problem of communicating with those who lived in the rural areas was enormous, and many peasants did not truly grasp the nature of the liberation for a long time.

6 The largest trade fair of Imperial Russia.

7 The zemstvo was a local self-government body created in a reform of 1864. It acquired powers of taxation and was assigned a number of local responsibilities, including running the schools. The zemstvo attracted a large number of professionally trained teachers to its schools.

8 Populists (*narodniki*) – a group in the educated Russian society of the 1870s who tried to live among the peasants, either to help them move forward or to stir them to a socialist revolution.

9 Rus' – archaic and romantic name for the "true old Russia."

10 Varangians were Scandinavian warriors, Vikings; many historians consider them to be the founders of the Russian state.

11 *Raznochintsy* formed part of a layer of Russian society consisting of people from the peasantry, the clerical class, poorer city dwellers, small merchants, low-ranking officials, and destitute gentry who were often educated but without recognized rank in Russian society.

12 This sentence does not make good sense in the original. The section in square brackets is particularly garbled and has been reconstructed.

13 Sytin is using a printer's expression – to be "set in type." This was a process of assembling type by hand to create a printable version of a handwritten manuscript.

14 Kontrakty – local name for Kiev trade fairs.

15 These are titles of the most popular fairy tales from Russian folklore: "Bova the Prince," "Eruslan," "The Little Hump-backed Horse," "The Firebird," and "Prince Ivan." Sytin is, of course, being ironic here when he refers to the "benefactors of the people" who viewed with contempt the very works that the people loved to read.

16 Beginning in the 1870s, committees, responding to populist ideals to promote literacy among the lower classes, designed and published reading material for adults. They were most prominent in St Petersburg, Kharkov, and Moscow. Sytin teamed up with the Moscow committee and published some of their materials. For the Kharkov Committee he published a collection of readings in three volumes under the title *Book for Adults*. The first volume of this series went through sixteen printings. The activities of the literacy committees came to the attention of the political police and in 1895 I.I. Durnovo, the assistant minister of the Interior, warned that the firms Mediator and Sytin were engaged in publishing that could result in the "spiritual awakening of the popular mass" (Durnovo to Nicholas II, February 1895, TsGIA [State Central Historical Archive] 776-1-8, sheet 21). Sytin is referring to Leo Tolstoy's efforts to promote popular education on his estate, Yasnaia Poliana.

17 V.G. Chertkov, a Tolstoyan, is discussed in chapter 2.

CHAPTER TWO

1 The All-Russian Industrial and Artistic Exhibition was held in Moscow, 20 May to 30 September 1882. Sytin says elsewhere that the medal was bronze. It was awarded in recognition of the high quality of the pictures in Sytin's publications for the people.

2 See chapter 4.

3 Vlas Mikhailovich Doroshevich (1864–1922) was a popular Russian journalist. He was editor of the *Russian Word* from 1902 to 1912 and published a number of his best-known works there. This is the first mention of Doroshevich in Sytin's memoirs. When he refers later to

their long-standing friendship, perhaps he has this encounter in mind.

4 V.N. Marakuev was the owner of the publishing house Narodnaya
   Biblioteka (Peoples Library). In 1885 he began to publish quality
   reading for peasants by Russian and foreign authors (e.g., Hans
   Christian Andersen and Gustav Flaubert). His mistake was in not dif-
   ferentiating between children's reading material and simple books for
   semi-literate adults. Children were interested in magical tales often
   including personified animals. Adults especially liked stories based on
   the daring knights of French romances.

5 In the mid 1870s a group of St Petersburg aristocrats, dissatisfied with
   the official Orthodox Church, invited Lord G.W. Redstoke to teach
   Evangelical Christianity. Under his influence, a retired Guards colonel,
   V.A. Pashkov, founded a Russian Protestant sect in St Petersburg.
   He was eventually forced to leave Russia. Evangelists, like Baptists,
   believe that only those who truly believe in Christ will be saved and
   emphasize free will.

6 About 12 by 24 feet.

7 A contemporary, the artist Mikhail Nesterov, observes that Chertkov,
   when appearing in a group, "at once introduced an atmosphere of his
   own: where the company may have been noisy and boisterous, when
   he came onto the verandah everything became very still, such was
   the effect of his quiet methodical, all-forgiving speeches" (http://art-
   nesterov.ru/durilin133.php).

   As for Chertkov's conversion, Nesterov cites these lines from his
   autobiography, when as a twenty-two-year-old guards officer, he
   wrote, "I used to live fast … I lived as if in a daze with rare intervals
   of sobriety. Lord, if you exist, help me, for I am perishing. That was
   how I prayed one day and opened the New Testament on the page
   where Christ calls himself the path, the truth and life. I was relieved
   and I cannot describe the joy that I felt at that moment." This feeling
   of exhultation had led Chertkov to conversion long before he met
   Tolstoy (Nesterov, 68).

8 Sytin uses "we" when he speaks of his firm, a Russian peasant and
   merchant way of connecting himself to a group and establishing
   himself as part of a whole.

9 At 80 kopecks Sytin was offering a very good price. However, once
   the booklets were printed he increased his charge from 80 to 90
   kopecks per hundred He was still setting the price to the peddler at

less than a kopeck for each book. The peddler could then charge one kopeck and make a small margin of profit on each sale. Sytin estimated direct publishing expenses at 65 kopecks per hundred.

A printer's signature in Russia was eight pages. As the printer's sheet was printed on both sides, each signature had sixteen pages of text. The Mediator books were made up of two signatures. Russian authors were paid a certain sum for each signature. In time Sytin paid the honoraria to authors and artists from his profits which depended on volume of sales.

10 Sytin is referring to the popular publications that he was already publishing and marketing. (He mistakenly wrote thirty-six pages instead of the actual thirty-two pages or two printer's signatures. Each signature contained sixteen pages of text, the number resulting from printing on both sides of an eight-page sheet.) For these publications he was charging the peddlars the low rate of fifty kopecks per hundred and they were selling for eighty.

11 The financing of Mediator changed over the next few years. Initially, Chertkov promised to cover the fees for honoraria. He seemed to be assuming that all authors would be as altruistic as he was and contribute stories at little or no cost. However his assumption proved to be incorrect – he ran out of money for the honoraria and authors began to set higher prices for their work. At this point Sytin stepped in and his company paid the honoraria. Mediator did not copyright its publication, following the Tolstoyan idea that the stories, once published, were available to all for re- publishing without charge.

12 Russian publisher were required to submit all books to the censorship committee. Books intended for the peasants received especially careful scrutiny.

13 P.I. Biriukov (1860–1931), journalist and biographer of Tolstoy.

14 Konstantin P. Pobedonostsev (1827–1907), law professor at Moscow University, after 1880 head of the Holy Synod (Department of Orthodox Affairs) and member of the Imperial Council. Pobedonostsev was also a close advisor to the Emperor Aleksandr III and was opposed to western style political reforms such as jury trials and the free press.

15 N.S. Leskov followed Tolstoy's example and donated his story "Christ Visits a Peasant" to Mediator. He wrote to Chertkov, "if we cannot sacrifice everything, we still can donate to the People 'the predestined portion,' a sort of 'tithe' … All of us can do it, and I think all of us

must do it ... so that Tolstoy would not feel isolated and would see that he has followers" (Leskov to Chertkov, 8 March 1887, in N.S. Leskov, *Sobranie sochinenii v odinadtsatikh tomakh*, Moscow, 1958), 11:355–6.

16 Vsevolod M. Garshin (1855–1888), one of the most important Russian authors of the 1870s.

17 Ivan I. Gorbunov-Posadov (1864–1940). Gorbunov had been a follower of Tolstoy from an early age. He dressed like a peddler in a short coat, high boots, a cap, and a bag over his shoulder and often sold or gave away Tolstoy's books. With Chertkov and Biriukov, Gorbunov-Posadov was Tolstoy's closet collaborator during his last years. Chertkov eventually lost interest in Mediator and Biriukov became its director. He invited Gorbunov-Posadov to participate in the project and, eventually, in 1897, Gorbunov became its director. He wrote a popular "Pictorial ABC" and many collections of stories and poetry. We have been unable to track down Al'demirova . Clearly, she was one of the many persons who helped out in one way or another.

18 Varvara Ivanovna Uxkhüll (Ikskul) von Gildenbrandt (1850–1928), a well-known St Petersburg society hostess and philanthropist.

19 Viktor A. Gol'tsev (1850–1906), journalist, critic, and social activist with populist tendencies; Nikolai V. Remizov (1855–1915), author and critic.

20 Garshin is usually considered to have committed suicide, as Sytin says. But Sytin's description of the meeting with Garshin suggests another explanation for his death: the writer, who was known to have been a heavy drinker, could have fallen through the flimsy railing from the fourth floor while intoxicated.

21 Eight miles.

22 A.I. Ertel' (1855–1908), noted populist novelist whose work was distinctive because of its descriptions of Russian social life.

23 Desiatina is a Russian unit of land measurement. It equals about 2.7 acres. Chertkov's estate was very large.

24 Gubernia is the Russian word for province.

25 Obviously, Sytin meant Chertkov.

26 Maria E. Kleinmikhel (1845–1931), Petersburg society hostess.

27 Roman R. Golike – owner of one of the best Petersburg printing businesses, founder of the first printing school in Russia, sponsored by the

Russian Technical Society, and co-founder of the Russian Printers Society.

28 Ivan N. Durnovo (1834–1903), from 1889 to 1895 deputy minister of the Interior.

29 Chekhov's pseudonym.

30 Nikolai I. Pastukhov (1831–1911) – publisher, journalist, owner of *Moskovskii Listok* (*Moscow News Sheet*) newspaper.

31 Abram Ya. Lipskerov (1851–1910) – editor and owner of the Moscow daily *Novosti* (*Daily News*).

32 Aleksei S. Suvorin (1834–1912), an outstanding Russian journalist and entrepreneur, owner of the influential *Novoe Vremia* newspaper.

33 At one of the entrances to Red Square was the popular Chapel of the Iberian (Georgian) Virgin, considered the protectoress of travelers. It was the custom on arriving in Moscow to visit the chapel and light a candle as thanks for a safe journey. Sytin also describes this encounter with Chekhov in chapter 4 on the founding of *Russian Word*.

CHAPTER THREE

1 The peddlers (*ofeni*) purchased pictures and chapbooks from the publishers and travelled through the countryside, selling them to individual peasant families. They also carried other useful items, such as needles and thread. The peddler system operated seasonally, avoiding times of ploughing and harvesting when the peddlers would be out working on the land. Sytin used these itinerant peddlers with great success as a means of distributing publications and the Mediator books to the peasants.

2 As editor of *Russian Messenger*, M.N. Katkov (1818–1887) had no official position, although he was extraordinarily influential in the government. It is surprising to find him threatening Sytin as though he were a censorship official. Still, Katkov's passionate involvement in issues of education was so well-known that N.S. Leskov called him "the main source of inspiration for the minister of popular education" ("Na smert' M.N. Katkov" ["M.N. Katkov's Demise"] in N.S. Leskov, *Sobranie sochinenii* [Moscow: GIHL, 1958], 11).

3 I.Ye. Repin (1844–1930) was a well-known painter of the Wanderers School of Russian artists, fourteen graduates of the Academy of Art who had protested the requirement that they paint a classical subject

for their graduating assignment, preferring to focus on art with a social message. Repin's favorite subject was the Russian peasant. His best-known picture is "The Volga Burlaki [Boatmen]." K.A. Savitsky (1844–1905) was another member of the Wanderers group.

4 Pobedonostsev was visiting Moscow. Normally as procurator of the Holy Synod his principal office was in St Petersburg.

5 Russian Orthodox priests wear robes made of brocade and a contract for supplying brocade to the church was as profitable as getting a contract on supplying footwear or uniforms to the military.

6 Pobedonostsev uses the familiar "ty," a demeaning form of address under the circumstances as the two had just met for the first time and Pobedonostsev treats Sytin as he would an inferior.

7 Sytin is saying that the popular *lubochnaia* literature is no more dangerous to the state than the Mediator publications and that neither is a threat to the government.

8 "Bova Korolevich" was a frequently published fairy tale which Sytin issued in many editions. It was based on a French romance but without the romantic elements and was a favorite of peasant readers. Katkov is using it as an example of what is acceptable for the village reader.

9 In July 1881 a new law required peddlers to obtain permits from local authorities and this requirement opened the way to banning certain titles. In the late 1880s Mediator abandoned its distinctive red borders and motto to help protect sales of its books from opposition by local priests. Despite this, increasing government attention to Mediator books discouraged sales through the peddler system and drove the peddlers from the field. Sytin then began to emphasize distribution through bookstores, village markets, reading rooms, and book warehouses run by local zemstvos.

10 Sytin seems to mean that these were the size of his usual press runs and that he produced these editions at half of their former cost.

11 V.K. Sablin is a mistake – Sytin is actually referring to Vladimir K. Sabler-Desiatovsky (1845–1918). From 1892 to 1905 he was deputy procurator of the Holy Synod.

12 P.S. Damansky, director of the Synodal Control, senator.

13 Sytin's collaboration with the Holy Synod had been lengthy and extensive. His critics would later use it to argue that he would publish

anything if it involved profit. In the episode described here, Sytin was clearly playing politics and collaborating with Pobedonostsev in order to avoid any damage that the procurator might inflict on him.

14 Mikhail E. Saltykov (1826–1889), a great Russian satirical writer who published under the pseudonym "Shchedrin."

15 Dmitry N. Mamin (1852–1912), an outstanding writer from the Urals His fiction, focusing on the life and customs of his native region, was published under the pseudonym "Sibiriak" (The Siberian").

16 Ignaty N. Potapenko (1856–1929) A playwright and novelist popular in the 1880s for his depictions of middle-class urban society and peasant Russia.

17 Sytin appears to be referring to his own recent experience in dealing with the Holy Synod. Those relations were a trap that he believes he escaped, thus avoiding becoming a creature of the Synod. He goes on to say that it took the functionaries of the Holy Synod who took over the book publishing enterprise a year to learn how difficult the trade was and then they failed.

18 This part of the manuscript opens with a sentence fragment.

19 The Deeds of the Apostles is a part of the New Testament that has traditionally been published in Russia for popular reading. It was the first book printed in Russia by Ivan Fëdorov (1525–1583) during the reign of Ivan the Terrible. Fëdorov is considered to be the first person to employ movable type in Russia and on the territory of modern Belarus and Ukraine.

20 There were individuals outside the official church who, like Sytin, believed that services and holy books should be translated into modern Russian, as lay Russians did not understand the old Bulgarian – that is, Church Slavonic – unless taught. The church successfully prevented all attempts to translate the holy books, because it held a monopoly on printing and distributing them in the empire.

21 Sytin understands that tsarist censorship policies have a class basis and make a sharp distinction between works for a popular audience and those for educated society.

22 Nikon (1605–1681), the sixth patriarch of Muscovy, initiator of a reform to eliminate mistakes in Church rites and books and to harmonize Russian church forms with Greek ones.

23 When those who dissented from the Nikonian reforms, the so-called

Old Believers, were forced to accept them, they responded with self-immolation. Many Russians still refer to the official church as "Nikonian."

24 As the serfs had been liberated in 1861, 1907 was almost fifty years later.

25 Maksim M. Kovalevsky (1851–1916) was a scholar, law expert, and social activist; Vladimir I. Kovalevsky (1848–1934) was a well-known economist and social activist, a namesake of M. Kovalevsky; Varvara A. Morozova (1848–1917) was a member of the famous Muscovite merchant clan, a businesswoman, philanthropist, and patron of arts.

26 Vladimir M. Purishkeich (1870–1920) was a conservative monarchist, a deputy elected to the State Duma and one of the founders of the Union of the Russian People, an extreme nationalist party on the political Right.

CHAPTER FOUR

1 Sytin uses the plural for cultural reasons, as explained in chapter 2, note 8.

2 A.S., publisher of *New Times* and Chekhov's publisher and friend

3 Anatoly Aleksandrovich Aleksandrov (1861–1930) was an associate professor at Moscow University and publisher of the right-wing nationalist *Russian Review* (*Russkoe Obozrenie*). Ivan L. Shcheglov (1856–1911) was a well-known author and playwright and Grigory P. Georgievsky (1866–1948) a professor of archeography (the collecting and publishing of historical documents and bibliographies) and director of the manuscript department of Rumiantsev Museum.

4 At this time, newspapers in St Petersburg and Moscow could be published without preliminary examination by censors. Papers were, however, subject to post-publication penalties.

5 The Grand Duke Sergei Aleksandrovich (1856–1905), governor-general of Moscow and the Tsar's uncle.

6 Vladimir A. Gringmut (1851–1907), a journalist, apologist for autocracy, and extreme nationalist, had been the editor of *Moscow Bulletin* since 1896 and in 1905 was founder of the Russian Monarchist Party. Sytin is suggesting that he will draw up a contract for the printing of his paper with Gringmut, who operated a publishing plant owned by Moscow University. Lev Tikhomirov was a one-time populist revolutionary who made his peace with the tsarist regime, returned to

Russia from abroad, and became a religious thinker. Nikon
(Rozhdestvensky [1851–1918]) was archbishop of Murom and Fedor
N. Plevako (1842–1908) was a celebrated Moscow lawyer and tal-
ented speaker.

7 That is, could the license be transferred to someone else.

8 As Petersburg was called at this time.

9 Vladimir K. Sabler was assistant to Pobedonostsev. In 1911, he was
named procurator of the Holy Synod.

10 Sytin says that Aleksandrov stole the catalogue "*ot soblazna*," which
means that he wanted to prevent Pobedonostsev "from the tempta-
tion" to punish them or scold them for something in the catalogue.

11 Sensationalist tabloid newspapers in Russia were referred to either as
"the yellow press" or "the boulevard press," while prostitutes were
called "the boulevard girls."

12 Mikhail P. Soloviev (1842–1902) who had headed the Main Press
Affairs Office since 1896.

13 The word "henchman" is the term the democratic opposition used to
refer to the monarchists. Prince Vladimir P. Meshchersky was publisher of a fiercely monarchist conservative newspaper, *Grazhdanin*
(*Citizen*), that enjoyed the endorsement of Nicholas II. Meshchersky
himself had the privilege of direct contact with the emperor and therefore his support or his enmity could be decisive in any affair that
needed imperial authorization

14 Meshchersky was singularly interested in fashionable ladies' dresses.
He imported them and sold them out of his apartment. By buying
a dress, Sytin was paving the way to ask for Meshchersky's help.

15 This refers to Sytin's policy of giving away a large number of papers
to keep his circulation up and to promote interest in the paper.

16 Yu. M. Aderkas, an employee of *The Citizen* (*Grazhdanin*) who
became the second editor of the *Russian Word*.

17 E.N. Kiselev, a journalist who had been serving as editor of Sytin's
magazine *Around the World* (*Vokrug Sveta*).

18 A modest and easy-going man, a doctor who had never practiced
medicine and Sytin's son-in-law, F.F. Blagov was the managing editor
who let Doroshevich do as he wished.

19 Sytin is being disingenuous. Clearly, he went to Odessa to try to
recruit Doroshevich as editor of his paper. Sytin does not make clear
when Doroshevich became his "friend." Earlier he says that they were

acquainted, but not sufficiently to acknowledge one another in public. Relations between the two men were not always smooth, as shown in Doroshevich's letters to Sytin in chapter 11. It is possible that a series of books published by Sytin in 1883–87 under the name of Valentin Volgin were written by Doroshevich. Doroshevich is also known to have written two books for the *lubok* publishers.

20 The *feuilleton* was a long article on the bottom half of the front page of a newspaper on cultural or political subjects. The writer affected a lighter tone than in other sections of the newspaper and sought to amuse the reader.

21 Grigory S. Petrov (1867–1925), author, priest, preacher, he held a position close to Tolstoy's in his insistence on the importance of spiritual perfection rather than outward ritual. He was soon to write for *Russian Word*.

22 *Rossiia* – St Petersburg newspaper directed by A.S. Suvorin's oldest son and rival, Aleksei.

23 "Piter" is the Russian familiar name for St Petersburg.

24 The name of the restaurant is actually "Cuba's." Georges Cuba was a French chef who opened several restaurants in Russia. This one was a particular favorite of ballet dancers. Sytin seems to have forgotten the precise name of the restaurant and added a "t."

25 Aleksandr V. Amfiteatrov (1862–1938), author, journalist. Amfiteatrov's connection with Sytin proved to be a long one. In his memoirs he recounts that during World War One he was in Italy attempting to spread propaganda to persuade Italy to leave the Triple Alliance and join the Entente. He writes, "The *Russian Word* of Moscow helped me a lot, by inviting me to set up a wide network of correspondents from Italy and the closest destinations on the Mediterranean. Doroshevich, Blagov, and Sytin gave me quite a large sum of money for this: between six thousand and thirteen thousand liras a month." He says that despite this he could not compete with the well-funded British and American agents (Amfiteatrov, *Zhizn' cheloveka neudobnogo dlia sebia i dlia mnogikh* [Moscow, 2004], 2:176). This is a striking example of Sytin's serving the tsarist regime in the realm of high politics. We have seen no evidence that the tsarist government either initiated or approved this venture in Italy.

26 He might mean either A.A. Suvorin or Amfiteatrov himself.

27 Amfiteatrov.

28 This article was "The Obmanov Family," a satirical piece written by
     Amfiteatrov on the imperial family. He included many details that
     came straight from the royal household. The Emperor was incensed
     and closed the paper and exiled Amfiteatrov on his own authority,
     without proceeding through the controls system

29 A distant Russian province in the region of the Enisei River in Siberia.

30 Not literally true but a jocular allusion to the hurried dispatch of
     Aleksander Radishchev, author and social critic, to Siberia by Cather-
     ine II in 1792.

31 The legal agreement covered the terms of Doroshevich's employment
     as editor of *Russian Word*, including his salary. Doroshevich
     demanded and received a high salary from Sytin, along with many
     additional privileges. The writer Leonid Andreev advised Kornei
     Chukovsky, who had been offered the job of editor of the literary sec-
     tion of *Russian Word*, to ask for one hundred thousand rubles and a
     villa in the Moscow suburbs. "Otherwise he will decide that you lack
     talent and will not pay anything. Duke Vlas Doroshevich and other
     Muscovite marquises have established the price list for him and he
     can only think according to its terms" (Chukovsky, *Sovremenniki.
     Portrety i etiudy* [Moscow, 2008], 216). Kolyshko says that Sytin
     feared Doroshevich and even hated him. The record presented by
     Sytin in these memoirs suggests otherwise. Doroshevich was a highly
     marketable journalist. Sytin understood that *Russian Word* depended
     on him and feared losing him to a rival (Kolyshko, *Velikii raspad:
     Vospominaniia*, 211–15.)

32 Upon arriving in Paris, Doroshevich began to write letters to Sytin
     concerning the editing of the paper. He made it clear that he had
     assumed full control of the editorship. His letters are published for
     the first time as chapter 11.

33 Stanislaw M. Propper (1855–1931) – was publisher of the St Peters-
     burg daily *Stock Market Bulletin* (*Birzhevye Vedomosti*).

34 February 1904–August 1905. It sparked the first Russian revolution.

35 A popular restaurant, named after its owner, whose clientele was from
     the affluent upper class (from Grand Duke Sergei Aleksandrovich
     down).

36 The Japanese attacked Russia without a declaration of war and
     Nicholas II issued a manifesto officially proclaiming war a few days
     after the fighting began in the Far East.

37 Vasily V. Nemirovich-Danchenko (1844–1936), an author and war
    journalist who had become famous for his reports from the front
    during the Russo-Turkish war of 1877–78.
38 Sytin is here addressing the spirit of Chekhov, who had died in 1904.
    As a permanent reminder of Chekhov's influence on the founding of
    the newspaper, Sytin hung a portrait of Chekhov right above the table
    in his boardroom.

CHAPTER FIVE

1 S.M. Tolstoy, *Drevo Zhizni. Tolstoy i ego semiia*, 188–9.
2 Nikolai K. Muraviev (1870–1936) was one of the best-known Russian lawyers of his time. A political activist, he often provided pro
   bono defences for those he considered victims of political persecution
   by government authorities. He became one of the guarantors of Leo
   Tolstoy's will.
3 The rights of ownership applied to all of them jointly.
4 The Marks team (representing *Niva*) eventually worked out a contract
   with Muraviev – which violated an agreement with the committee –
   then broke off negotiations and returned to St Petersburg. Sytin then
   signed the contract they had negotiated and acquired the rights to
   Tolstoy's works.
5 Adolf D. Marks (1838–1904) was a Russian publisher and editor of
   the popular magazine *Niva*.
6 One of the villages on the Tolstoy estate.
7 In these matters, the family is usually seen as being on one side and
   Chertkov and Alexandra Lvovna n the other. Sytin reports that they
   agreed on this point.
8 This is the most forthright admission from Sytin that he counted himself among the Tolstoyans. He had only implied a earlier passages.
   The letters to Muraviev are undated and it is not clear that they were
   actually sent. Sytin is probably using the epistolary form to express
   his ideas.
9 Sofia Andreevna writes that on 21 April 1912, " I finished my business
   with Sytin; I received 100,000 rubles for the books" (*The Diaries of
   Sophia Tolstoy*, 721). "Of course," Sytin says elsewhere, "our publishing company made no profit. But in October, 1913, Sytin would write
   to the company stockholders about the "colossal flow of subscribers to
   World (*Vokrug Sveta*) his popular magazine. He said subscriptions had

tripled, thanks to published supplements of Tolstoy's works, to make *World* one of the best-selling magazines in Russia. He also predicted that advertising in *World* "will bring greater results than all Russian journals taken together." Sytin would also issue Tolstoy premiums with subscriptions to his daily paper *Russian Word*, helping to boost readership by 13 percent in 1913 (Sytin, *Zhizn' dlia knigi*, 180; Dinershtein, "Vo imia blagogo," 96–7.) Sytin's claim to the Rozeners that their mass-marketing possibilities exceeded his is belied by the use he made of Tolstoy's works in *World* and *Russian Word*.

CHAPTER SIX

1 P.A. Stolypin (1862–1911) was president of the Council of Ministers and therefore prime minister from 1906 to 1911. The documents on pages 120–9 and 145–8 of this chapter are reprinted from, "I.D. Sytin. Vstrechi: P.A. Stolypin, P.A. Kropotkin, A.S. Suvorin," 139–44. Those on pages 129–44 are from the Sytin Exhibition Centre.

2 A.A. Makarov (1857–1919) was one of Stolypin's subordinates. Stolypin at this time was serving as both prime minister and minister of the Interior.

3 Stolypin had embarked upon what he called the "wager on the strong and the sober" to enable peasants to buy and consolidate their own lands, freeing them from the commune. His goal was to create a class of sturdy, independent farmers who would be bulwark of the government.

4 P.P. Zubovsky, official of the ministry of Interior, editor of the ministerial daily *Sel'ski Vestnik* [*Countryside Messenger*] (1881–1917) and of its free supplement, *God Will Help* (1901–11).

5 Stolypin was shot by the terrorist Dmitry G. Bogrov during a gala performance at the Kiev opera theatre in 1911.

6 Moscow's' most famous cemetery.

7 Sytin's comments on the visit to Novodevichy underscore his piety.

8 N.K. Roerich (1874–1947), artist, designer of stage settings, and archaeologist. Roerich worked in vivid colors and his pictures have an emotional and mystical quality.

9 Toward the end of the nineteenth century Chekhov developed liberal political views; this was the main cause of his anger toward Suvorin.

10 The high bank of the Moscow River from which one can have a wide view of the city.

11 This is a reference to a Russian village tradition. If it became known or rumoured in a village that an unmarried girl had lost her honour, self-appointed and anonymous guardians of public chastity smeared the gates of her house with tar to let everyone know that there was a woman of ill-repute in the house. It was an invitation to shun and ridicule the girl.

12 In November 1916 the Duma was in continuous uproar against Rasputin-influenced ministers appointed through the interventions of Empress Aleksandra.

13 Boris V. Stürmer (1848–1917), statesman, prime minister in 1916, appointed through the influence of Empress Aleksandra.

14 Admiral I.K. Grigorovich (1853–1930), naval minister, 1911–1917, took an interest in Sytin and his publications. He backed the *Military Encyclopaedia* and provided a military telegraph aboard a Russian military vessel in the Black Sea to send war correspondence to *Russian Word* during World War One.

15 The city in Belorussia where the headquarters of the Russian Army was located.

16 Fr. Georgy Shavelsky (1871–1951), chaplain of the Russian Army and Navy during the First World War.

17 This was M.K. Lemke, the historian and journalist who was serving as head of military censorship at Military Headquarters.

18 Vladimir N. Voeikov (1868–1941), major general, chief of Nicholas II's security.

19 Sergei I. Witte was minister of Finance from 1892 to 1903 and then president of the Council of Ministers (premier) in 1905–06. He was an effective statesman and took the lead in the economic reforms of the late nineteenth and early twentieth century. His premiership was the first under the new constitutional order.

20 Sytin's School and Knowledge Society, described in chapter 5.

21 Sytin is offering to put his book printing plant on Piatnitskaia Street and other resources at the disposal of the Society. To acquire working capital, the Society would issue shares to raise 180,000 rubles. The shares are a small sum relative to the value of his printing plant and could easily be bought back in the future.

22 Sytin has in mind V.A. Sukhomlinov (1848–1926). In 1909 he became war minister, in 1911 he was appointed to the State Council. After the beginning of the First World War, Sukhomlinov was commonly

blamed for Russia's military failures. The naval minister was Adm. Ivan K. Grigorovich.

23 Sytin had published ten volumes of the *Encyclopaedia* and wished to have the Emperor's endorsement. There were officials in the Ministry of War who were opposed to associating the Emperor's name with a publication that might be seen as "liberal." The volumes were divided into four parts and included 1) military science, 2) military technical information, for instance on armaments, 3) general information about the army and military legal system, and 4) information about the navy.

The volumes contained many tables, maps, and other illustrations. The scope was broad and covered worldwide trends and social developments that related to the military, including military budgets in other countries and pacifist movements. Although Sytin had in mind as one of his purposes preparing the Russian military for the anticipated conflict with Germany, he produced a work that was not sufficiently "patriotic" to satisfy elements on the right wing, politically.

24 The military editors.

25 Not "in tune" with the current situation.

26 The intention had been to publish twenty volumes, but only eighteen were completed with two remaining unfinished. The third volume refers to the concluding volume which contained annexes and other supplementary material. Three thousand sets of the eighteen volumes were completed. An additional three thousand remained in the form of unbounded signatures.

27 Sytin was worried – and his officer-editors probably agreed – that the lower ranks of the military would never have access to the full encyclopedia. If they didn't, one of Sytin's purposes would not have been achieved.

28 A disparaging term for a radical newspaper.

29 A popular St Petersburg newspaper (1901–02) that attracted some of the leading Russian journalists. It was closed by the Emperor after a few months because of the publication of an article about the Imperial family. The incident is discussed in chapter 4.

30 Aleksandr D. Protopopov (1866–1917) was a member of the Duma (Octobrist Party) and a monarchist. As minister of the Interior in 1916; he became a member of the Empress's intimate circle on the eve of the February Revolution. As minister, Protopopov tried to start a

newspaper that would promote official policy but appear to be in the hands of a private publisher. He persuaded a number of bankers to put up funds for this venture. It is clear from several sources that Protopopov wanted Sytin to assume public control of the paper in order to give it credibility. Later, others tried to enlist Sytin's support.

Zinaida Gippius, the poet, noted in her diary for March 1917 that "Sytin has talked with the Gorkists and heard Bolshevik tones in their words. I suppose nonetheless, that they were buttering up to Sytin in various ways ... Sytin was shaken, was frightened, and more so because he is so smart that he is quite capable to outsmarting himself. He is swearing to support Kerensky's newspaper [A.F. Kerensky was prime minister under the Provisional Government from July to November, 1917] and at the same time he let it drop that he will not abandon the Gorky-[N.N.] Gimmer [N. Sukhanov, a moderate socialist, was Gimmer's pseudonym] newspaper. I suspect that he has already committed himself to giving them a hundred or more thousand rubles (Whether he actually gives it to them is another question)" (Gippius, *Zhivye litsa*, 1:312).

31 It was rumored that Protopopov was Rasputin's candidate.

32 A Russian way of saying that the main business had been decided.

33 Protopopov was planning to give his profits back to the government.

34 A Russian measure of land equivalent to 2.7 acres.

35 Sytin visited England in 1900, but we have been unable to find any record of the trip.

36 Kropotkin had been imprisoned in 1874 for spreading socialist propaganda among workers and peasants and, in a widely known jailbreak, his comrades from the recently organized Land and Liberty organization freed him and assisted him to flee abroad in 1876. The Peter and Paul fortress, located in central St Petersburg across the river from the Winter Palace, was used by the government for incarcerating those charged with political crimes.

37 Kropotkin was born into an aristocratic Russian family. His father owned a huge estate with more than one thousand serfs. The male line of Kropotkins traced their origin to the founder of Russia, Riurik, and thus merited the title prince, but Peter abandoned it at the age of twelve. He became a well-known Russian zoologist and geographer and a widely known and influential anarchist. He advocated a communist society free from central government and based on voluntary

associations among workers. By all accounts, Kropotkin was an especially warm and kindly individual who loved to argue his ideas.

Sofia Grigorievna Kropotkina (1856–1941), born Ananieva-
Rabinovich, the wife of Prince Peter Kropotkin, met the exiled revolutionary in Geneva where she was studying biology and zoology at
the university. She was Kropotkin's assistant throughout his life
and wrote popular science books.

CHAPTER SEVEN

1 Epic folk songs about heroic episodes, either mythical or from
  Russian history.
2 Sytin is here writing of a brutish mass that is good only for hard
  work.
3 The zemstvos were local government institutions established in the
  reform of 1864. They featured many elements of self-government and
  became beacons of liberal reform in the countryside.
4 The Solovetsky Monastery was built on an the Solovetsky archipelago
  in the White Sea in the fifteenth century. It was one of the centres of
  Russian Orthodox religious life and in the seventeenth century a
  centre of resistance to ecclesiastic reforms of the Moscow Patriarch
  Nikon. Under the Soviet government it became a notorious
  concentration camp.
5 An essay by the journalist Nemirovich-Danchenko, who was a war
  correspondent for Sytin's *Russkoe Slovo*, seems to have been a source
  for Sytin's comments on the Solovetsky monastery. For one thing the
  rhythm of the prose is similar to Nemirovich-Danchenko's work and
  would explain why this section of the memoirs is the most fluidly
  written. A major Sytin addition is his placing of the account about the
  importance of Solovki into the larger context of his view of Russians
  and Russian values (Vas. I. Nemirovich-Danchenko, "Solovky," in
  Na kladbishchakh: Vospominaniia y vpechatleni'ia [Moscow, 1874,
  424–0; reprint 2001]).
6 Sytin, as he often does, is actually discussing with himself about this
  subject, upbraiding himself for holding or not holding certain ideas.
  Here he is debating with someone who led a life that included
  spending time at the Solovetsky monastery.
7 Galich and Soligalich are two ancient towns in Sytin's home province
  of Kostroma, about 500 km from Moscow. Their names indicate their

traditional industry, mining for salt. "Sol" is salt in Russian and "galich" is the Russianized pronunciation of the Greek word for salt.

8 *Kvas* is a drink made of fermented bread, yeast, and sugar. It is popular among Russian peasants.

9 There appears to be a break here between what someone told Sytin and his own narrative.

10 The liberation of the serfs took place in 1861. Sytin is writing in 1924.

11 Maksim Gorky

12 A small monastery erected in distant, uninhabited areas. Sometimes it was the work of a single monk.

13 The *bezpopovtsy* were one of the sects of the Old Believers that formed in the seventeenth century at the time of the Schism in the Russian Orthodox Church. They deny the legitimacy of the Orthodox Church and its hierarchy and reject priests, replacing them by elected elders.

14 Manuscript text is unclear here.

15 Nikolai A. Bugrov (1837–1911) was a millionaire owner of steam mills from Nizhnii Novgorod. An Old Believer, he was known for his public works and for supporting Old Believer settlements.

CHAPTER EIGHT

1 The abbreviation used to refer to the State Publishing Enterprise of the Russian Soviet Socialist Republic, founded in 1919 under the aegis of the Bolshevik government. Sytin also dealt with the Council of People's Commissars created in 1917, which he misnames as the All-Russian Council of People's Deputies.

2 Sytin says elsewhere that the approach was made in 1920.

3 "Kushnerev & Co.," a large printing business founded by Ivan N. Kushnerev (d. 1896).

4 Sytin is referring to his efforts in 1910 to start a paper manufacturing plant at Kem in the Russian north, inland from the White Sea on the Kem river. A technical specialist estimated that a waterfall there could produce 20,000 horsepower. Surrounding forests could be the source of wood pulp.

5 Mikhail V. Sabashnikov (1871–1943), the survivor of two brothers who owned a Moscow book publishing company and were well-known philanthropists.

6 Vladimir V. Dumnov (1854–?), head of a large Moscow publishing

company, Salaev Brothers' Heirs.(He had married the niece of the owners.) Prior to the revolution he published school and university textbooks.

7 Sytin felt that if he was to argue or differ from the other members of the new board, they would all side against him on political grounds. He wanted support from someone who would see things the way he did.

8 Otto Yu. Schmidt (1891–1956), professor at Moscow University, Soviet mathematician, geographer, astronomer, and Arctic explorer. At the time he was the head of Gosizdat.

9 G.I. (Sergei V.?) Chefranov (1872–1952), teacher, graduate of Moscow University, and M. Sabashnikov's classmate.

10 Stinnes's representative from Germany.

11 A *pud* is a Russian measure of weight equivalent to 16,38 kg or about 36 lbs.

12 Hugo Stinnes (1870–1924), one of the largest German industrialists, creator of the Stinnes concern, which merged over a thousand companies dealing in everything from mining to shipbuilding. Sytin is referring to a government-authorized trip that he made to Germany in 1921–22 to try to persuade Stinnes to back his paper-making project. Stinnes agreed, but his death in 1924 ended the prospects for German backing.

13 One of the first Soviet trading organizations (1921). In 1922 it became Moscow State Shareholding Society and took charge of Soviet commercial ventures abroad.

14 Soviet Narodnykh Komissarov – Council of People's Commissars – equivalent to the Council of Ministers.

15 State Bank of Russia.

16 Vaclav V. Vorovsky (1871–1923), professional revolutionary, Marxist literary critic, diplomat. Shot in Lausanne by a former White Army officer.

17 Narodnyi Komitet Vnutrennikh Del – Ministry of the Interior.

18 There were rumours that Sytin had been jailed for illegal business dealings, but he denied that they were accurate. His grandson Mikhail I. Sytin writes in an unpublished memoir on file at the Sytin Exhibition Centre that they were not true (MS "Vospominaniia Starshego Vnuka," 3).

19 All are important pre-Revolution paper-making companies. The

Kuvshinov dynasty was one of the largest paper-making enterprises in Russia with a fortune that classed them with such magnates as the Morozovs in textiles. The Riabushinsky family were textile and paper manufacturers and bankers. Vargushin was a St Petersburg paper-mill owner. We could not identify Govard and Protas'ev, but are assuming that they are important because Sytin has named them as important manufactures. All of these enterprises were nationalized in 1918.

20 Leonid B. Krasin (1870–1926), revolutionary, member of the Bolshevik party. After 1917, diplomat, minister of foreign trade since 1923. Krasin proved to be an opportunistic revolutionary. He sent members of his family abroad on well-supported business trips that concealed the holiday-like character of their travel. He told his wife not to worry about him for he was receiving gifts from various Soviet organizations, including a five-pound jar of caviar from the Armenian trading organization Armentorg which arrived at a time of severe famine in Russia.

21 There was a Ginzhe printing business in 1834 – this might be a descendant. Eynem was the former owner of the famous chocolate factory in Moscow which still exists under the no less famous name Krasnyi Oktiabr' – Red Oktober.

22 Petr A. Bogdanov (1882–1939), economist, head of VSNKh, the All-Russian Union of National Economy, one of the active proponents of New Economic Policy, which temporarily allowed private enterprise in Soviet Russia. Nikolai I. Bel'sky, synoptic engineer, also studied the properties of waterfalls.

23 He was posted to Britain as the Soviet ambassador.

24 Andrey M. Lezhava (1870–1937), chairman of Zentrosouyz in 1919–20, economist.

25 Nikolai I. Bel'sky, synoptic engineer, also studied the properties of waterfalls.

CHAPTER NINE

1 Vladimir G. Korolenko (1853–1921), a well-known author, journalist, and political activist. He was exiled to Nizhnii Novgorod, Gorky's native town, for his revolutionary activity and lived there from 1885 to 1895. The Fair referred to is the famous Nizhnii Novgorod Fair that attracted buyers and sellers from all of Russia and beyond. Sytin describes his boyhood experience there in his introductory chapter.

2 Sytin may be referring to the trial of Mendel Beilis, an event that created a sharp division in Russian society between those who accepted
   Beilis's guilt and those who saw the trial as an unspeakable act by the
   tsarist government in which it was subverting its own judicial system
   in a transparent effort to discredit Jews. Mendel Beilis, a Jew, was
   accused of having committed a ritual murder of a Christian boy.
   Sytin's newspaper gave extensive coverage to the trial and called into
   question the impartiality of the proceedings. Although Beilis was
   acquitted, the jurors stated pointedly that they believed that a ritual
   murder had taken place. The prudent Sytin, while deploring the
   actions of the government, must have feared for his newspaper.

3 Gorky's Capri stay, sometimes attributed to his tuberculosis, began
   during the revolution of 1905–06 when many Russian intellectuals
   left for abroad in order to avoid government reprisals. The colony of
   Russian political exiles in Capiri existed between 1906 and 1913,
   when the government declared an amnesty to mark the 300th anniversary of the House of Romanov.

4 Mikhail K. Pervukhin, a Russian journalist, author of a book about
   Russian visitors to Capri.

5 The word is Russian for "country house." It suggests the modesty of
   Gorky's dwelling.

6 Gorky's former wife, a prominent member of Lenin's Bolshevik Party,
   who remained on good terms with Gorky after their divorce and visited him in Italy.

7 Ivan Ivanovich Petrov (1861–1892) was a Gorky disciple and likely
   the I.I. Petrov who was a Sytin company editor and worked on Mediator.

8 The son of Sytin's son Vasily.

9 A Russian unit of length equivalent to 3,500 feet.

10 Sytin is alluding to his need to stay on good terms with the censors.
    Sytin's accounts of the visits to Capri say nothing about the tough
    business negotiations that he and Gorky conducted. These are dis-
    cussed in the Introduction.

11 Nikolai P. Gorbunov (1892–1938), revolutionary, secretary of the
    Council of People's Commissars, and Lenin's personal secretary in
    1917–20. His father, Pavel I. Gorbunov, was an engineer and manager
    of paper factory in the vicinity of St Petersburg.

12 Actually Pavel Ivanovich or P.I.

13 According to accounts by Sytin's children, Dmitry Ivanovich and
    Anna Ivanovna, V.I. Lenin's decree assigned Sytin and his family the
    apartment in the building of the newspaper *Russian Word*. Following
    Lenin's death in 1924, the authorities seized the five rooms of the
    apartment for the "Pravda" publishing house and moved Sytin to
    his last apartment in Moscow, Gorky Street 12, apartment 274 (the
    name of the street was later changed back to its pre-Revolution name,
    Tverskaia). That apartment is now the location of the Sytin Exhibi-
    tion Centre.

CHAPTER TEN

1   In peasant fashion, Sytin maintained a strict hierarchy at the table.
    His sons' seniority determined how close they sat to their father.
    The same rule applied to his daughters and their mother.
2   A *kasavorotka* is a traditional Russian dress shirt with a high collar
    and buttons running down the side to the left of the neck. The tail
    hangs outside the trousers below the belt line. The use of
    "Mamochka" and "Papochka" – that is, Mama and Papa – was
    common in urban, middle-class families but not in peasant families.
3   Fruit-flavoured hard candy.
4   A large, heavy carriage. Because it was a farm carriage it was built
    with no concession to comfort and had no springs.
5   A wide sledge built low to the ground. Bitiugi were initially bred
    in Voronezh province by peasants as powerful work horses. They
    excelled at pulling heavy loads for great distances. Their origin
    appears to have been in the region of the Bitiug River, a tributary
    of the Don River.
6   Sokolov inserts a footnote here that does not follow from the
    discussion of his mother. Thinking of her death reminds him of Sytin's
    end, and so he writes, "And in general at the end he was forgotten
    by everyone to the time of death. Only his close relatives took care
    of him. Even now after his death the *Life for the Book* was published
    with great difficulty. Because of his contributions to Mother Russia
    a museum, a Museum of Book Publishing, should be opened in his
    honour and a monument worthy of such great man should be erected
    at the cemetery." The I.D. Sytin Exhibition Centre at 12 Tverskaia
    Street in Moscow and a monument at Sytin's grave in Vvedensky
    Cemetery in Moscow have realized Sokolov's ideas.

7 Black Hundreds were mass organizations of low- and middle-class Russians and included many urban unemployed. They sprang up during the social turmoil associated with the Revolution of 1905 and could be incited to anti-Semitic violence and pogroms. The name can be traced to self-selected organizations of peasants and townspeople in medieval Russia.

   Sytin blamed officials for the destruction of his book publishing plant on Piatnitskaia Street. The plant had become a centre of workers' agitation, with printers playing a prominent role. To root out the organizers, the Moscow authorities sent the army to surround the plant on the night of 11 December 1905. An exchange of gunfire between persons in the plant and soldiers surrounding it led to a fire that consumed most of the plant by morning. Live ammunition could have ignited the flamable materials in the plant. Witnesses asserted that men, allegedly Black Hundreds, were running through the plant setting fires. The tardy response of the fire brigade also suggested the complicity of the authorities, at least at a low level. Sytin hastily left Moscow for St Petersburg on the night train because rumours had reached him that he might be a target of the Black Hundreds. He returned several days later and set to work to restore the destroyed printing plant.

8 The number of candles for which saint, the amount of money required, and the change to be given.

9 "Kerenky" was the popular name for the banknotes issued by the Provisional Government under Alexander Kerensky. By 1918, they were virtually worthless although still in circulation. Sokolov does seem a bit put out that he was paid in such miserly fashion.

10 "Honorary citizen" was a privileged status that had been bestowed on non-noble city dwellers since 1832 for their contributions to the welfare of their town. The nominaton was personally approved by the Emperor. An honorary citizen could not be subjected to corporal punishment and had the right to stand for election to the town council. "Orders" refers to medals received from time to time by Sytin from the government.

CHAPTER ELEVEN

1 N.I. Rozenstein was one of a group of able journalists who joined *Russian Word* about the same time as Doroshevich. Doroshevich had

failed to see Brut for what he was. It is possible that Rozenstein was aware of Brut's dubious credentials. According to S.G. Svatikov, who was commissioned by the Provisional Government in 1917 to investigate the activities of the Russian secret police abroad, the name Efim Karlovich Brut was a pseudonym for Efim Simhov Broad. Brut's literary alias was Belov. He had been a solicitor in Odessa and chairman of the professional licensing association. In 1897 he gambled away 3-4,000 rubles of the association's funds at Monte Carlo. To escape prosecution Brut fled to France,where he made a living by writing for various Russian newspapers, including Sytin's *Russian Word*. In 1916, Brut wished to return to Russia but, fearing prosecution, volunteered his services for a fee to the Russian secret police abroad while petitioning the Emperor to grant him a pardon. The secret police, the Okhranka, turned him down. The next year, in 1917, following the February Revolution when anyone connected with the Okhranka was subject to prosecution, Brut explained himself as a searcher for truth who had tried to penetrate the inner working of the Okhranka in order to expose it to the public (S.G. Slatikov, *Russkii politicheskii sysk za granitsei*, [Moscow 1918, 114–18; reprint 2002]).

2   *S vami piva ne svarish*, lit., "I can't make beer with you."

3   The circulation of *Russian Word* was lower than it had been earlier in the year, creating great consternation at the paper.

4   The byline for the column "The Russian."

5   Doroshevich's wife.

6   Doroshevich is referring to the new press regulations forthcoming on 21 November 1905. In the new rules, the Emperor Nicholas II declared the establishment of freedom of the press in Russia.

7   The first elected representative assembly in the history of Russia would meet from April to July 1905, a little over two months. It would not be "long" but short because the Emperor Nicholas II closed it and called an election for the next Duma.

8   Lit. "their curiosity will be blunted."

9   Peter D. Boborykin (1836–1921) was a novelist, journalist, and playwright, Ivan Kh. Ozerov (1860–1926?), a professor of financial law and taxation at Moscow University who wrote for Sytin's paper, and Vasily V. Rozanov (1856–1919) a well-known philosopher, critic, and journalist. Doroshevich was right: they were not only well known but popular. Rozanov is read in Russia even today. Rozanov was a

journalistic pioneer and the first major Russian newspaperman to write for an allotted space.

10 Doroshevich is referring to his plans to advertise the paper during the coming subscription campaign.

11 Doroshevich is referring to the fire that gutted Sytin's book-publishing plant on Piatnitskaia street in December 1905, and to the railway and postal strikes during the same months. Sytin later said that he recovered quickly from the financial losses.

12 "Administrative situation" is a euphemism for the system of press controls. Doroshevich and other editors and journalists kept a close eye on the ebb and flows of restrictions and waited for times of lessened controls to publish works that they thought might encounter restrictions.

CHAPTER TWELVE

1 Al. Altaev, pseudonym of Russian Soviet author of historical fiction and biographies Margarita V. Yamshchikova (1872–1959). The recollections on Sytin are from "Moi starye izdateli: Iz vospominanii," *Kniga: Issledovaniia i materialy* 26 (1973): 176–82.

2 The exact title is *Razorennye Gnezda* (*Ruined Nests*), a seventeenth-century tale of Boyaryna Morozova, Stepan Razin, Nikon, and Avvakum. Theodosia Morozova (1632–1675) and Archpriest Avvakum (1605–1681) were Old Believers who suffered cruel persecution for refusing to accept the ecclesiastic reform of Patriarch Nikon (1605–1681), Stepan Razin was the leader of the Cossack rebellion in 1670–71.

3 Elena N. Tikhomirova, wife and collaborator of a well-known Russian pedagogue, Dmitry I. Tikhomirov. They are the authors of the best and still popular alphabet books in Russian.

4 Metropol was one of the most luxurious hotels in Moscow, built in 1905 across from Red Square by the millionaire Savva Mamontov. The hotel had a first-class restaurant and was the venue for the first cinema theatre in Russia in 1906.

5 Altaev refers to the fact that she belonged to those who, with the Soviet authorities, were anti-capitalist and would support the nationalization of Sytin's enterprises.

6 Lysates was a mixture of organic substances touted as a rejuvenating elixir in the 1920s.

 7 Daniel Defoe's novel was widely popular in Russia.

 8 Adolf F. Marks (1838–1904), Petersburg publisher of great renown,
    editor of the popular illustrated magazine *Niva*. After his death,
    according to his will, his business became a shareholding company
    and in 1914 I.D. Sytin bought a majority of the shares. The business
    ceased to exist in 1917.

 9 Mavriky O.Wolff (1825–1883), publisher and bookseller, owner of
    model bookstores that catered to affluent readers. He is reputed to
    have been the first millionaire publisher in Russia.

10 Nikolai A. Nekrasov (1821–1877), Russian poet and magazine pub-
    lisher of democratic and populist sympathies. Motylkov is referring to
    Nekrasov's long narrative poem "Who can live happily in Russia?"
    about the Russian peasantry. A free-verse translation of the stanza in
    question expresses Nekrasov's hopes that "a time will come when the
    peasant will be taught to know the difference between worthwhile
    and worthless books, when he will bring back from the market Belin-
    sky's or Gogol's books rather than Bliucher's portrait [he was a field
    marshal] and the silly tale about Milord …" Quoted from "Komu na
    Rusi zhit' khorosho?" in N.A. Nekrasov, *Sochineniia v trekh tomakh*,
    3:103.

11 Russo-Turkish war of 1877–78.

12 Aleksandr S. Pushkin (1799–1837), Russia's national poet.

13 "English Mylord," "The Story of Adventures of the English Mylord
    Georg Brandenburg and Markgrafin Frederika Louise" appeared in
    1782 and became a staple in Russia's book market, "Frol Skobeyev,"
    a sixteenth-century Russian novel and one of the first secular literary
    works.

14 Nikolai V. Gogol (1809–1852) Russian and Ukrainian author, author
    of the play "Inspector General" and the novel *Dead Souls*.

15 As publications for common people.

16 "The Minor," a satirical comedy by Denis Fonvizin (1744–1782) that
    mocked the attempt by upper-class Russians to mimic the French.

17 "Woe from Wit," a comedy by Aleksandr S. Griboedov (1795–1829).

18 *Captain's Daughter*, *Dubrovsky*, and *Tales of Belkin* are popular sto-
    ries by Pushkin.

19 Ivan A. Krylov (1769–1844), Russian fabulist, translator of many of
    Aesop's and Lafontaine's fables, to which he added some of his own.

20 "The Song of the Merchant Kalashnikov," a poem by Mikhail Yu.

Lermontov (1814–1841), Russia's most influential poet after Pushkin's death.

21   Historical novels by the French Victor Hugo (1802–1885) and the Polish Henryk Senkiewicz (1846–1916) were popular in the late nineteenth and early twentieth century.

22   New editions of the *Children's Encyclopaedia* were published in the 1960s and 1980s.

23   Hugo Stinnes.

24   This assertion is contradicted by Sytin's readiness to travel to Germany and negotiate with Hugo Stinnes over investing in the paper-making industry.

25   A mysterious Siberian hermit whom many mistakenly believed to be Tsar Alexander I (1777–1825) who had abandoned the throne in order to expiate his sins by dedicating his life to God.

26   S.V. Iablonovsky [S. Potresov], *Illiustrirovovannia Rossia*, 51 (Paris, 1934): 4–5.

27   One of the two brothers who were dramatic actors of the first half of the nineteenth century.

28   Count Sergei S. Uvarov (1786–1855), minister of Public Education, 1832–48 and author of Nicholas I's "Official Nationality," the ideology of the regime.

29   Ironic allusion to "fibbing," the second meaning of the word "fable" in Russian, implying that the minister of Education often lied, while the fabulist was a true educational influence.

30   Literally, "On the Other Side of the Moscow River," a largely commercial section of the city across the Moscow river from the Kremlin.

31   Vladimir V. Korolenko, (1853–1921), a writer and social activist, sometimes called "The Embodiment of Russian National Honour."

32   This is an error – Sytin was eighty-three when he died.

33   *Gentleman* was a comedy by A. Iuzhin lampooning a Moscow millionaire merchant Mikhail Morozov, who was an anglophile. The playwright poked fun at the pretentiousness of the wealthy and their authoritarian mannerisms.

34   A character from Aleksandr N. Ostrovsky's play *Your Drink – My Hangover* about a despotic merchant whose real name is Tit (Titus), but another character mispronounces it.

35   Aleksei I. Putilov (1866–1937?) was a prominent Russian entrepreneur and financier.

36 The Gordons appear to have been brothers. Noi Abramovich or
    N.A. Gordon was a member of the board of directors of the Russko-
    Aziatskii Bank, the Baku Oil Company, chairman of the board of
    directors of the company, Lafarm[e] a director of the Petrograd Car
    Building Company, and a Moscow timber company. The latter would
    appear to be his link to papermaking.

37 Boris I. Katlama was a Petersburg entrepreneur.

38 Arkady V. Rumanov (1878–1960), journalist, head of the Petersburg
    office of *Russian Word* since 1906. In 1916 he became editor of the
    popular magazine *Niva* after Sytin bought it. The personal relations
    between Rumanov and Sytin were close.

39 Published in B.S. Utevsky, *Vopominaniia Iurista*, 255–8.

40 Other evidence contradicts this description. Sytin did not smoke.

41 Utevsky is given to repeating legends about Sytin. As Motylkov
    pointed out above, one of Sytin's motives in buying the Marks
    publishing company was to acquire Marks's copyrights for classical
    Russian authors.

42 Aleksandr N. Potresov and Yulii O. Martov were leaders of the
    Russian Social Democratic Workers' Party.

43 An individual or personal pension larger than average, granted to
    persons whose contributions to the Soviet state was considered
    outstanding.

BIBLIOGRAPHY

Altaev, Al. [M.V. Yamshichikova]. "Moi starye izdateli: Iz vospomina-niia." *Kniga: Issledovaniia i materialy.* 26 (1973): 154–82.

Amfiteatrov, Aleksandr V. *Zhizn' cheloveka neudobnogo dlia sebia i dlia mnogikh.* 2 vols. Moscow, 1924.

Brooks, Jeffrcy. *When Russia Learned to Read: Literacy and Popular Literature, 1861–1917.* Princeton: Princeton University Press, 1985.

Bukchin, S.V. *Sudba feletonista: Zhizn' i tvorchestvo Vlasa Doroshevicha,* editcd by F.I. Kushelov. Minsk, 1975.

Chukovsky, Kornei. *Sovremenniki. Portrety i etiudy.* Moscow, 2008.

Dinershtein, E.A. "Vo imia blagogo dela (L.N. Tolstoy, I.D. Sytin i 'Posrednik')" *Kniga: Issledovaniia i materialy* 37 (1978): 70–97.

"I.D. Sytin. Vstrechi: P.A. Stolypin, P.A. Kropotkin, A.S. Suvorin," *Kniga: Issledovaniia i materialy,* ed. I.E. Matveeva. 61 (1990): 139–44.

Kolyshko, I.I., *Velikii raspad. Vospominaniia.* St Petersburg, 2009.

Mendeleev, A.G. *Zhizn' gazety "Russkoe Slovo" izdatel. Sotrudniki.* Moscow, 2001.

Motylkov, A.M. "Moia rabota u I.D. Sytina (Iz vospominanii bukinista)," *Issledovaniia i materialy,* 37 (1979): 157–66.

Nekrasov, N.A. *Sochineniia v trekh tomakh.* Moscow, 1959.

Polveka dlia knig: Literaturno-khudozhestvennyi sbornik, posviashchennyi piatidesiatiletiu izdatel'skoi deiatel'nosti I.D. Sytina, edited by N.V. Tulupov. Moscow, 1916.

Ruud, Charles A. *Russian Entrepreneur: Publisher Ivan Sytin of Moscow, 1851–1934.* Montreal: McGill-Queen's University Press, 1990.

Sytin, I.D. "Iz perezhitogo. Avtobiogaficheskie nabroski iubiliara."
    Polveka dlia knigi, 11–28.
– "Iz perezhitogo" *Russkoe Slovo* 41, 19 February 1917.
– *Zhizn dlia knigi*. 1st ed., Moscow, 1960; 2nd ed. Moscow, 1978, supp.
    1985.
Tolstoy, Sofia. *The Diaries of Sofia Tolstoy*. Edited by. O.A. Golinenko et
    al., translated by Cathy Porter, introduced by R.F. Christian. New York:
    Book Sales, 1985.
Tolstoy, S.M. *Drevo Zhizni*. Moscow, 2002.
Uspensky, Boris. *Raskol i kulturnyi konflikt XVII veka*,
Utevsky, B.S. *Vospominaniia Iurista*. Moscow, 1989.

INDEX